THE HORSE GOD BUILT

Also by Lawrence Scanlan

The Horse's Shadow
Harvest of a Quiet Eye: The Cabin as Sanctuary
Grace Under Fire: The State of Our Sweet and Savage Game
Little Horse of Iron: A Quest for the Canadian Horse
Wild About Horses: Our Timeless Passion for the Horse
Horses Forever
Heading Home: On Starting a New Life in a Country Place
Big Ben

As Coauthor
Healed by Horses: The Carole Fletcher Story
The Man Who Listens to Horses
Riding High: Ian Millar's World of Show Jumping

THE HORSE GOD BUILT

The Untold Story of Secretariat,
the World's Greatest Racehorse

LAWRENCE SCANLAN

Thomas Dunne Books
St. Martin's Press New York

THOMAS DUNNE BOOKS.
An imprint of St. Martin's Press.

www.thomasdunnebooks.com
www.stmartins.com

All photographs are by Raymond G. Woolfe, except those on pages 143, 187, and 223, which are by Lawrence Scanlan.

ISBN-13: 978-0-312-36724-4
ISBN-10: 0-312-36724-4

First published in Canada by HarperCollins Publishers, Ltd.

First U.S. Edition: May 2007

10   9   8   7   6   5   4   3   2   1

For Edward "Shorty" Sweat

It's like God said, "You just think you've seen horses. I'm gonna show you a horse." Then he built Secretariat.

—Jim Reno, sculptor, Kerrville, Texas,
in *Equine Images* magazine, 1991

Charles learned quickly that working at a racing stable is an unforgettable experience, and it quietly threatened to become a life—of oneness with nature and communion with horses, of incurable wonder.

—Edward Hotaling,
on the life of Charles Stewart (1808–1884),
a black jockey and trainer from Pocahontas, Virginia,
in *The Great Black Jockeys,* 1999

Contents

~ Photographs ~

THE HORSE GOD BUILT

A HORSE AND HIS GROOM:
SECRETARIAT AND "SHORTY" SWEAT

A MAN APPROACHES THE STALLION BARN at Claiborne Farm, near Paris, Kentucky, intent on one stall where a horse—bright as an orange, shiny as brass—is anxiously circling and examining his new digs.

"Hey, Red," the man says to the horse. The late-fall day is chilly and bright, as good a day as any for a parting.

The horse is Secretariat and the man his longtime groom, Edward Sweat, though everyone calls this low, muscled man "Shorty." Secretariat nickers at the sound of the man's voice, as Eddie has come to expect. They are old friends, almost beyond greetings. The chestnut's eyes soften and his ears swivel forward to take him in.

"Did you know, Red, you're in your daddy's old stall?" Eddie asks the horse. "Bold Ruler lived here. What do you think of that?" Eddie runs his right hand over the brass nameplate, then falls silent. He looks up and admires the lofty ceilings, the expansive stalls, the wide corridor, how the little ten-stall barn opens to the sky at each end. The place is airy and neat, a fitting home for a fine, fine horse. The first thing the horse had done—once his shipping bandages had been removed from his legs—was to inspect his new apartment, then roll in the straw.

Eddie thinks of his two great charges, Riva Ridge and Secretariat, and how different they were in their stalls. He used to call Riva "Pea-head" because of his small cranium. The horse—named after a battle between American and German soldiers in the mountains of Italy in 1945—would go into his stall after an early-morning workout, lie down, and fall asleep. If you wanted to brush Riva, you had to get in there before he dozed off. Eddie could have lain down on top of him, knocked down the barn; Riva wouldn't have budged. The horse wanted, and got, his nap. He had won the Kentucky Derby in 1972, and with that victory came a privilege or two.

Secretariat, on the other hand, would sleep standing, facing a corner; only at night, when quiet had settled over the barn, would he lie down. But he never stretched out. The imperious horse would fold his front legs beneath him and listen, always listen, for strange sounds. And the second he heard one, he was up. Eddie knows all this because he has spent untold hours watching this horse, listening from his cot outside the stall, monitoring his moods and cycles. No need now for such vigilance.

It is Sunday, November 11, 1973. The day marks the end of something, the beginning of something else. Everyone close to the horse feels unbearably sad. Trainer Lucien Laurin was teary-eyed back at Belmont Park in New York when the horse was loaded, and now, at Claiborne, he is still teary-eyed. Exercise rider Charlie Davis stayed in his bunkhouse bed at Belmont, for he could not bear to watch the horse leave. The horse's owner, Penny Chenery, normally available to the press, declines all interviews. For a long time, she just stands in the barn at Claiborne and stares at her horse. "It's been a rough day for her," Elizabeth Ham, Chenery's secretary, tells a reporter on the scene. "This is the end of a lot of things. This means a big change for a lot of people."

Eddie looks stricken at the prospect. He stares intently at the horse with the three white feet and the star and the stripe on his forehead, and the horse returns the gaze, trying to fathom his groom's mood. Eddie knows that a horse—certainly a keenly intelligent and spirited horse such as Secretariat—reads his handlers constantly. His eyes and ears are fixed on Eddie Sweat, for the horse knows something is amiss. His head is high; his tail snaps out annoyance. Why am I here in this new place, he wants to know, far from the track and home? Where is the man's prattle, which I always find such a comfort? Why isn't he in here putting a halter on me, the great horse thinks, and setting me up in the cross-ties for a rubdown? Eddie is always saying or doing, or both, and now he just stands there. The horse has never seen the man so still, so silent, so removed, and the stall door between them now feels like a wall.

The work of a groom is constant, with its own rhythms and rituals. When the horse was out breezing on the track, Eddie and his cohorts were mucking out his stall, taking away sullied bedding, filling hay nets, hauling buckets of water. How many times has Eddie hand-walked and hand-grazed Secretariat? He has lost count. And though Eddie has never been *on* the horse, he has spent many, many hours at his side, behind him, before him, beneath him—strapping on the big chestnut's shipping boots and leg wraps, laying a wool blanket over his back, checking his legs, reaching for his oh-so-ample girth, doing up horse-blanket straps, picking his feet, brushing on hoof paint. Eddie

Sweat has cleaned his tack, has bathed the horse and cleaned his privates, given him worm paste, cut up the carrots he loves, poured into his feed bucket the grain and hot mash he adores. Man, this horse loves his supper.

"Don't worry, Red," Eddie says, "I told them how much you love a good feed. You won't be missin' any meals here."

Eddie Sweat takes no comfort this day in his small claim to fame: He is the only groom in history to have handled Kentucky Derby winners two years in succession—Riva Ridge in 1972, Secretariat in 1973. Born in 1939, the sixth of nine children to a poor black family of tenant farmers near Holly Hill, South Carolina, Eddie was briefly a boxer in his youth, hard-bodied, with powerful thighs and massive forearms.

Geraldine Holman, Eddie's youngest and favorite sister, remembers her mother, Mary, telling her that even as a child, Eddie was obsessed with horses. Because of the age gap between them, Eddie and Geraldine only got to know each other later. She once asked him, "Why did you leave home so early?" And Eddie told her, "I was just fascinated with horses."

As a boy, he would board a school bus that passed Lucien Laurin's Thoroughbred operation, Holly Hill Farm. Some days, Eddie skipped school to hang around Laurin's farm, and Eddie's mother would be furious when she learned of it. Eddie landed work at Holly Hill in the early 1950s—first as an exercise rider and then, when he got too heavy, as a groom. In time, he became the farm's most trusted and most valued groom, the one given the prize horses to rub and brush, to load into vans and drive to faraway meets, the groom with "the touch."

"Lucien practically raised Eddie," says Geraldine. "Lucien was his second family." Laurin had taught him the basics—how to apply poultices and powders and all the rest. But Eddie's father—part black, part Cherokee Indian, with white blood as well coursing in his veins—also taught Eddie some things.

David Walker, a longtime racetrack groom who learned his craft at the feet of Eddie Sweat, his uncle, told me, "Eddie's father, David Sweat, knew a lot about animals. He would go into the forest and gather herbs for his poultices. Eddie was the same way. For a damaged tendon in a horse, he would make a little potion, wrap him up, and the next thing you knew, that horse was walking. Eddie was the greatest groom who ever lived. He had a way with horses. He could get them to do things that no one else could."

Eddie's first horse, one he loved very much, was a Thoroughbred called Lake Erie. The horse was not sound, but Eddie kept working on his legs. "The little horse ran good for me," Eddie would later say. "He won every time I turned him loose, he must have won four or five straight. So that sort of gave me 'the spirit' of rubbing horses." Then came Count Amber, and a son of his called Amberoid (winner of the 1966 Belmont Stakes), and Traffic and National, Tumiga, Bronzerullah, Lord Quillo. Eddie remembers a great many of the horses he has rubbed and much about them.

But this day, he cannot quite grasp the fact that the horse who stands before him, who continues to look at him expectantly, will never run again. The horse will tear around his paddock when he has a mind to, but he will never again best other Thoroughbreds on the track, in front of a grandstand with every man, woman, and child standing up, screaming. Almost as bad, thinks Eddie, as clipping a hawk's wings and confining him to a cage.

"That ain't right," Eddie says to himself. "Makes no sense." Then he pauses and wonders whether it makes any more sense that he will probably grieve till the day he dies over the loss of this horse.

Eddie's manner around horses is casual, yet protective and watchful, and he brooks no nonsense. What Secretariat loves about Eddie Sweat is that this man does not fear him (though he does, at times, fear *for* him, but that is another matter). Even a trace of fear in a human begets fear in a horse; calm usually begets calm. Attending to this horse has never been easy, yet they have come to an understanding, this horse, this groom.

The difficulty, one that may well have stymied other grooms, is the horse's princely air. He has had it since he was a foal roughhousing in the paddock, and he has it yet, a haughtiness to go with his coiled-spring athleticism. Secretariat is big-boned to boot—not overly tall, about 16.2 hands fully grown and shoes on, but imposing since he weighed two hundred pounds more than most Thoroughbreds. "He has muscles in his eyebrows," the venerable racing scribe Charles Hatton once observed. Others were struck by the horse's fearlessness in races, how he would burst through openings between horses—like a bruising halfback splitting linebackers, some said. In his early days, he was clownish and awkward and high-strung. One time after a race, a fan reached out to touch him and the horse scooted forward, driving Eddie into some ceremonial ropes near the winner's circle and leaving burns on Eddie's neck. Secretariat was a handful. And so smart that sometimes his jockey pretty much let the horse decide the winning tactic in a race.

Eddie was never cowed by the horse he calls "Big Red," but simply went about his business, as though he were brushing Billy Silver, the gentle Appaloosa gelding and track pony who was besotted with Secretariat.

Brush in one hand, cloth in the other, Eddie used to lay on each as if guided by a metronome: brush and rub, brush and rub. As he worked from the front of the horse to the rear, Eddie would stand a little to the side. Any farther would have been construed by the horse as a sign of wariness or weakness, which would not do; any closer, Eddie knew, was pure recklessness. The horse would issue little kicks (warning shots across the prow, but more playful than menacing), swing out to the side, lean into Eddie's body, and bob his head in protest or try to bite the brush.

So much adrenaline, so much mischief, thinks Eddie, and he shakes his head in wonder and amazement as he looks into Secretariat's eyes. He calls up all the times during handling when the big stallion reared up on him. Not because the stallion was mean or hot-tempered or crazy, but because he was so fit and primed and energized. "Hot to trot" did not begin to describe this horse. Secretariat could barely stand still when he wasn't sleeping or eating. He was the boxer who could not stop shadowboxing.

Jim Squires, who wrote *Horse of a Different Color,* talked about how hard it is to be a stallion's keeper, especially a Thoroughbred stallion's keeper. "Presumably because they are so valuable," he wrote, "Kentucky horses are in general the most protected, pampered, and undisciplined animals in existence. As a result, many of them—stallions in particular—are prone to bite, strike, kick and eat the very 'hardboots' who care for them."

Eddie laughs to himself, thinking of Secretariat when he was a brash two-year-old colt who would run from the sound of motors, as if someone had struck a match and set the flame against the horse's skin. Time and miles cured this horse, as they do most horses. But even now, thinks Eddie, every motor—when it purrs but especially when it starts—stirs up in Secretariat the memory of that first encounter.

Eddie can see it now. They were at Saratoga, in upper New York State, and exercise rider Jimmy Gaffney was walking Secretariat along the backstretch after a workout. Through the dawn mist, Jimmy could see someone get into a truck, and he knew what was coming. "Don't start the truck!" he screamed, but the driver was already inside the cab and was beyond hailing. Jimmy could feel his horse tense beneath him, but there was nothing he could do. In the moment that engine fired, the horse he was riding all but vanished. Secretariat was so strong, so quick, and he could drop and shy sideways faster than a man can blink. Jimmy hit the ground, but, bless him, thinks Eddie, never lost his grip on the reins. The left hand held as the big horse dragged him over the track, onto the wet grass, and back toward the stable. Eddie conjures that red tail raised like a flag, that clipped mane aswirl in the wind, Jimmy skimming alongside like a human sled. Eventually, he did let go, and a groom caught the stallion between barns, but it was a long time before the pulses of everyone in Secretariat's circle abated.

Eddie knows the power of idle talk to calm a troubled horse. And brushing-time chat never much varied. "Stop it now! C'mon, Red. C'mon, Red. I'm gonna brush you now," Eddie would plead. "You're steppin' on my toes. You tryin' to put a foot in my pocket?"

Bill Nack took down that banter while researching his book *Big Red of Meadow Stable,* and while the words were all uttered in English, they were delivered tonally—as if Eddie were speaking Vietnamese. "I spent many hours watching Eddie work," Nack told me. "He talked to the horse, but it was all a singsong to keep the horse's mind busy. Secretariat, of course, didn't understand English, but he did understand tone. So Eddie spoke in diphthongs."

Nack was once asked by a racing fan to name some of the most fascinating personalities he had encountered in his many decades around racetracks. He named Eddie Sweat first, calling him "one of the most memorable characters I've met in racing." Then he named Angel Cordero, Jr., whose signature move was the leaping dismount. Finally, Nack named the groom Sloan "Duck Butter" Price. I admire Nack—for his writing, and for his unsentimental view of the track, and I found it telling that two of his choices were black grooms, and that Shorty Sweat topped his list.

Marvin Moorer, Eddie's firstborn son (Marvin had decided in his youth to take on his mother's name, for personal reasons), is a former racetrack groom who worked with his father at Belmont between 1983 and 1987. Marvin watched him work with Secretariat a lot. What Marvin later remembered was that Eddie spoke to the horse in a southern Creole language known as Geechee, or Gullah.

A blend of English and several West African languages, including Yoruba and Ibo, Gullah can still be heard on the coasts and islands of South Carolina and Georgia. Gullah culture formed centuries ago when people from Barbados and West Africa were brought as slaves to the islands to grow rice, indigo, and cotton. Depending on what's being said, the singsong oral language can sound like an English dialect or be almost incomprehensible to an English speaker. Here are a few samples: *Uh yeddy um but uh ain sheum,* which means "I have heard of him, but I haven't seen him." Or this, from the translation of the New Testament into Gullah, a twenty-five-year project that was just completed in 2005: *"Fo God mek de wol, de Wod been dey. De Wod been dey wid God, an de Wod been God."* ("In the beginning was the Word, and the Word was with God and the Word was God.")

Marvin recalled watching his father in the stall as Eddie asked Secretariat to pick up his left front foot, and the horse did it. "I thought," said Moorer, "Is this a trick they've put on for my benefit?" There came from Eddie a constant chatter, delivered in the firm belief that this horse was grasping every word and nuance. And the measure of his trust in the horse, said Marvin, was that Eddie would sometimes brush him in the barn corridor—without cross-ties. I liken it to holding a hawk on your arm without leather protection and relying on trust and instinct to spare you from the talons' squeeze.

"I know what you want," Eddie would say to Secretariat. And, of course, Eddie *did* know. Heaven for a horse is a handler who speaks your language, and fluently.

Sometimes, the ritual between them would take a sour turn. As if his patience had finally been exhausted, Eddie would bark at the horse and just glare at him. Secretariat took it like a needed slap in the face. He would retreat, lower his head, even step back some and make little licking and chewing motions with his mouth. It is what horses do when they offer peace.

Eddie insists on, and gets, respect. A horse needs to know that his handler understands him and will not be intimidated. Secretariat would want what all horses want: a worthy leader to trust and follow and count on. In Eddie Sweat, Secretariat has gotten that, and much more.

A handler can be too cocky or too careful, and Eddie has found the middle ground. No one understands this horse like this groom. On matters of feeding and workload and routine horse doctoring, the horse's trainer has often deferred to Eddie. And Secretariat leans on him, too, as many on hand this eleventh day in November of 1973 will attest.

Secretariat was flown earlier in the day to this, his new home in north-central Kentucky. Eddie swallows hard as he remembers the trip. The L-188 speeding down the runway, engines loudly droning, Eddie in the hold with the horses—Secretariat and his running mate, Riva Ridge. Eddie had taken up a position directly in front of Secretariat, like a stewardess holding a nervous passenger's hand. Man and horse faced each other, pressed into each other, a small human forehead touching a massive equine brow. Eddie had seen a hint of worry in the horse's eyes; Secretariat, with his teeth, had taken a grip on Eddie's ski jacket. Eddie closed his eyes and, with his mouth open slightly, breathed in the very essence of the horse, as if to store the memory somewhere deep inside him.

Eddie led Secretariat off the plane at Lexington and onto a van and finally passed him over to the stud-farm managers at Claiborne. He had to explain the great horse's likes and dislikes, in the manner of a worrisome mother listing to a new baby-sitter the salient and partic- ular needs of her only child. How this horse hates motors and having his ears touched. Loves oats and cut-up carrots more than sweets or hay. Loves to play with his doffed halter like a dog tugging on his own leash. Can tire of adoring crowds but actually likes having his picture taken. Eddie thinks of all the times he has held the horse on a lead shank before a circle of photographers and fans come to see the leg- end in the flesh.

Secretariat is still fresh off dramatic victories in the Derby, the Preakness, the Belmont. Named Horse of the Year, he is a champion racer with $1.3 million in earnings, the first Triple Crown winner since 1948, and now he will take on new duties at this farm as a breed- ing stallion with six million dollars' worth of work lined up for the rest of his days. At this moment in time, the fall of 1973, no stallion on earth is worth more. Owner, trainer, and jockey have all shared in the Secretariat windfall. Old track traditions and hierarchies have meant that the groom—the one human the horse seems to cherish— has gotten only one or two apples of the many golden ones that have fallen in Secretariat's considerable wake. The most celebrated groom of his day, a virtual security blanket to a champion horse, Eddie is still just another backstretch gypsy, traveling from barn to track, barn to track, where he has often slept on a cot by Secretariat's stall, rising be- fore dawn, shoveling horse manure, earning base wages. He is an em- inently skilled horseman earning an unskilled laborer's wage and living a migrant worker's life.

Eddie is only sad now. If he should experience moments of bitter- ness later on, they will be years, decades, down the road. For now, he still sups on privilege. And yet no one has borne the burden of Secre- tariat as Eddie has.

The horse's racing career spanned some seven hundred days, only twenty-one of them actual race days. All the others were rest days, workout days, travel days, days of fending off the press and adoring fans. The pressure sometimes wore on Eddie. "If anything goes wrong," he would say, "it's my responsibility."

No more. This afternoon, a new handler, Lawrence Robinson, had a go at leading Secretariat, but the horse immediately declared his allegiance to Eddie Sweat. The horse's magnificent hind end, the one that a racing writer once likened to the motor on a Sherman tank, swung around and, in a blur, he nailed his new handler in the rump with a cow kick. The new man, the caretaker of stallions at this legendary stud farm, is neither green nor unthinking—far from it. This was all the horse's doing. At one point during his little tantrum, Secretariat turned and looked directly at Eddie, who appeared small and uncomfortable in his new role as bystander. The horse's look said, What is going on here? Why him and not you?

Eddie stays a week at Claiborne to help with the transition. He knows, as does Lucien Laurin, that Secretariat will not tolerate the sudden loss of his beloved groom. The horse is weaned off his handler slowly, like a foal from a mare.

Eddie later tells a reporter why he's so sad. "I guess a groom gets closer to a horse than anyone," he says. "The owner, the trainer, they maybe see him once a day. But I lived with him, worked with him." Then, while staring into Secretariat's new stall, Eddie makes a chirping sound, and the horse responds instantly by pricking his ears and moving closer to Eddie.

"Well," says Eddie, in a voice soft and tinged with unspeakable mournfulness and aimed at the horse, "it's all over now. They'll never forget you, big fella. Never."

What the man really means is that *he,* Shorty Sweat, will never forget this horse. Eddie has never encountered a horse like this one and he will sorely miss Secretariat's kindness, his curiosity, his heart. God, such a heart. "This is a hurting thing to me," he will later tell a friend, understated as always. "I'm so sad I didn't even want to bring him over here. It's been a wonderful two years. Now it seems like my whole career has ended." Eddie is thirty-four years old.

He ponders leaving the track. He considers, only briefly, becoming a truck driver—with steady wages and hours. His wife, Linda, wants him to quit the track. But the horses are in his blood, and the shed row, for all its vagaries, calls to him.

He puts it this way to a reporter: "I've been at it a long time. Like I told my wife before I married her, 'Before I met you I was with the horses and I'll still be doing it long after you're gone.'" It's as if he thinks himself blessed by a life with horses—so blessed, he will out-live Linda.

Eddie remembers the first time he saw Secretariat, and how he dis-missed the colt. A song by Roberta Flack comes to him, a song he heard often that year on barn radios: "The First Time Ever I Saw Your Face." Too pretty, he thought then of Secretariat. Too damn fat. Eddie and the other barn rats started calling him "Ol' Hopalong" for the way the young colt devoured oats, put on pounds, and gracelessly took to the track.

Eddie had told *Canadian Horseman* in 1973, when he was in Toronto for the Canadian International Stakes, "I didn't think much of him when we first got him. I thought he was just a big clown. He was real clumsy and a bit on the wild side, you know. And I remem-ber saying to myself I didn't think he was going to be an outstanding horse." The Meadow, the farm in Virginia where Secretariat was born, had seen a few Bold Ruler colts, and they had a reputation for running three-quarters of a mile and then quitting. Eddie thought the pretty red horse was in that mold.

Two years later—and Eddie smiles at the thought—Ol' Hopalong has joined Nixon and Watergate, Vietnam and Woodstock on the front pages of every newspaper in the land. There is only one hero in 1973, and he is "The People's Horse," the one who still eyes his groom at Claiborne with an air of expectancy.

Eddie Sweat has been around horses most of his life and he has never come so close to perfection. Everywhere Secretariat has gone, people have wanted to touch him—before the race, after the race, even, on occasion, during the race. Every day for two years, thinks Eddie Sweat, that's been my job: to touch greatness. And now it's over. He turns his back on the stall and walks away, fixes his gaze on the lush fields at Claiborne and discreetly wipes a tear from his left eye. He does not, dares not, look back.

No one could have predicted Secretariat's greatness, or that of Seattle Slew, Seabiscuit, or Man o'War. It is what keeps every trainer in the game—the hope that the next superhorse is, at this very moment, out in the middle field, the dark bay foal, say, sucking hard on his mare's teats.

Gus Gray, a trainer I met in Ocala, Florida, early in 2005, told me then he had a colt who was going to win the 2006 Kentucky Derby. "You can lay down your bet right now," he assured me. "The horse"—and Gus owned half of him—"got these big eyes, like a eagle. When you see him, you done seen the champion." The colt's name was John in the Cloud, and his ancestors included Tri Jet, Tom Fool, Storm Cat, Swaps, and Bold Ruler (the sire of Secretariat).

But the odds were massively stacked against his winning (and sure enough, he did not make the entry list): Derby winners are exceedingly rare, and only eleven horses in history have ever won the Triple Crown. I remember a European rider's term for the Canadian show jumper Big Ben, a term he used with affection: "That horse," he told me, "is a freak." Just as Secretariat was a freak.

Secretariat's owner, Penny Chenery, would be the first to admit that breeding horses is a genetic crapshoot. She told me that Secretariat, "next to having my children, was the most remarkable event in my life. But he was not my creation or accomplishment. We just got lucky." Secretariat's full sister, a filly called The Bride, was a fine broodmare but did nothing on the track.

When a great one like Secretariat comes along, we feel as if a blessing has been bestowed upon us. And it has. A great comet has streaked across a black sky and we happen to have been walking along a dark country road and seen the celestial rarity in all its brilliance. We will tell our grandchildren what a marvel it was, one that made us feel both small and exalted at the same time. While that comet burned and cast its shimmering light, the world seemed a more beautiful place, and it felt good to be alive.

~ 1 ~

RED HORSE, BLACK ANGEL

EIGHT IN THE MORNING north of Lexington under a bright summer sun, and this corner of the sprawling theme park in Kentucky already has the feel of a lively small-town fair. A long row of white domed tents—spires on top, blue pennants flying—offers shade to the peddlers setting up their wares. Strange to say, given the breakfast hour, but the smell of grilled burgers and hot dogs is in the air, the sno-cone sellers are doing a brisk business, and it seems like every hawker of Secretariat memorabilia in America has booked kiosk space here under that hot Confederate sun. It's Secretariat Day at Kentucky Horse Park.

Kentucky Horse Park is a twelve-hundred-acre working horse farm and theme park, with more than fifty breeds on display and all manner of horse shows running from February to December. The big Rolex eventing competition takes place here, along with dressage and rodeo and hunter/jumper shows and Pony Club rallies. The park is a mecca for the horsey set and will be the site of the 2010 World Equestrian Games.

Earlier, a volunteer at the entryway dropped into my hand a keepsake—a Secretariat button. Inside a white circle is the head of a red horse wearing blue-and-white blinkers, red for the horse's chestnut coat, blue and white the colors of Meadow Stable. From trees inside the park hang oversized blue pennants with the same image at the top and, below, these words:

SECRETARIAT
BRONZE STATUE

UNVEILING

JULY 17, 2004
SECRETARIAT.COM

Browsers are cruising the tents and filling up their shopping bags, apparently undeterred by the lofty prices of almost everything. The only free thing here is Big Red gum, with packets going to anyone who can answer this skill-testing question. (Warning: If you didn't get "Who's buried in Grant's Tomb?" you may not get this one, either.) "What was Secretariat's nickname?" a cheery woman in a red T-shirt asks me while offering a pack of Big Red gum. A huge poster at her kiosk announces the 2004 Secretariatfest and the prospect of "officially licensed merchandise"—Secretariat teddy bears and key chains, little plastic Secretariat snow globes, Big Red pens. I pass the test, get the gum, and try some. It's awful. Awful pricey describes some of the art here, and I am reminded of this fact: Many are drawn to the memory of a great horse and many are trying to capitalize— sometimes artfully, sometimes in a tacky way.

I, too, am drawn to the memory of a great horse. My mission—to paint a fresh portrait in words of the great Secretariat—has brought me to this unveiling thousands of miles from home. I've caught wind, you see, of a curious fact: The bronze we are about to see will feature not just the horse, with his jockey up, but the groom. Think of all the bronzes, paintings, even photographs of legendary horses. In most, the horse alone is captured for posterity, and in some works of art, the jockey has a place on the great runner's back. The groom, the lowly groom, is almost never depicted.

I have hardly begun my journey, but already there's a theme for the book cooking in my brain. The theme is connectedness between a human and an animal, and day by day I'm realizing that the exquisite horse whose story I would tell had forged a profound connection with the man who cared for him—cared for him in every sense of the phrase. And it seems that Secretariat's sculptor and I are of the same mind. We want to honor the one rarely honored: the groom.

Ron Turcotte has arrived at the park in his wheelchair. He has driven all the way from New Brunswick, Canada, in his van and hooked up in Lexington with his brother, Aurele, who has flown down from his home in Quebec. Air travel, Ron Turcotte tells me, is a nightmare for those who use wheels to get around. He gave up on it a long time ago. He's wearing a blue blazer with a round decal over his heart that shows a stylized horse and jockey in a Stars and Stripes motif. The jacket is the one they gave him when he was inducted into Thoroughbred Racing's Hall of Fame at Saratoga in 1979. On Turcotte's right lapel is a pin that depicts the Secretariat postage stamp issued in 1999.

The memorabilia buyers soon suss him out and line up to have him sign their framed photos of Secretariat, bobble-head dolls, posters, framed art, T-shirts, and ball caps. Turcotte is wearing a sea blue cap of his own. BREED MORE SECRETARIATS, it reads.

A vendor is trying to persuade Turcotte to sign a ceramic jockey's boot—a replica of the one he wore during his Triple Crown rides, black, with wide brown trim at the top. Vendor and jockey seem to be negotiating. This is what baseball, football, and hockey players complain about: merchandisers who use an athlete's signature to jack up the price of their wares. I am astonished by the range and the sentimentality of some of these wares, and I wonder, Who buys these trinkets? And do china-shop rules apply? If Turcotte drops the ceramic boot, is it, de facto, his?

An old jock like Turcotte is used to autograph hounds and he doesn't mind keeping them waiting while he poses for photos with some track cronies. One is another ex-jockey, Bobby Ussery, who rode against Turcotte umpteen times and Secretariat a few times. He is wearing a U.S.A. ball cap and a blue shirt with the top three buttons undone to reveal a hairy, fleshy chest and about a pound of gold jewelry at his neck. The two old jocks are laughing, with Turcotte telling some tale from decades ago—something about wrestling in the tack room with another jockey for possession of a wallet.

The old jocks reminisce in the way that war veterans do: They never talk of actual fighting, only of the jolly stuff before and after battle. Jockey Jerry Bailey (he rode Cigar and retired in 2006) once said that his work is so dangerous that jockeys count themselves lucky if they come through a race unscathed. Imagine what it's like to be a jockey. Imagine bending your knees as if you were sitting in a chair (without the support of an actual chair), and maintaining that crouch for minutes, your calves and thighs straining while a great deal happens all around you. Other riders and their horses advance and recede;

they may jostle and bump your horse, and there is the ever-present risk that your horse will catch the heels of the one in front—with catastrophic results. Your saddle is tiny, the perch precarious, and you'd better have fine balance. You need soft hands to feel the horse through the reins, you need great strength to hold him, and you need dexterity to switch the crop from one hand to the other. You need, above all, guts. Did I mention that your "chair" is five feet in the air and moving along at forty miles an hour?

"It's not really if you're going to get hurt when you become a jockey," Bailey said, "it's how many times, how severe, and you hope that you don't take the big hit, which is being paralyzed."

In his official biography, *The Will to Win,* Ron Turcotte concedes that it was not death he feared on the racetrack, but paralysis. His worst nightmare unfolded in the eighth race at Belmont, July 13, 1978, when he was aboard a filly named Flag of Leyte Gulf. The filly clipped the heels of another and down he went—slung like a stone from a shot, as he later drew the picture. It was the jockey's last race, number 20,281.

Ron and Aurele Turcotte take time to pose for a five-minute-sketch artist who—for nine dollars—will capture your likeness and set it on a cartoon horse. "Put a little wrinkle in my forehead," Ron tells the artist. "It was always there." Or was it? He seems playful with his brother and his old pals, somewhat wary and bored with strangers. He was a gifted and much-honored jockey, whose fortune, and misfortune, was to ride a perfect horse. When that horse lost the odd race, the second-guessers came out of the woodwork. Turcotte's face is puffy and pale, and I'm told he battles chronic pain, heart trouble, and all manner of infection, yet there is mischief in those eyes, too.

Early in his career, Ron Turcotte learned that a young groom was helping himself to the jock's supply of Chiclets. On another occasion, a groom was nicking his doughnuts. Turcotte's cure, in the first instance, was to fill a Chiclets box with Feen-a-mint, a laxative, and, in the second instance, to bait a jelly doughnut in the same manner. In the tack room or on the track, Turcotte played for keeps.

Down the way, the still-youthful Eddie Maple, in black wraparound sunglasses, blue jeans, and a blazer the color of racetrack turf, has similarly been circled by fans clutching shopping bags teeming with Secretariat trinkets. Maple was the last man to ride Secretariat in a race, at Woodbine, in Toronto, more than three decades ago.

"Why do we still care about Secretariat?" I ask him as he signs.

"The fact," he replies, as if reading off a shopping list, "that he was the first horse to win the Triple Crown in twenty-five years, the way he won the Belmont, the fact that he was a beautiful horse."

"Was he smooth?" a young girl asks him before handing him her eight-by-eleven poster to sign. Maple asks, and receives, permission to borrow the back of another girl as he affixes his signature. "One of the smoothest horses I ever rode," he replies while signing, an answer that seems to please both girls immensely. The girls are wide-eyed, and I would bet the house they are Pony Clubbers. In the ample paddocks behind them, dozens of sleek horses and elegantly attired riders are trotting and cantering through their warm-ups. All those horses and riders act as if *they* are the thing and we are the backdrop, but from the vantage point of the tents, it is the other way around.

Inside the largest of the white tents, with the Secretariat bronze hidden behind a tall white curtain, several hundred people have gathered to witness the moment of unveiling. Some have lined up in the sun for an hour or more to get choice spots near the bronze.

Donna Brothers—an ex-jockey whose face and voice would be familiar to anyone who takes in globally televised broadcasts of the Kentucky Derby, the Preakness, and the Belmont (mounted on a track pony, she interviews the winning jockey right after each race)—acts as master of ceremonies and introduces speakers as they approach the lectern. The lineup is impressive: Secretariat's owner, two jockeys and an exercise rider, and one of the horse's biographers.

Jimmy Gaffney, one of the big chestnut's old exercise riders, says, "Secretariat was the greatest racehorse that ever lived." Gaffney started galloping horses when he was sixteen years old and rode horses at tracks all over the country. Age and emphysema and, more recently, throat cancer have put a halt to all that. Until just a few years ago, he worked at the track as a pari-mutuel clerk. If, for example, you put five dollars on Woebegone to win the fourth, a clerk such as Gaffney will punch in the data and give you your ticket—which you will crumple in your fist when Woebegone comes in last.

Gaffney tells the throng what they want to hear, but I take from the emotion in his voice that he means what he says when he declares, "Secretariat changed my life forever. Every time I had the privilege to get on his back, I felt the incredible, awesome sense of power. It's a feeling I'll never forget." His voice breaks as he declares that while we may yet again see another Triple Crown winner, "We will never ever see another Secretariat."

Jimmy Gaffney was among the first to realize that Secretariat would be a great one. He used to brag about the horse on shed row—to fellow riders, to writers like Bill Nack, to his own wife and his mother. His mother sent him a pommel pad (sometimes inserted under the saddle for extra comfort) with SECRETARIAT knitted in blue letters on a white backing. Then Gaffney himself bought two blue saddle pads (the quilted cloth on which the saddle sits) and had SECRETARIAT stitched onto them, as well. Finally, he took home the exercise saddle he normally used with Secretariat and, with his leatherwork kit, hammered SECRETARIAT into its side. All this naming and heralding long before the horse had won his maiden race.

Up next is Eddie Maple, who talks about the pressure he faced going into that last race at Woodbine for the Canadian International Championship on October 28, 1973. "I figured," he says, "this would have been the end of my life if something happened." He means that had Secretariat lost, a black cloud would have hung over the name of Eddie Maple until his dying day.

The rider gives way to the sculptor, Ed Bogucki (pronounced Bo-*gook*-ee), who describes a brush with death while working on the bronze. He was outside when a gust of wind blew down a heavy ladder, which would have crowned him had it not crashed onto Eddie Sweat's bronze head instead. The sculptor thanks his "black angel," but strangely, no one from Sweat's family is here. In fact, I do not see a single black face amid the hundreds here.

Ron Turcotte gets laughter and applause when he thanks Penny Chenery for holding the event on his birthday—his thirty-first. (He is, in fact, five days away from his sixty-third birthday.) He thanks the owner for putting him up on "the greatest horse who ever lived. I could talk about him all day long," he says. "He was a charming horse, a lovely horse, and we used to fight over who was going to get up on him."

Turcotte makes an interesting point about the blinkers that Secretariat wore. The horse did not actually need them, but he came to associate them with work, and this was a horse who loved to work. The blue-and-white blinkers, like the number 1A on the saddle pad he wore in the Kentucky Derby, would come to identify him. Today, reveals Turcotte, he is getting more mail about Secretariat than he did in 1973.

Last to speak is Penny Chenery, who remembers the exhilaration of the Belmont. "I would love to know what he was thinking that day," she says. "Why did he keep on running when he'd passed everybody by almost an eighth of a mile? My gut feeling is that it was his home track and he was ready for that race. I just think he got out there and put away Sham early and just felt 'Okay, I feel good, I'm just going to show them how I can run.' He was in the zone. There was no acceleration, no deceleration. It was the same stride. You had the feeling that he could just keep on going."

Chenery thanks the horse's trainer, Lucien Laurin, who, she says, "made all of us. He made Ronnie, he made Jimmy, he made me." She observes, as she has many times before, that perhaps only a "tough-minded" trainer like Laurin could have brought out the greatness in a horse like Secretariat.

"The other, really important part of his life," says Chenery, "was Eddie Sweat." She explains that either Eddie or exercise rider Charlie Davis ("they were great buddies," she notes) would sleep outside the horse's stall when Secretariat was shipped from track to track. "I'm sure," Chenery says, "they were a very important part of his sense of well-being." It seems a great pity that Charlie Davis is not here, either.

Finally, to fanfare, the tall white curtain falls away from the thirty-foot-high scaffolding and there are gasps and applause from the audience. Ed Bogucki's fifteen-hundred-pound creation is life-size and up on a pedestal, so the horse we would have looked up to at least figuratively now looms over us literally. A battery of strategically placed floodlights on the scaffolding illuminates the upper portion of the bronze, but everything below is cast in shadow. The effect, strangely, is to make the horse seem more real, a step closer to flaming into being. The most striking aspect of the piece are Secretariat's eyes. Eddie Sweat's eyes are cast in shadow, and Ron Turcotte looks to be squinting. The horse's eyes, on the other hand, are wide and blazing.

The bronze jockey has a tight grip on the reins, and Eddie Sweat has his right hand on the horse's side and a firm grip on the chain at the horse's mouth. But Secretariat appears so muscled, so taut and ready to explode, that even frozen in this bronze pose he looks like he could carry us all into the next life.

In 1937, when Ed Bogucki was five years old, he clipped a photo of Man o' War from *Life* magazine. Growing up in Racine, Wisconsin, the son of Polish immigrants, the boy was revealing a gift for fine art and an intense interest in animals.

"I know it doesn't make sense," he would say fifty-four years later, "but I just felt there was something that was going to be done. I just liked him very much. I don't know what it was, maybe destiny."

That year, 1991, the Kentucky Horse Park invited Bogucki—who was by then a prominent name in the world of equine art—to create bronzes of both Man o' War and Secretariat. The park invited fifteen artists to contribute art for a show that would be called "Man o' War and Secretariat: Thoroughbreds of the Century."

Fred Stone, a California artist, contributed a watercolor he had done in 1982. The work, called *The Final Thunder,* shows groom Will Harbut out in a paddock, holding and facing a still-robust Man o' War, who looks out to the viewer with keen interest. Above them, illustrious horses race toward that great finish line in the sky. Inspiration, says Stone, came from the 1948 Vaughn Monroe song "Ghost Riders in the Sky." The idea behind the watercolor, Stone later explained, "is that the old man and the horse are standing out in the sun just before they died." Groom and horse died within a month of each other. The artist's aim was to depict the close relationship between that man and that horse.

For the art show at Kentucky Horse Park, Stone did a watercolor called *The Final Tribute*. This one likewise deploys the ghostly horse in the sky (Ron Turcotte up in the clouds, the distinctive 1A on the saddle pad, Secretariat wearing the Derby wreath of roses). The watercolor feels a little over the top, not least because it puts the poor jockey in the hereafter long before his time. On the other hand, the lower portion of the watercolor—depicting a youthful Secretariat in his paddock—is riveting. His tail is aswirl, his mane is up and flying, and the power in his stride has been vividly caught.

Christine Picavet, a French-born artist now living in New Mexico, saw Secretariat often at Claiborne. "Most of the time when they turned him out," she told *Equine Images* magazine, apparently laughing as she told the story, "he would run around the paddock and then come back by the fence and roll in the mud puddle. So, if you wanted to see him clean, you had about five minutes." He was like a little kid playing in the mud, she said.

Someone once sent Penny Chenery a photograph of the horse covered in mud, an image that delighted her. She called the photograph "a gloriously human picture of a champion." On the track, he was all business, Chenery said, but at Claiborne "his personality developed. . . . He was always doing something."

Picavet's oil on linen shows the horse running freely in his paddock, and he looks to be floating across the grass against an almost impressionistic backdrop of trees. He looks smooth and silky, as fluid as water. You can imagine that sitting on him would be like sitting on a cloud pushed across the sky by a wild wind.

The artist first saw the horse at Claiborne in the mid-1970s, just a few years after he had retired. She thought him a bit overweight, but he still struck her as one of the most beautiful horses she had ever seen.

"His body was just perfect," she said later. "He had the most gorgeous head, so broad and kind. He had incredible hind legs, especially from the hock to the ankle, set well beneath the mass of his hindquarters. It is something you rarely see."

Jim Reno, a sculptor from Texas, produced a life-size bronze of Secretariat for that show at the horse park. It stands just outside the entryway. I like what Reno said about the horse more than the work itself, which struck me as stolid. The irony is that less than a hundred yards away, high on a lofty pedestal and surrounded by a moat of water, is the almost one-quarter-larger-than-life-size bronze of Man o'War. I met several Secretariat admirers in Lexington who expressed deep disappointment that the Reno bronze was so flat—as dull as the Man o'War statue was noble.

In the Man o'War versus Secretariat sweepstakes, it seemed to them, the horse park had weighed in on the former's side. I had to admit that it felt that way. The Man o'War bronze stands at the end of a long walkway, a little like the Arc de Triomphe at the end of the Champs-Elysées. The circular moat and the fountains grant Man o'War even more grandeur, and the viewer feels compelled to walk all around the statue and see the horse from every angle. As you walk, you pass bronze plaques that capture moments in his life and bear testimony to his greatness. You look up to the statue and feel only awe. Knowing that Man o'War's bones lie below him only heightens that sense.

Secretariat, meanwhile, has a lesser location. He stands off to the side by the entryway and is partly hidden by a low hedge. Even though Man o'War is farther from the gates, you cannot miss him; Secretariat, you can easily miss. He seems, by comparison, small, an afterthought. His polite admirers are disappointed; the less courteous ones are outraged.

This is what Reno, who saw the horse in the flesh three times, said of Secretariat: "It's like God said, 'You just think you've seen horses. I'm gonna show you a horse.' Then he built Secretariat. He just stood out like a diamond—beautiful conformation. He had the look of an eagle; he'd just look right through you."

Reno also did a bronze, twenty inches tall and thirty-two inches long, of Secretariat being ridden flat out by Ron Turcotte during a morning workout. Late in July of 1973, Reno had gone to Saratoga to take measurements for the bronze. Reno is a former hot walker (one who walks horses after races and workouts to cool them down), exercise rider, jockey, show jumper, horse breaker, and trainer, so he comes to equine art from a world of hands-on horsemanship. He remembered how effortlessly Secretariat moved, and how he would look off in the distance—"like he could see something far away that we couldn't—it was almost eerie. There was no question in his mind. He knew he was great."

Eddie Sweat held Secretariat while Reno took the three dozen or so measurements he required. The only one he didn't get was the width across the gaskin (a horse's so-called second thigh), since Reno's incursion to that area prompted a kick. Eddie also warned Reno not to touch Secretariat's ears. "He didn't like anybody messing with his ears," Reno recalled.

Reno's measuring offered him some insight into the horse's power and stride. For one thing, Secretariat measured thirty-one inches from his withers (the highest part of the back) to his bottom line (the belly) and thirty-five inches from that line to the ground. And while his shoulder measured twenty-seven inches, his head was twenty-five inches. On almost all horses, those measurements are all the same. (Humans, Reno pointed out, have a similar synchronicity: We are all eight heads tall—multiply the height of your head by eight and, invariably, that's your height.) Secretariat also had four more inches on his legs than is normal, yet despite that length of leg, he had an extremely short cannon bone, at nine inches. (The cannon is the long, straight bone above the horse's fetlock, or ankle.) Reno believed that the horse's long forearm, long shoulder, and short cannon bone lay behind his extraordinary reach and long stride.

The artist Richard Stone Reeves was commissioned by Penny Chenery in June of 1973—not long after the Belmont—to paint Secretariat. He drove to Belmont Park a week after the race to do some preliminary work on the painting. "I don't think," recalled Reeves, "any horse I've ever painted posed with more elegance. He seemed to enjoy being brought out into the early-morning sun and stood patiently in various positions for me until I was finished. Then he was reluctant to be taken back to his stall. His groom, Eddie Sweat, was wonderful with him. The two obviously were good friends and Eddie was just as patient as Secretariat."

Reeves's oil on canvas, fourteen inches by eight inches, shows Eddie in his porkpie hat on the left, holding the lead shank in his right hand, with the remaining length folded neatly into his left. Eddie's focus is all on the horse, and he is holding the shank at chest level, presumably to keep Secretariat's head up and off the tempting grass below. A horse blanket lies on the ground between horse and man, and the gorgeous young horse has his head turned to the painter with a slightly resigned look, as if his pal Eddie has asked him to do this thing, to stand and pose, and he, as any good friend would, has complied.

Ed Bogucki is a stickler for conformational detail, and he hunted down rare archival footage at the Arlington International Racecourse of Man o'War competing at the height of his career. He also borrowed photographs from fellow artist Helen Hayse, who had seen the original Big Red in person when she was a child and again when she was sixteen years old.

Like Bogucki, Hayse made a point of including the groom in her art. Her oil painting of Man o'War, completed in 1987, shows the proud horse with Will Harbut, the horse looking somewhat tense but undeniably awesome, his groom so relaxed that you would think he were holding an old two-dollar-a-ride pony.

Helen Hayse told *Equine Images* in 1991 that she never got over her first encounter with Man o'War. "He was magnificent," she said. "He looked like an emperor should ride him at the head of a conquering army. In his middle years, when he was at his physical best, he was more muscular with a high head that looked out over the world, like he was the king of everything he surveyed."

A well-known equine artist, Hayse, who died in 2003, did five paintings of Man o'War before she was satisfied that she had captured him. In 1987, the same year she painted Man o'War, Hayse painted Secretariat and found herself comparing the two horses. Secretariat was pretty, Hayse maintained; "Man o'War was magnificent."

Ed Bogucki, who takes a different view, saw Secretariat in 1989. Bogucki pronounced him plump (in the rich archival literature on Secretariat, you can find ample testimony to back that observation). But even then, in his dotage, the horse had stature. "My impression," Bogucki recalled, "was that he was carrying a lot of weight. I thought he was too heavy. I didn't want to show him as he was then. I wanted him light and active and in the prime of his career. Still, for all that, I was impressed. He still had a lot of power, yet he was easy. You feel a stallion's power even though he's not running and you feel the great-ness. He oozed it."

The sculptor, with the blessing of a stud groom at Claiborne, ran his hands over Secretariat. Bogucki checked out the horse's cannon bones, fetlocks, knees, shoulders, withers, gaskins, the set of the tail. He watched him walk and run.

"He *did* have the look of eagles," said Bogucki. "It was a pleasure to run my hands over him, and he was so patient for all this."

Bogucki's task for the Kentucky Horse Park show in 1991 was to create a one-third-life-size version of the horse. Like many sculptors, he was inclined to include the jockey. So, during the spring of 1990, Bogucki traveled to Saratoga Springs, New York, to meet with Ron

Turcotte, who was there for celebrations to mark the fortieth anniversary of the Racing Hall of Fame. Bogucki photographed him, measured him, and videotaped him for the sake of accuracy. The sculptor had by then chosen the moment—just seconds after the Kentucky Derby win—he would immortalize.

At that point, Eddie Sweat did not figure in the bronze that was forming in Ed Bogucki's head. But as he pored over archival material, which he later admitted was "overwhelming" in size, he spotted one photograph that changed everything. It was a shot that Raymond Woolfe—author of a very fine photo essay entitled *Secretariat*—had taken the day that Eddie Sweat handed his horse over to the stud manager at Claiborne Farm. I had seen the photograph early on in my research and it immediately drew me to the character of Eddie Sweat. It struck me that here was a man of substance and great feeling. The image was of Eddie seen from behind and standing by a low wall while wiping a tear from his eye with his left hand. (Woolfe later told me that this black-and-white shot, and a similar one on the plane—of Secretariat gripping Eddie's ski jacket with his teeth—are his two favorite images of the hundreds in the book. Many of the images are in color, and many are splendid, so his comment is telling.)

"I knew Eddie liked the horse very much," Bogucki told me, his comment purposely understated. "I knew he *had* to be in the statue and that the combination would make a good presentation. No one is closer to a horse than a groom. Eddie really loved that horse. To exclude him wouldn't have been proper. The combination—Eddie and Secretariat—was essential to the Derby win."

In 1991, Bogucki asked Eddie Sweat—then rubbing horses, as ever, at Belmont in New York—to come to Wisconsin and check the nearly completed clay model for accuracy. Bogucki sent him plane tickets in the mail, but Eddie had to fit in the trip between morning and evening feedings at the track. It must have been a hectic day: from the airport in New York to the one in Milwaukee, then whisked out to Bogucki's small farm in rural Wisconsin, three hours with the sculptor, and then back to New York and the track.

The sculptor recalled how moved Sweat was to see himself included in the work. "You got my boots and my hat!" Eddie enthused when he got closer to the model. Sweat talked at length about what was happening in those adrenaline-filled moments after the Derby win. He confirmed what Ron Turcotte had earlier told Bogucki: The horse was still so wired, so "on the muscle," that he practically dragged his groom all the way to the winner's circle. The race had siphoned off only a portion of his drive.

"Secretariat," said Bogucki, "had a ton of energy left. His blood was pumping. For the bronze, I wanted the horse really collected and ready to burst out."

The groom has his right hand on the horse for a reason. "Eddie's touch would have been a calming influence," Bogucki said. "They're talking. It's almost a mental thing. You hook into an animal." Then Bogucki told a story about training one of his Arab horses and how the horse would lose focus the instant Bogucki lost his. I heard him say that the connection between human and horse can be lost in a heartbeat, like a telephone connection. Suddenly, the line is dead. Eddie Sweat's arm and voice—that and his intimacy with this horse—afforded such a connection.

The other reason Eddie Sweat would have laid his hand on the horse, said the sculptor, was to get a sense of his intentions. The horse was so energized, and yet so caught in the crush of well-wishers, that the groom must have feared for their safety as well as his own. The horse would have instinctively moved into the groom's rigid arm, offering Eddie Sweat at least a little control over a potentially dangerous circumstance.

Eddie Sweat impressed the sculptor as a kind and gentle man.

They connected immediately and talked, in a loose and amicable way, about buying a horse together. It was not idle talk, and it was a measure of how comfortable and trusting each was in the other's company. "I had the pleasure," Ed Bogucki said, "of having a very good friend very quickly. I genuinely liked and admired him. He was not a big man, but short and powerful and considerably strong. He was very dedicated in everything he did, and I wished I'd had the pleasure of knowing him longer."

For Ed Bogucki, the Secretariat bronze represents the contributions of all grooms, exercise riders, and hot walkers, the people who work on, and sometimes live on, shed row (or the backside, as some call it). They do so much, he told me, and get no credit.

By this time, all my instincts as I researched my book were pointing me toward the backstretch. I was interested, of course, in Secretariat's owner and trainer and jockey, but it was the so-called bottom echelon of Secretariat's circle that now called to me. Eddie Sweat, his bond with that horse, how Eddie saw the horse, and, as best I could determine, how the horse viewed Eddie: That's what I wanted to explore.

It bothered Bogucki that Eddie was so subservient. "Hat in hand and all that crap" was how Bogucki put it. It was one of the first things the sculptor talked about when I met him outside an art gallery in Lexington in the summer of 2004. "Eddie would say, 'Yes, boss' when I'd ask him something," Bogucki said. "'I'm not your boss,' I'd tell him. 'Yes, boss,' Eddie would reply."

Ed Bogucki was wearing blue jeans and a fashionable striped shirt. His white hair fell over his forehead in bangs, and he struck me as an older, thinner version of that TV performer from my childhood, Captain Kangaroo. Bogucki was seventy-two years old, though he looked far younger, and I thought of what an old horseman had once told me: "Horses keep you young."

Sweat told Bogucki many stories about his old charge, including a funny one about why the horse was late arriving to the paddock for the Derby. It seems that Secretariat had nodded off and lain down in his stall before the race. Eddie had to rouse him, clean away the bits of bedding that were stuck to him, and make him presentable to the world of racing.

The original small bronze from the art show at Kentucky Horse Park found, naturally enough, an admirer in Penny Chenery. She liked its vitality and spirit, and she set about organizing a fund-raising committee to commission another bronze by Bogucki. This one would be slightly different in some details. But more importantly, it would be life-size.

In 1999, the fund-raiser got the kick-start it needed. Chenery contacted Sotheby's and organized an international sale of Secretariat memorabilia through Amazon.com. Fans and admirers of the horse were also invited to contribute to the fund, and many did.

Bogucki, meanwhile, also made a detail of the bronze—just the horse's head and shoulders—and set it on a wooden base. He signed it "To Eddie Sweat, a friend." But getting the minisculpture to Sweat proved difficult, for he could not be found. Finally, Bogucki got in touch with a racing broadcaster in New York named Andee Brown, who was able to find him. Brown organized a conference call, linking the sculptor and the groom. Sweat was recovering from open-heart surgery, and he seemed happy to know the statue was coming his way.

This was late in 1997, when Eddie was also ill with leukemia, kidney disease, heart disease, and asthma, ailments that finally forced him to leave the employ of Roger Laurin (Lucien's son) the following year. He died at North Shore University Hospital in Manhasset, New York, on April 18, 1998.

Jimmy Gaffney knew that Eddie and his family were in need of help in the days before he died. Through a mutual friend, the exercise rider sent the groom a check. But the friend brought it back. Eddie did not have a bank account and therefore could not cash the check. Gaffney sent him cash instead.

"Can you imagine?" Gaffney said to me. "No bank account."

Gaffney had read somewhere that Eddie Sweat had gambled away a lot of the money he had earned while grooming Secretariat. Gaffney was simply lofting a clay pigeon in order to shoot it down, and this he did quickly and with alacrity, the anger rising in him as he spoke. Cancer has destroyed Gaffney's saliva glands, so that sometimes, on the phone, there would be a pause while he took a drink of water to lubricate his throat.

"Eddie never gambled in his life," said Gaffney. "He never bet the horses." It irked Gaffney that some reporter had besmirched the reputation of a friend, a good and honest man. Pity that Eddie Sweat did not possess Jimmy Gaffney's entrepreneurial spirit. Gaffney, you see, had saved some of Secretariat's horseshoes—forty of them—and fortified his track pension by selling them. One shoe, worn in the horse's first race, was recently auctioned off for thirteen thousand dollars.

Gaffney knew when he rode Secretariat that he was going to be a great champion. "Right away," he told me, "I noticed his power. He was a little rough and hard to hold and he had a habit of ducking left on the track when a rider would pull him up after a gallop, a habit we corrected with a full-cheek snaffle [a type of bit]. But there was just something about him. It's hard to explain, but even in the walk you could feel his power."

Gaffney told Bill Nack, "Start taking notes." Nack was then a track hound hard on the trail of Riva Ridge, and he must have heard many hot tips in his days on the backstretch. This was one he acted on. "I've been on good horses all my life," Gaffney said. "I was the first one to recognize Secretariat's greatness. And I rode him just about every day for thirteen months. I told my mother, 'This is going to be a great horse.' I knew that sucker could run."

Raymond Woolfe's book contains several shots of Jimmy Gaffney up on the two-year-old Secretariat. In one, the rider is up out of the saddle and perched over the horse's neck and flying mane. "Galloping in the early days," the caption reads. All of the horse's feet are off the ground, and there is great symmetry in the image. I am jealous of the rider's position; I want to be up there, feeling all that power under restraint.

In another shot, likely taken right after the gallop, the rider has stopped his horse and turned him sideways to pose for the camera. Exercise rider Charlie Davis is on another horse behind, but he looks nowhere near as pleased as Gaffney. The eye is drawn first to his horse, to the slight tension in him, and the undeniable look of pride on Jimmy Gaffney's face. He has strong arms, strong eyebrows and hawkish features. His smile does indeed seem to say, This sucker I'm on can run. One day you'll read about him.

In other images, these in color, Gaffney is seen in his red riding helmet, the goggles attached, and a bright yellow cardigan—"Perry Como sweaters," we used to call them—which seems at odds with his brown leather riding boots. Gaffney is holding Secretariat, facing him as someone else hoses him down. The veins are popping at the horse's neck and shoulder. Another shot shows Gaffney hot-walking the big horse after that same bath. A big red blanket, edged in black, with LL (for Lucien Laurin) at the haunch, drapes the horse. Secretariat has a soft look in his eye and, with the blanket tucked up close to his head, reminds me of an infant swaddled and ready for sleep.

Gaffney said he cried when Secretariat won the Triple Crown, and he cried again on those few occasions when the horse lost. He is most bitter about the Wood Memorial on April 21, 1973, when Secretariat finished third, four lengths back.

Gaffney rode the horse three-eighths of a mile the day before the race and found him sluggish, so much so that he had to kick him into gear. He knew there was something wrong with the horse, and he reported that fact to Henry Hoeffner, an assistant to Laurin. Meanwhile, there had been a death in Laurin's family—that of his father-in-law. The result was high stress in the Meadow Stable's barn and also confusion, and it's unclear whether Laurin was actually aware of the dramatic change in the horse's condition. A vet, meanwhile, had discovered a small abscess in Secretariat's mouth just before the race, but he didn't believe it was problematic. In any case, wisely or not, Secretariat ran in the Wood Memorial.

Laurin and Gaffney then had what the latter called "a big blowout," and Gaffney quit Laurin's employ just before the Belmont.

If Eddie Sweat had died penniless, Jimmy Gaffney blamed the trainer. He remembered Laurin saying to him, " 'Stick with this horse, Jimmy, and I'll take good care of you.' " Gaffney told me, "I worked my ass off. I really made Secretariat into a champion racehorse. But my bonus was nothing like what I expected. 'I'll make it up to you,' Lucien told me. Well, he never did."

Jimmy Gaffney has a vivid memory of sitting on a bale of hay, drinking a can of beer, with Eddie Sweat after one of Secretariat's victories. The owner and trainer were heading off to a champagne dinner, and Eddie and Jimmy looked on as the limousines pulled up.

I offered the opinion that nowhere is the disparity between the haves and have-nots played out quite so dramatically as it is on the racetrack. The winner's circle inevitably excludes the very ones who know the horse best and love him most. I told Gaffney that although I had never met Eddie Sweat, I did have a powerful sense of the man, and the more I learned about him, the more outraged I was that he had died so poor. Ed Bogucki had included him in the bronze, but the process of exclusion continued in other ways. "Where," I asked, "was Eddie Sweat's family at the time of the unveiling? Were they not invited? Where was Charlie Davis, the black exercise rider who also rode Secretariat? Where, for that matter, were the African-American admirers of Secretariat? Are there none?"

"It's funny you should say that," Gaffney replied. "My wife was there, and she said the exact same thing." Then I told Gaffney about something I had read, somewhere among all the clippings at the Keeneland Library: that Eddie Sweat had somehow squandered his earnings.

"Are you kiddin' me?" Gaffney shot back. He was practically spitting rage at this wild untruth that had found its way into print.

During a long telephone conversation just before he died, Eddie Sweat had apparently complained to Jimmy Gaffney that he had been badly treated. I'm not sure that Eddie used those precise words, but that, apparently, was the sentiment. Did Eddie mean that his contributions as a gifted groom had not been fully recognized? Did he mean that the wages of a groom—even the groom of the great Secretariat—don't amount to a hill of beans, and that only as he lay dying did he fully grasp that fact? Or was he voicing, finally, a lament on behalf of all on shed row whose love for a horse begets them that horse's love, and precious little else?

The night before the unveiling, there was a black-tie dinner in Lexington, to which Gaffney and his wife were invited. "*Now* I'm invited to some of these parties. I wasn't then," he said, meaning the early 1970s, when he was part of backstretch society. The beer/champagne divide was, and is, as tall as some horses.

But for all his bitterness, and he is palpably bitter, Jimmy Gaffney loved the work of exercise rider. "I did it all my life," he said. "I miss the smell of a horse, right now. And I loved Secretariat. Despite anything you may have read, he was not a dangerous horse. He might nip Eddie if Eddie was working around the horse's testicles, but he wasn't mean; he was playful. He had this unique way of accelerating; he'd pull his legs up and out. It was very unusual, but it sure worked."

As for Eddie Sweat, Gaffney has an image of him driving Lucien Laurin's red horse van—to and from Belmont, to and from South Carolina, to and from Florida. For Gaffney, the image of Eddie behind the wheel of that van speaks volumes of the great confidence that owner and trainer had in him. In the barn, on the highway, night or day, Shorty Sweat, they knew, would always do right by the horses entrusted to him. "He had a way with horses," said Gaffney. "He knew how to manage them. It's hard to say what distinguishes a good groom from a bad groom, but Eddie was Lucien's best groom. He was reliable; he was there all the time."

There is a saying on the backstretch to describe a groom preparing a horse after a race—rubbing him down, bathing him, organizing his food, blanketing him, making him comfortable: "Do him up," a trainer will say, and the groom will know, or should, precisely what that means. By all accounts, Eddie could do a horse up as well as, or better than, anyone else in the business.

Groom to a multimillion-dollar horse, he died a pauper. In an author's note to the 2002 edition of *Secretariat: The Making of a Champion,* Bill Nack wrote that Eddie Sweat's handling of Secretariat had made him "the most renowned groom in America." That groom lives on in Ed Bogucki's bronze, but bronze is cold. Cold comfort.

⌒

Bill Nack spoke longest that day at the Kentucky Horse Park when the bronze of Secretariat was unveiled. He seemed an old hand at the lectern, relaxed and chatty. He linked his stories together in a neat garland, as if he had told these tales a thousand times before, which, no doubt, he had, for more than thirty years had passed since the first telling.

What impresses me most about William Nack—elegantly dressed that day in a gray tweed jacket and a yellow tie dappled with variously colored profiles of jockeys' torsos—is how lyrically and yet how quickly he wrote, always to a magazine's deadline, about Secretariat. He seemed to be on the scene for every critical moment in the horse's life: every race, many of his workouts, every critical passage. Nack had the sense, and the good fortune, to be there and to get it all down.

Nack even compiled, with the aid of Lucien Laurin and his assistant Henry Hoeffner, a log detailing the horse's training regimen for every single day from January 20, 1972, when the horse arrived at Hialeah from the Meadow Stud, to November 12, 1973, when he was shipped from Belmont to Claiborne Farm.

I had seen a copy of the log at Keeneland Library. The type clearly emanated from a typewriter—a Corona, it turns out—and it speaks volumes of Nack's mission that he would set out to compose such a logbook, like a courtier following in a king's footsteps as he walked in sand day after day, the courtier measuring and recording in his book the depth and size of the print, the length of stride, the weather and circumstances of the day.

"Walk," the log might read, or "Jog," "Gallop," "Half mile in 47⅗." Every race, too, was listed. Sometimes there was an asterisk, as for September 16, 1972, when Secretariat won the Futurity Stakes at Belmont. Beside the asterisk is this note: "Ron Turcotte hit Secretariat and went faster than Lucien wanted him to go. 'He's just a baby,' Lucien scolded. 'You're asking too much of him.'"

Nack's long features in *Sports Illustrated* on Secretariat's life and, especially, his death are some of the finest sports journalism I have ever read.

It has been said of Bill Nack that he was to Secretariat what James Boswell was to Samuel Johnson: chief biographer (though Raymond Woolfe might have something to say about that). Nack told a magazine reporter in 1998 something of his own biography: In the summer of 1958, he was a hot walker at Arlington Park in Chicago. He had a notion then of not going to college. "I want to go off with the horses," young Nack told his parents, who reacted as if he had announced his intention to join the circus or become a hobo. Eventually, he did go to the University of Illinois, then fought in Vietnam in the 1968 Tet Offensive. Later, he was hired by *Newsday* (Long Island), where he reported on politics and the environment.

At the magazine's Christmas party in 1971, the eggnog no doubt flowing, Bill Nack stood on a table and recounted every Kentucky Derby winner from 1875 (a horse called Aristides) to the present. That remarkable bit of theater won him the job as *Newsday*'s racing writer.

"I couldn't stop smiling," he said of the time. "They made my hobby my job."

He also had good luck. What if he had picked Sham as the horse he would follow and chronicle? But Nack knows bloodlines, and the Bold Ruler/Princequillo "nick," or combination of bloodlines, was a notable one. Nack was following his own instincts as well as Gaffney's tip when he started taking notes on the young Secretariat.

Nack began his address at the unveiling by citing the ancient Greeks, who thought that the horse, along with the human form, was perfection itself. And in all his years at the track, the sixty-something Nack said he had never seen a horse's conformation to match that of Secretariat. He marveled at the horse's enthusiasm for competition and he called the horse's Triple Crown victory the greatest feat in the history of Thoroughbred horse racing, and one of the greatest feats in the history of sport in America. "He remains," said Nack, "a platonic ideal of the racehorse."

Nack recalled a particular assignment in the wake of Secretariat's dramatic win at Belmont on June 9, 1973—this was the race he had won by thirty-one lengths, setting an American record. Nack's task was to find out where certain prominent people had been during that race.

"I had some fun with it," he began. "I found out from my friend [sportswriter] Heywood Hale Broun that Jack Nicklaus, the great golfer, was watching the Belmont Stakes at home. He ended up on all fours on his den floor, pounding on the floor, as this horse turned for home. Friends looking on were perplexed or aghast, or both. He said, 'I don't know anything about horse racing, but for some reason I was pounding on the floor and tears were coming down.' And he said to Heywood Hale Broun, 'Woody, I don't understand it. Help me understand it.' And Broun said to him, 'Jack, your entire life as a golfer has been a search for perfection. And on June the ninth, you saw it and you recognized it for what it was.'"

In the press box that day at Belmont, there was what Nack called "pandemonium." Meanwhile, up on the third floor—in the track's dining room, in fact—Pete Rozelle was also watching the race. Nack described Rozelle, the commissioner of the National Football League, indeed the father of the modern NFL, as "a very distinguished man."

Rozelle told Nack that what he remembered most about the race was that during Secretariat's spine-tingling stretch run, he felt someone's hands around his ankles. His first thought was that someone had collapsed at his feet. "And I realized," said Rozelle, "I was standing on my table! I have no idea to this day how I got there."

Everyone who had been inside that sprawling, high-ceilinged tent in Lexington laughed, all doubtless remembering where *they* had been when that race was run.

Later, Nack told us, he asked Ron Turcotte what it was like to be on the great horse's back in the last seconds of the Belmont, what he heard and saw. "I heard Sham's hooves disappear behind me," replied the jockey, referring to the horse who finished fifth and last that day after vying for the lead right up to the homestretch. "And then there was nothing," Turcotte went on. "All I could hear was Secretariat breathing and his hooves hitting the ground. It was very quiet."

⌒

Many racing fans assume that all the noise of the grandstand, all that thunder of the hooves, is as loud for the jockeys as it is for spectators. Not so, says contemporary Canadian jockey Chantal Sutherland. She likens that minute or so during a race to entering a tunnel where all is quiet. "You could whisper to the jockey beside you during a race," she once said, "and he could hear you."

What Ron Turcotte heard as he headed for the finish line that day in June of 1973 was an almost surreal quiet—just his horse's breathing and the drumming of his hooves. There was another sound, that of bedlam in the stands as the rafters shook, but Turcotte said it sounded like ocean surf to someone walking just out of sight of the sea. At the mile-and-an-eighth pole, the jockey heard a voice at the hedge yelling, "Ron, go on with that horse!" But when Turcotte looked, there was no one there. "I think," Nack told us, "Ronnie assumed it was God," and we laughed.

In the Belmont, all the horses carried 126 pounds, so Turcotte was able to use his favorite saddle—not one of those flat, tiny leather things, but a heavy cushioned saddle. The jockey once said that riding a racing saddle is like sitting on two rods; riding this big saddle on that big striding horse, he said, was like sitting on a comfortable sofa.

⌒

"He was such a nice horse to gallop," Ron Turcotte was saying, reminiscing on the phone one morning from his home in Drummond, New Brunswick. The unveiling was months away.

"I've heard all kinds of stories about Secretariat," he told me, stories about how mean or spooky the horse was. "The truth is, he never did a thing wrong. He was the kindest horse in the world." Turcotte did remember that morning in New York early on in schooling when Secretariat dropped his first rider. But that was nothing. Jockeys fall off young horses; it's as common as rain dripping down windowpanes.

"Ask anyone," Turcotte went on, pleading Secretariat's case. "Charlie Davis and I used to play around. With me on Secretariat and him on another horse, we'd grab each other, goose each other." The big red horse did not blink an eye.

As for Eddie Sweat, Ron Turcotte heaped praise on the man in the same way that everyone who knew him did. "Eddie was special," the jockey said. "He was special to me. Horses were his life. He was a dedicated, good horseman. That day at Claiborne, he just sat there crying. He just broke down. He had a deeper feeling for that horse. You don't see a dedicated horseman like that anymore. Before the Derby, Eddie slept on a cot in front of Secretariat's stall to make sure no one got to the horse. You didn't have to worry with Eddie. Any horse he looked after was well monitored and guarded."

How was he with horses? I asked Turcotte. He replied that a mean horse would start the day trying to take a chunk out of Eddie, but by day's end, Eddie had that horse eating out of his hand. "He would never scold a horse," the jockey said. "Even if a horse were to rip his pants or take a nip out of him, he would *never* slap a horse. He'd raise his voice a little and he would stare him down. My brother, Noel, and I, that's how we learned. The mean horses, you just leave them alone and stare them down. He ignores you; you ignore him.

Those stories about horse whisperers? Eddie was beyond that. The horse would come to him."

Ron Turcotte likewise had a reputation for getting along with horses. When he worked with his father cutting lumber in the bush around Grand Falls, New Brunswick, he had a favorite workhorse, a Canadian (the breed, I mean) called Bess. "I loved her," he once said. "She was almost human." When his father sold the horse during a long period of unemployment (there were eleven children to feed), Turcotte's feelings were hurt and he headed off to Toronto, hoping to find work as a roofer. But a carpenters' strike put that notion on hold and he survived by digging worms at golf courses during the night. One day, as he paid his rent at the boardinghouse where he was staying, he noticed the Kentucky Derby being shown on television, and his landlord suggested he get a job at the track.

At Woodbine, he was hired on as a hot walker for Pete McCann, trainer for Windfields Farm. Run by E. P. Taylor, Windfields was the most prestigious Thoroughbred farm in Canada and one of the great racing operations in North America. The pay was thirty-five dollars a week; accommodation was a cot in the tack room. Then Turcotte became a groom, and a demanding former jockey named George Thompson was soon showing him the ropes as exercise rider. Turcotte's was a tough apprenticeship: After the first day of riding he was so tired and sore, he could not climb the stairs to his room. Later, on the advice of another jockey, he ate with his left hand for months so the crop would feel natural in either hand. He was not afraid to use the stick, but he never used it needlessly. The muscled rider with the tree-trunk legs got on with his mounts.

I reminded Turcotte of that greeting he used to give Secretariat: He would reach into the horse's mouth and grab his tongue as if shaking a hand. "Eddie would do the same thing," Turcotte said. "He'd grab the tip of Secretariat's tongue to wish him good morning.

Before you knew it, every time Eddie passed his stall, the horse stuck out his tongue."

Ron Turcotte says he used to dream of horses from his early youth, as far back as he can remember. "All boys drew cars," he said. "I drew horses." But not even in his dreams could he have conjured up a horse like Secretariat.

"Riding him," he told me, "it was like a pleasure ride. He was so *agréable* [agreeable]. It was something you dream of. I'd be on him, thinking I was Roy Rogers on Trigger. I'd teach him something one day, and the next day he would do it."

⌒

In the days leading up to the unveiling of the bronze, I feel the need to see those Triple Crown races once again. Jenifer Stermer, the curator of collections at Kentucky Horse Park, takes me into a small room off the museum; then she wheels in a television on a high metal cart, a VCR, and a mittful of videos on Secretariat. I will watch the races in their entirety all by my lonesome in that tiny, high-ceilinged room.

There, in the minutes before the Derby, is Eddie Sweat, looking cool in a red hat. Charlie Davis is up on Billy Silver, providing company and solace to Ron Turcotte and Secretariat. I get a chill seeing the pair move from last at the first turn and then charge for home. In the Preakness, it is the same. Last at the first turn, then the charge from behind. Here comes Secretariat. I am taping all this, so I can replay, if I wish, the audio. The machine also records my awe as the horse charges. "Jesus, Jesus," I can be heard to say.

And then the Belmont. The voice of the announcer, Chic Anderson, saying, "He's moving like a tre-*mend*-ous machine. . . ." And overlaid is my own voice on the tape I will take home—"Oh, oh"— sounding as if I have been hit in the belly by a fist. I am not on the floor, like Nicklaus, nor on a tabletop, like Rozelle, but I am moved all the same, even though I know precisely the choreography of these races. I have read all the books, the racing charts, pored over all the literature, and I knew where and when Secretariat will make his move. And yet I am totally unprepared for what I feel. The heart gives over to exhilaration, the frissons play up and down the spine, and the eyes get wet. I am alone in a room, overcome by something I struggle to define.

As my viewing of the 1973 Belmont draws to a close, I write in my notebook, "Power power power. Flow, flow, flow." But the words seem absurd on the page, and they do this horse no justice, no justice at all. I insert more videos, watch Secretariat getting a bath at Claiborne. He looks so relaxed, his skin so smooth, and the water runs off him as if he were already made of bronze.

I have a friend who lives near Ocala, Florida, a lifelong horse-woman named Carole Fletcher, who is teaching several of her horses to spell—to pick out wooden block letters of the alphabet on voice command. She is a trick-horse trainer, and as kind and patient, and as demanding, as any horse trainer in the world. We had both read a remarkable book called *Beautiful Jim Key,* about "an educated horse" who performed feats of spelling and simple math onstage (he would use his lips to make correct change out of a National Cash Register). This was in the late nineteenth and early twentieth centuries.

Much taken with the book, Carole sought out its author, Mim Eichler Rivas, and visited the horse's grave in Tennessee. The story of Jim Key defies belief, though it's well documented. My question to Carole was this: "Why would a horse like Jim Key even *try* to attempt spelling?"

"It's something we don't understand," said Carole. "When my horse picks out the letter *h,* for example, I can see him thinking. But maybe he's also picking up some message from me, some kind of telepathy." So the horse is perhaps using not only his brain but also some sort of equine receiver in his brain that's sending a message from Carole—"That's the block; pick that one, that one there." Or maybe what the horse sees is an image of the right block, and then his formidable memory kicks in and allows him to complete the task. We may never know.

In her book, Rivas speculates that what motivated Beautiful Jim Key was the desire to please his master—a black man named Dr. William Key, a self-educated veterinarian, a former slave, and the greatest horse whisperer of his time. "The secret," wrote Rivas, "of Beautiful Jim Key's extraordinary abilities was something more than 'simply education.' . . . It was both more than that, yet also more basic. It was love. The love between human and nonhuman was so powerful it had bridged the language divide."

My own speculation is that Eddie Sweat and William Key had both discovered the same secret: that the love of a horse can have particular and spectacular rewards, and one of them is a connection beyond words.

~ 2 ~

THE BACKSTRETCH: EDDIE'S WORLD

HOME FOR A RACETRACK GROOM living on shed row is typically a twelve-by-fourteen room with a concrete floor and a single lightbulb overhead, that classic symbol of penury. Two or more grooms might share this space. There might be roll-out cots, a cheap radio, a little TV with bunny ears. There might be a hot plate and a tiny fridge, though local fire regulations sometimes forbid the use of appliances. Chilly at night, a hot box by day, invariably noisy and smelly and dirty, such accommodation—if one can call it that—often lacks privacy, security, and comfort.

There are no laundry facilities. The window might be carved out of a cinder-block wall, with a blanket over it. The shower and washroom down the hall may not have been cleaned in a long, long time, and some grooms cannot bring themselves to use them. Your neighbor may be a drifter strung out on drugs or alcohol, so petty theft is rampant. There is no rent, which is a small blessing, and references are rarely sought, but you can also be evicted without recourse.

Wages for grooms and hot walkers can be as low as a few hundred dollars a week—for twelve- and fourteen-hour days. Migrant workers, especially, might earn minimum wage but aren't always paid for every hour worked, never mind overtime. The best some grooms can hope for is one day off in thirteen; smaller outfits offer even less. Classier stables may offer a groom up to six hundred dollars a week, with a day or two off every week and bonuses when the horse being rubbed wins a race. All attempts at unionizing grooms have failed: Turnover is too great, and there are always teenage runaways and migrant workers at the gate willing to work for a pittance.

Only a few states in the United States offer pension programs to backstretch workers. Medical coverage is hit-and-miss, although California's Santa Anita Park has an enviable setup: a medical clinic for backside staff, who pay only two dollars a visit, with free hospital and emergency care. The cost is covered, in part, by a share in uncashed pari-mutuel tickets. (Such tickets are issued each time a bet is made at the track, but some tickets are not cashed in—through oversight or the desire for a keepsake or souvenir.) But most grooms felled by accident or illness must depend on charity doled out by the Horsemen's Benevolent and Protective Association.

There is money at the track, lots of it. Churchill Downs, for the Kentucky Derby in 2005, had a new look—a $121 million face-lift, with luxury boxes selling in the quarter-million-dollar range. But, contrary to theory, the wealth does not trickle down to lowly grooms. According to the Jockey Club, some $1.1 billion in purses was won at more than one hundred tracks in North America in 2005. Meanwhile, more than $15 billion was wagered on those same races. Backside workers not only see precious little of this money but get even less than they once did.

That's because the track is facing competition from lotteries and casinos, and attendance at races is declining. Too many trainers are chasing too few owners for work, so the squeeze is put on the men and women at the bottom of the track hierarchy. Trainers charge owners a daily rate to exercise, feed, and house horses (about forty-five to seventy-five dollars a horse), but some trainers will charge far less than their actual costs: They gamble that winnings will make up the shortfall. In the meantime, the only place to trim costs is in labor. And track labor has always been cheap.

Bill Nack described the groom's life in *Sports Illustrated* in 1991. "In New York," he wrote, "the cradle of American racing and the citadel of the sport's eastern establishment, some of the housing for backstretch workers is a scandal." He described how in 1989, Charles Clay, the California-based groom of Sunday Silence (the horse had won the Derby and the Preakness), was appalled by the housing he was offered at Belmont. When he saw his dorm at "the citadel," he scrubbed every inch of it with bleach, set off two cockroach bombs, and put forty roach traps along the walls. "They expect people to live in that kind of filth?" said Clay. "It was a disgrace."

A student at the University of Maryland studied backstretch life for his Ph.D. thesis in 1995. Anthony J. Schefstad called his paper "The Backstretch: Some Call It Home," and he concluded that the backside of the track is "one of the last operating serfdoms in the United States." He documented the low wages, the isolation and boredom, the deplorable housing, but he also noted that grooms' "genuine love of horses" often serves as a substitute "for other satisfactions."

Schefstad found—this was in 1993—that resident grooms in Maryland earned an average of $1,009 a month; hot walkers got $544 a month. Most had little education or training and lacked even a driver's license. Some had entered the United States illegally and were ripe for exploitation. And while several organizations offer help to grooms, the charity is meted out on a case-by-case basis.

Schefstad had worked at the track since 1990 and thus had special access to the private and guarded world of the backstretch. It is a world, he wrote, in which stories circulate about the generosity of trainers who keep sick grooms on full salary, bestow cars on them, pay for their children's operations. "We take care of our own," the stories say. The stories are true, but they are also rare.

Schefstad detailed "a personal communication" he had had in November of 1991 with the president of a racing communications firm who was describing what he saw at a prominent Midwest track. "While the track is probably the nation's nicest," the president wrote, "the backstretch situation is the worst. . . . Instead of single men and women you see in most backstretches, [it] seemed to have entire families living there. It was, in a word, depressing, especially when you look across the road to a facility that cost upwards of $200 million to build." The correspondent *had* to be describing Arlington in Chicago.

"Of all the racetracks I've been to," said my track-rat friend David Carpenter, "Arlington is the most beautiful—even more beautiful than Saratoga. It was so clean that when people ripped up their losing pari-mutuel tickets, they didn't drop them on the floor like they do at other tracks. That would have been unseemly. No, they dropped the tickets in the waste bin." David remarked on the landscaped grounds, the flowers, and, at the entry, a life-size bronze of a six-year-old John Henry, with Willy Shoemaker up, edging a horse called The Bart by a nose in the first Arlington Million stakes race. Arlington, then, features a lavish entry and a Third World backstretch.

Judy Jones, an equine artist who grew up in Chicago, calls Arlington "the Taj Mahal of racing." When fire burned down the old track in 1985, the new one was built to a majestic standard and even won an Eclipse Award for its design. "But nothing," Jones said, "was done for the backside. There was a lot of controversy about it. That backside looks like the ghetto."

More recently, there have been changes to the Arlington backstretch, though not enough for some. In the fall of 2005, a spokesman for the track cited four-million dollars' worth of improvements to backstretch housing and said, "Arlington Park provides the highest quality of backstretch living standards at any racetrack in America." The occasion of the comment was a court case brought against Arlington by the U.S. Department of Justice involving violations of the Fair Housing Act.

Jeffrey Taren, a lawyer representing the HOPE Fair Housing Center—a nonprofit organization seeking to improve backstretch housing at Arlington—told me he's had "the royal tour" of the backstretch. "If that's the highest quality," he said, "it's a sorry statement for the industry as a whole." There have been "marginal improvements" to housing at Arlington, said Taren, and the Illinois legislature has earmarked millions of dollars in casino royalties to improve conditions at the state's backstretches. In the meantime, he said, there are still areas on the Arlington shed row where one communal bathroom serves 140 people. "When all is said and done," said Taren, "it's still going to be the kind of housing that you and I would never want to call home."

I have not seen Arlington, but I have been to Saratoga, and I remember feeling there what I felt when I first went to Fenway Park in Boston and Wrigley Field in Chicago. The memories of great events in sport seem to have been etched into the fabric of these places. I remember a wooded area on the grounds at Saratoga where families were picnicking in the shade as the race card played out on a warm spring afternoon. The backstretch, that other world, is close by at both Arlington and Saratoga, but hidden and cordoned off.

Schefstad reported that everyone he talked to on the backstretch liked horses more than people. Asked what he would miss most if he no longer lived and worked at the track, one groom told him, "The horses. The people, most of them, not all of them, aren't worth a damn." On the other hand, few horse-care workers spoke disparagingly of the backstretch. For all its indignities, it was home—maybe even an improvement on previous arrangements (a dumpy motel, a homeless shelter, a jail cell).

The language in Anthony Schefstad's paper is often academic and detached, but I could sense his sympathy for "racetrackers." This man clearly knows the track, knows the fragility of horses and what happens to unsuccessful or injured horses, and how rare is the great horse with heart. "Such is the dream of the resident horsecare worker: to work with such a horse," Schefstad wrote. "All dream of rubbing a Secretariat, Northern Dancer, Ruffian . . . that one horse that will set them apart and provide a defining moment in their life."

Racetrack grooms are like carnival workers. They pull up stakes every thirty days, as the meet at one track ends and another begins elsewhere. They go north and south according to the season, or maybe west, hoping for a kinder life. On to the next shanty in the next city or town, maybe hitching a ride with a trainer or getting in the van with the horses. When you spend any amount of time with a horse, you begin to smell like one. I like that smell, though not all do. It is a tincture of hay, straw, and leather, all manner of horse emanations, and the dander and dust that come off a horse when you brush him and that settle on your hair, your skin, in your ears and nostrils.

A groom's tools are few and simple. A cloth in a back pocket, brush and curry comb, a broom and manure fork—those are the main ones. Each stall has to have its soiled straw removed daily and replaced with fresh stuff (for a horse should not breathe the vapors of soiled bedding, nor should we, for that matter). Each horse—and one groom may be responsible for three or four horses—has to be rubbed and brushed, bandaged and tacked up and led to the track on race day, maybe rubbed with liniment to loosen his muscles in cool weather, and afterward bathed and sponged, the excess water removed with a metal scraper. Feet must be cleaned before and after every workout and feet painted to prevent cracking and splitting. Elaborate mixes of oats, sweet feed, vitamins and supplements must be prepared individually for each horse and fed each horse twice daily, along with hay. There is wormer to be administered, medication to be given, cuts to be tended to. The groom must check the feet and legs for heat and other signs of injury, apply poultices as necessary, soak feet in tubs of Epsom salts or ice or menthol brace, take a rectal temperature if the horse seems out of sorts. Water tubs have to cleaned daily and filled. The horses must be hand-grazed and, when there are fields for them, led to and from the paddocks. Horse blankets need cleaning, as do saddles and bridles with saddle soap and beeswax.

A groom is there before dawn to wake the horses and begin the day, with work winding down before noon. The resident groom faces a long and mostly boring day—maybe the groom goes to the track and loses precious pay—before more work in the evening and turning off the lights at night.

Eddie Sweat would start work with Secretariat and the other horses at 5:30 A.M. and continue to 6:00 P.M. each evening. He saw little of his wife and children, even while he was based at his home track of Belmont, and when he was on the road with the horses, he would be gone for months at a time. "I don't mind the hours," he said just before the Belmont Stakes in 1973. "The racetrack is home to me. It is the only life I know."

A groom is moving constantly, and the good ones follow a precise rhythm, so that each job occurs in its most natural order and never at the expense of another. The horses are led to track and bath stall and paddock, with no one kept waiting. Eddie would have known all the little tricks—putting cayenne mixed with Vaseline on bandages to discourage a horse from chewing them off, blowing into a horse's eye to dislodge dirt, adding vinegar to a poultice for healing a wound. Eddie was entrusted with the best horses; he was given the keys to the horse van when the horses shipped on to the next meet; he was the groom who knew what to do without ever being told. He was loyal, punctual, dedicated, the groom's groom.

He knew, really knew, Secretariat, Riva Ridge, Chief's Crown, and every horse in his care. He could tell by watching them if they were bored or angry, sour or tired, feeling playful or pained. He knew the spots each one liked to have scratched—under the jaw, just behind the ears, along the back. Maybe one horse preferred not to have his mouth touched; another might have found it heavenly to have Eddie massage his gums and nostrils. He would have done all he could to keep his horses happy and ambitious.

"I respect my horses and my horses respect me" was one of Eddie's favorite expressions. What a beautiful word is *respect*. Implicit in that word—at least in the context of the horse–human relationship—is a host of other words: *confidence, humility, decency, understanding, openness*. Eddie brought all those qualities to his dealings with horses, and you cannot put a price on that.

Phyllis Rogers, a librarian at Keeneland, told me she was sure that Eddie Sweat had given a talk one year to a Thoroughbred owners' association in Lexington, and though she made inquiries on my behalf, no one seemed able to find the video taken of his lecture. What a pity. We will have to imagine that scene: the most celebrated groom in North America, his name forever linked to the immortal Secretariat, humbly urging the rich and powerful to be kind to their horses. It would never have occurred to him to suggest that they be kind as well to their grooms.

⁓

At a French restaurant in Lexington, Le Deauville, the owner ostentatiously greets patrons at the sidewalk terrace between puffs on his Gauloise. He is there blowing smoke as we enter, and then again as we leave—a cigar-store Indian with a Parisian accent. Inside his establishment, over escargots and steak frites, Amy Gill is describing what it's like to walk the track at a packed Churchill Downs, in Louisville, just moments before the Derby.

"A friend of mine is an equine physiotherapist, and she sometimes works on horses on Derby day," Gill says. "I often join her down there on the backstretch. It's so amazing to be that close, to look up at those twin spires from the track, to be so close to the horses that you can touch them. It's very emotional."

Gill is an equine nutritionist who makes her rounds of bluegrass farms, advising on blends of grain and vitamins and minerals to promote health, prosperity, and speed in her clients' horses. Slim, dark-haired, and effusive, she is herself a rider and a horse owner. Gill grew up in Connecticut and as a child spent summers at a cottage near Chaffeys Locks, a place close to my own home in southeastern Ontario. That curious geographical connection means that when she talks about Derby day, the scene seems both real and surreal, as if a girl from a village down the road were detailing all that she has seen and heard on a visit to another galaxy.

"Why *emotional?*" I ask.

Gill does not romanticize horses or a life with horses, unlike some horsey women. She comes to the horse with science in one pocket and detachment in the other. But she has also been around good horses all her life and is clear-eyed when she talks about why some of us find the horse so attractive.

"Horses evoke emotion in us," she tells me in the restaurant over our shared entrée, which she barely touches. "It has to do with the curvature of their bodies. Their sleek shape, their softness. It's the beauty thing. What sells the horse is the beauty. They're sensual, erotic. And when you see them up close, all these great horses just before the Derby, you see their determination. That combination of power and intelligence."

As he walked on to the track at Louisville, leading Secretariat—the fastest, the most beautiful, the most admired horse of his time and maybe of all time—Edward "Shorty" Sweat would have felt everything that Gill was describing. He would have enjoyed that same view of those nineteenth-century spires that Gill finds so enticing. Twice, Eddie walked winners toward the Derby circle and a waiting garland of roses—in 1972 and 1973. I imagine that for many years the thrill of that walk, with the copper horse especially, must have sustained him, given him a sense of pride and self-worth. This, too, is a form of wealth.

Being at the Derby must be a little like hobnobbing with movie stars. No, better. These stars are purer than those others—and beautiful, and they shed purity and beauty as they walk among us. This must be why so many people wanted to touch Secretariat, to run their hands over his body.

⌐⌐

At 5:45 A.M. at Keeneland Race Track, the lights are all on in the grandstand, and so are the tall skylights on the roof. The track before me is cast in their stark light, the sky above still black as licorice. I sit on a bench at trackside, eager with notepad, camera, and tape recorder, and I wait. There is no one about and I am beginning to wonder if my source at the Keeneland Library has misled me. Where are the sleepy-eyed grooms, the exercise riders on twitchy young colts and fillies, the squinting trainers with their stopwatches?

And then I hear it, faintly at first but unmistakable, the two-one, two-one, two-one beat of a galloping horse. Iddle-oop-iddle-oop-iddle-oop-iddle-oop. Black horse and black rider explode from the darkness like a fast boat darting out of fog. They are sprinting flat out across that wide expanse of light, racing toward the pitch-blackness beyond the finish line. The rider is tucked in behind the horse's neck, and I can hear the horse's loud breathing, or "high blowing," *brrrapppp brrrappp brrrappp,* and the sweet mythic thunder of his hooves. Then horse and rider are gone, black into black, and the sound of them fades. I miss them immediately. "Do it again," I say to no one.

This is as close as I will get to a dream I have had for many years: to be on the back of a Thoroughbred coming down the stretch, tucked in behind my horse's neck and holding back nothing, feeling that wind in my face, that sense of floating and flying at the same time.

I have galloped horses, and I remember many of them: a little palomino mustang and a big red quarter horse on weeklong wilderness treks in Wyoming; a Thoroughbred–quarter horse cross on a cattle drive in southern Alberta; a Selle Français in the Saumur region of France; a bony bay gelding in Costa Rica; a roan on a beach in southern Spain; my own horse, countless times, on the old railway bed near the stable. In Wyoming, I raced in quarter-mile sprints, one-on-one, against other riders. But I have never galloped a Thoroughbred a mile, flat out, on a racetrack.

More riders and horses now dot the track. A lovely black horse moves past at a slow gallop, the rider, in black chaps, up out of the saddle and leaning on his knuckles at the horse's withers. Two women riders trot against the flow on the outer rail.

Every exercise rider at every track in North America obeys the same traffic laws: You walk and trot clockwise on the outer trail; you hard gallop, or "work," counterclockwise on the inner rail. Riders on galloping horses are to stay in the middle of the track. Likewise, the middle zone is meant for horses being "ponied": a riderless horse being led in a walk, trot, or gallop by a mounted rider (this is done for several reasons, but the main one is to relieve pressure on the horse's legs while still getting in training miles). The track has virtually been divided into color-coded speed zones, so that a rider's speed always dictates place on the track and direction.

Some breezing horses (running at a fast gallop, almost top speed) snort like old trains; others are as quiet as computer fans. By the time morning light begins to cast long shadows over the track, several dozen riders are out there. Some are curious about this audience of one.

"Did you bring your breakfast?" one rider asks as she trots past and sends me a smile.

"What are you doing?" another asks cheerily.

Researching a book, I tell them. Walking a little in Eddie Sweat's shoes, to see what he and Secretariat and their crew saw and did on tracks like this one all over North America. I am also learning the language of the track: a *furlong* is an eighth of a mile; a *blowout* is a short, quick, two- or three-furlong hard gallop to condition a horse before a race; a *pipe opener* is a longer fast workout; a *two-minute lick* means covering a mile in two minutes; a *walkover* is when every other horse in the race miraculously scratches and the remaining entry need only cover the distance in a gallop to fulfill the rules of racing.

One rider with a bracing Scottish accent stops her horse at the rail where I stand. Our conversation goes like this:

"What time do you get up?"

"I rise at five."

"What time do you go to bed?"

"As late as I can."

"Do you like the speed?"

"The faster the better."

"How long you been doing this?"

"Seventeen years."

"Do you like your work?"

"Oh, I love it."

She has fat white stars on her round green crash helmet, the kind of thing you might see on a circus performer about to be shot from a cannon. Her cutoff T-shirt reveals a muscled back, a flat, flat belly, and nut brown skin. Whenever an exercise rider's arms are exposed, I notice, be the rider male or female, young or old, the muscles of the biceps and forearm are taut and ropy. Most riders wear flak jackets; some have whips stuck in the backs of their pants; some have walkie-talkies attached with strong elastic bands to the back sides of their helmets (trainers sometimes want a word before or after a ride, so this enables easy communication).

Now come more riders, and they are galloping more frequently. You can hear the Hispanic riders chirping to their horses (*¡Vámonos! ¡Vámonos!*), you can hear the odd crack of whip on horseflesh, a curse of displeasure at a horse's antics. This soundscape is available only to the trackside observer at dawn. During a race, the shouts of the thousands—that sound of surf that Ron Turcotte talked about—obscure the other, singular sounds.

When Secretariat was running and at the peak of his popularity, thousands of people would rise at dawn to watch him work. Eddie Sweat, Jimmy Gaffney, Charlie Davis, Ron Turcotte, Ted McClain, and the rest must have marveled to see their private dawn world so invaded. At Saratoga Springs one time, some daring entrepreneur—no doubt claiming to have risen early and done his spadework—was hawking Secretariat manure at two dollars a bag. (The red horse's poop continues to draw interest. In the late fall of 2006, the Miami Metrozoo was featuring a large exhibit called "The Poop on Scoop"— with stool samples from around the animal kingdom. Two local donors to the zoo had loaned a prize of their own: a lump of the great horse's excrement encased in a glass globe.)

Everyone at the track is selling something, but sometimes there are no buyers. One fresh-faced rider stands at the Keeneland in gate, his riding helmet in his hands, looking forlornly to the track, as if gazing out to sea. Were he to place a want ad in the newspaper, it might read, "Freelancer for Hire: Will ride any horse, any time, fee negotiable . . . very, very negotiable." He has come all the way from Ireland, hoping for work, and this, apparently, is how it is done. You stand where this man stands, he of the freckles and red hair, and hope to be noticed. You hope a trainer likes the look of your face and puts you on the work list and up on a horse, then another, and another. But the Irishman tells me he has been here for days, with no takers, and, with money running low, he may soon turn back for home.

Some riders are salaried and work for one trainer. The rider gets to know the horses in that stable, and thus experiences fewer surprises. Freelancers, on the other hand, can sometimes make more money by riding a dozen horses at the track in the morning and another dozen "babies" on farms in the afternoon: At $15 a pop, that's $360 a day. But a freelancer never knows what he or she is up against. Maybe the horse has been stall-bound for weeks, storing energy like a kid who cannot wait to free the contents of his piggy bank—all at once, by smashing it with a hammer. Maybe the horse is rank or sore or simply sour on the whole business, a ticking time bomb.

In *Blood Horses,* writer John Jeremiah Sullivan calculated that a typical Thoroughbred—from yearling to the end of his racing career—spends 91.7 percent of the time in a twelve-foot-by-fifteen-foot stall. *Before* that time, as foals, they are turned out to pasture, so they do know something of fresh air and space and the smell of grass. By comparison, a stall must feel like jail.

In my own barn, I've seen the look on horses kept in on stall rest to let an injury heal. They whinny to you as you pass; they look at you accusingly and pleadingly. What have we done? the horses seem to say, to deserve this? And I know from hard personal experience, and from reading far too many horse books, that a horse denied turnout and confined to a stall is less happy, and more wired, than one given extended daily romps in a paddock or even an hour of schooling every day. But racehorses are costly, and their health must be guarded. Riders, on the other hand, are cheap and easily replaced. This is the hard math of the racetrack.

I see a rider wearing Stars and Stripes gloves, her white saddle pad likewise festooned with red stars. A just-retired jockey named P. J. Cooksey, she was in a horrific spill at this very track the previous October, and a photograph in the *Lexington Herald-Leader* not only captured the dramatic moment but won an Eclipse Award—the highest honor for racetrack scribes and photographers. Three horses went down when the front legs of one horse clipped the back legs of another; the result was three riders down and three loose horses. The photo shows Patricia Cooksey on her back and unconscious, and a riderless horse galloping straight for her. Two track EMTs, Horatios at the gate, stand before her, legs apart, as if braced for a blow, the one in front with his arms high and wide. Both men are eyeing the horse. Come what may, they will stand their ground.

An outrider, Bob Landry, described to me how that loose horse bore down on the three figures and did not stop or sidestep them, but leapt over them all like some winged horse—"pretty as you please."

I encounter Cooksey on the shed row and walk with her to the barn, one at least half a mile from the track. She is up on a tall filly, a dark bay by Fusaichi Pegasus, the Kentucky Derby winner in 2000 and one of the great runners and potentially great sires of this era. On such a big horse, even this little woman towers over me, and I thrust my tape recorder as high in the air as I can to catch her words.

P. J. Cooksey was a jockey for twenty-five years. Only later will I learn what a trailblazer she has been: the second woman to ride in the Derby, the first woman to ride in the Preakness, one of only two female riders to record more than two thousand victories. As for "gettin' on horses in the morning," as she puts it, that she's been doing for twenty-eight years. I tell her, one, that I have yet to meet any exercise rider who does *not* love the work, despite the risks, and, two, what a thrill it has been to watch the dawn gallops. I want her to express what it's like, and Cooksey cannot stop smiling as she tries. "Oh, it's just a great feeling," she says. "It's just you and the horse. You hear the horse's nostrils flarin' and blowin.' They get into that rhythm as they're stridin', and when you're out there by yourself pretty much, it's real quiet then. It's just you and the horse. It's hard to describe but you just . . . you just *love* it!" There is no mention of the calamitous fall that left her with a concussion and two broken legs.

The nicest aspect of her work, Cooksey says, is being on a gifted horse like the one she's on now. "They're a different breed, the really good ones," she says, and my mind goes back to what Jimmy Gaffney said about Secretariat. How this experienced rider sensed, even in the walk and early on, the young chestnut's power.

What an astute rider can pass on to a young horse is trust, and it is what makes these dawn workouts so much more than fitness rituals. A young horse learns to stay calm and relaxed while running— whether in the lead, dead last, or being passed—and to let the jockey decide.

I tell Cooksey that I am struck by how little credit the backside workers—grooms, hot walkers, exercise riders—get for what they do to shape and educate, comfort and encourage young horses.

"Your grooms," she says, "they're the backbone of the industry. And the exercise riders, they're the extended hands and feel of the trainer. You have to have a good exercise rider who knows how a horse feels underneath him and can communicate that back to the trainer."

At that point, we arrive, finally, at the barn, and the filly's trainer quickly approaches. If this is a party, I am not on the guest list. The butler has pounced to show me the door.

"Can I help you?" he says gravely. Behind this thin veil of courtesy lie other, implied questions, such as "Who the hell are you?" and "What are you doing with a tape recorder in my rider's face?"

I tell him I'm just talking to the exercise rider, though what I really mean is, "What is your *problem*?" And he turns to P. J. Cooksey and asks her, "Do you know this man?"

"Oh sure," she says, giving me a sly wink, and the trainer, vaguely satisfied, retreats to the barn. He is, she says, a prominent trainer with expensive horses, and he is wary of snooping reporters. I thank Cooksey, for I truly am grateful, and I play a little of our recorded conversation as I walk back to the track. The filly's clip-clop is like music, a Greek chorus to the words of a woman who never tires of "gettin' on horses in the morning."

⌒

At 9:30 in the morning, Joe Riggs, Sr., has stopped for a late lunch—a fried-egg sandwich and a thermos of coffee. Riggs is something of a legend among outriders, the grand old man of the bunch. The *Daily Racing Form* once called the former jockey "one of racing's most respected outriders."

An outrider is a traffic-cop-cum-rescuer, there to see that exercise riders obey the rules and respect one another's space, there to save them when the horse gods rule against them during the faint light of dawn or the harsh light of a race. Every outrider has stories to tell of dashing to stop a riderless runaway horse, or about one dragging a rider with a foot caught in the irons.

"I don't know how you're supposed to feel at sixty-one," Riggs tells me. "All I know is I'm doing the same stuff I did when I was forty-one." And if he still had the pants he wore as a teenager, he could wear them, too, and make weight if he had a mind to go back to racing.

Helmet and goggles, leather chaps and jacket still on, he looks a little like a World War I fighter pilot as he sits at a makeshift counter in the tack room that doubles as the outriders' lunch room. I ask him about job satisfaction, and he offers terse answers, as if this were all so self-evident and beyond explanation. There is much on the mind of Joe Riggs, Sr.: He had a bout with cancer awhile back, he is casting about for a new horse to replace his gifted but aging track pony, and he is trying to seal the deal on a land purchase in Florida. "That's kinda layin' on me," he says.

But Joe Riggs, Sr., is here to tell me an outrider has the best job in the world. He loves the fact that his day is done at 11:00 A.M.—"and I don't mind gettin' up in the mornin'" (though I think he means the middle of the night, since for him it's rise and shine at 4:00 A.M.). He would say the money is pretty good, and when I tell him that a stockbroker would scoff at his wages, he has a counter. The stockbroker cannot say in the morning, "'I'm goin' horseback ridin' today.' I can." Every day, Riggs gets paid to go for a hack. (He would retire in 2006.)

Riggs's thin dash of a mouth gets a fraction wider, and he goes back to his egg sandwich.

Back at the rail is Joe Riggs, Jr., a farmer, trainer, and breeder who has breezed one of his own horses just minutes ago. His farm is outside Paris, Kentucky, close by Claiborne Farm. For sixteen years, he was an outrider at Keeneland, working early mornings alongside his father, then as an exercise rider at farms in the afternoon. He gives me his card, says he'll be home all day if I care to visit. I am reminded of the billboard I noticed outside Paris enticing visitors with its promise of "Horses. History. Hospitality."

It is a pleasant thing to be lost on Bethlehem Road in Bourbon County. I am lost often, and when it happens and I am my own navigator, I feel no particular frustration. To be lost is to be expected. Best to be lost alone (my wife, Ulrike, I think, will back me on this), free of that sometimes sour chemistry between driver and navigator.

I am looking for Joe Riggs, Jr.'s farm—Holly Valley Thoroughbreds. Meanwhile, there is the view. Trees over the road often link to form a canopy, black horse fencing follows every hill and dale, and the hills offer no end of broodmares and foals. The sight makes me sigh with pleasure. A field of clover compels me to stop in the shade, roll down my window, and take in the perfume. It's so invigorating, I get out of the car, and the scent's power increases tenfold. If I can smell the clover, the horses must be reveling in it (or pacing in frustration if the clover is a fence line away). I pass a farm called, optimistically, Winning Ways, others with rockers on the porch. Bliss is a view of rolling fields dotted with Thoroughbred horses.

Finally, I find the Riggs farm. A long, meandering driveway ends at an old stone house, or, more precisely, the shell of one. The house is windowless, doorless, and, at one end, roofless. Joe Riggs, Jr., as laconic a man as I have ever met, seems unsurprised to see me pull up. He is just bidding adieu to his wife, Elise, who is heading off to work. She is a horse broker, and her income is the only steady one on the forty-acre farm.

The farm was once part of a sixteen-hundred-acre plot allotted to a Colonel Matson from Virginia, who fought in the War of Independence and got the land in lieu of pay. A generation down the line, the land fell to a distant relation, a Union army general, whom local history would remember as "Butcher Burbridge" after he allegedly killed Confederate sympathizers and buried them in ditches on or near the farm.

The dark tale does not bother Riggs, who seems intent on restoring the house that dates from 1806 and has not been occupied since 1987. "I like that old stuff," he says.

Ask him what he does and he may say, "I breed a few, train a few, sell a few." The first bit of business is to take me out to the paddocks to meet the horses—he has about twelve broodmares and foals, all of whom come to us as we enter their field.

In the barn are more horses, including one very sick baby. This, too, is a fact of life for the breeder. A few years ago, a mysterious illness raced through this farm, killing foals, as it did throughout the American South. Mares would get just to the point of dropping their foals, then suddenly abort. The mysterious scourge (so-called mare reproductive loss syndrome, or MRLS) was blamed by some on pesticides, by others on tent caterpillars on cherry-tree leaves, which horses love to eat. Whatever the cause, the scourge seems to have gone.

Then we settle into plastic lawn chairs on gravel in the shade of an oak by the drive shed, my host procures two cold Mountain Dews from a fridge inside, and we chat for several hours. Riggs is a forty-year-old man wearing a white Keeneland ball cap, a short-sleeved shirt that hangs off his lean frame, and white cargo pants that somehow stay up despite no belt or the press of a belly. Joe junior has his father's dry wit and small, thin mouth, which opens to reveal a fine set of teeth. Too fine, I'm thinking, to be the originals, long ago lost to horses' hooves. But I'm wrong.

We talk about the horse he breezed that morning at Keeneland, how he let another horse come abreast of his filly—"so the beast can look into the eye of the beast." He was heartened by what he saw and felt. His horse—out of a mare he nursed back to health nine years ago—surged; the other folded.

"She left that other filly," says Riggs proudly, "like she was tied to a fence." There's nothing better, he tells me, than achieving success with a colt or filly that you yourself have pulled into this world from its mother's body. "You go through all the little sicknesses, the colt running into the fence. . . . Sometimes you think he's not worth the bullet to shoot him with, and that could be the one that makes you all the money. You gotta stick with it."

We talk, in part, about hope. It is what every horseman must have. BREED MORE SECRETARIATS was the note on Ron Turcotte's ball cap. If only it were that simple. Joe Riggs, Jr., talks of not getting a hoped-for price for a filly, of illness and injury and all that can befall horses. And so it is that home, for the moment, is a double-wide mobile home behind the drive shed.

"Trailer trash," Riggs jokes.

"So what keeps you going?" I ask him.

He sighs as he answers. "It's hard to put it on any one thing," he begins. "I wish I had a good quote for you. The only one I can think of—and old-timers used to say this all the time—'No man with a young horse in his barn ever jumped off any bridges.' Like you said, I'm gonna need luck, but if you know you need luck, that means you gotta have hope. That's what keeps you going. And if not this year, then next year."

The man leaning back in his lawn chair and swigging on his soda is angled toward the light. "We live on hope," he says, and here in the bluegrass country, hope springs eternal. Everybody here knows someone with a filly or colt who brought home the gold.

Riggs tells the story of Xtra Heat, relates it like a parable. Its lesson: Never give up on a horse until you see that horse run. Xtra Heat sold as a weanling, as a yearling, and as a two-year-old for next to nothing. Tried in cheap claiming races at Louisiana Downs, the filly won, and kept on winning, moving up in class every time and taking sixteen races in a row. Xtra Heat would earn $2.3 million.

I liken this to finding water in the desert: Everyone has an oasis tale. As for dying of thirst, that's just what happens in the desert. Now imagine discovering Niagara Falls in the desert (to bring this back to Secretariat).

Many owners and dabblers, therefore, own pieces of horses—10 percent of this one, 20 percent of some others. The racing game is a numbers game, and you try to spread your losses, never putting all your eggs in one basket.

"A commoner on the backside," as Joe Riggs, Jr., calls himself, does not know what it feels like to win a major stakes race. But he does know the feel of victory. "A win is a win is a win," he tells me, even if it's a claiming race. "At that moment in time, when your horse has been shown to be better than the other horses on the track, it's hard to imagine feeling any better."

I tell Riggs the story of Snowman, a story that seems a natural follow-up to his tale of Xtra Heat. In February 1956, Harry de Leyer arrives too late at a horse auction in New Holland, Pennsylvania. The decent horses have all been sold, and fifteen sorry dregs have been loaded into a slaughterhouse truck. But one, a dappled gray, catches Harry's eye. The horse's tail is caked in manure, his body bears bite marks and sores, and there is a crease across his chest from years of pulling a plow. Harry buys him for seventy dollars and calls him

Snowman because of the way he blinks when he emerges from the van's darkness. Inauspiciously, the horse trips at the bottom of the ramp.

Harry cleans him up, schools him a little, and sells him to a chiropractor down the road. But Snowman keeps leaping the five-foot fencing and running back to Harry, who realizes, one, the gray loves him and, two, he can jump. Snowman goes on to become the American national show-jumping champion for two years running. Harry declines offers to buy him for $400,000. Countless articles, and two books, are written about "the Cinderella horse." In my favorite photo, he is swimming with three of Harry's gleeful kids on his back. Snowman's mouth is open in a brown horsey smile and he still has what Harry saw that day in the abattoir truck—"a kindness in his sad eyes."

Joe Riggs has a rescue story of his own: Simply Bell was within an hour of boarding a meat truck. Riggs knew nothing about her, only that she was a sweet mare temporarily parked in his field, and he had no wish to see her go down that road. She repaid him with a foal that sold for $35,000, money that helped Joe and Elise buy the farm. "We'll keep her until she dies," says Riggs.

As I drive north to the Paris Pike and back to Lexington, what rings in my ear is his mantra: "We live on hope." Hope to sell a horse to put a roof on the house, to keep the farm going. And if Joe Riggs, Jr., were to strike it rich with a horse, what would he do? "The same thing," he said. "Only better. Better babies, better mares, better stallions." Bull Hancock—who plucked from Ireland in 1949 the great Nasrullah, who sired the even greater Bold Ruler, who, in turn, sired the immortal Secretariat—was famous for this advice: Breed the best to the best and hope for the best.

"The love of the horse." This racetrack phrase is uttered with the solemnity of a prayer—most of the time. The love between horse and human exists everywhere on the planet and has done so ever since one of our ancestors bravely backed that first horse, perhaps six thousand years ago on the steppes of Asia. Eddie Sweat, were he alive, would admit such love. And Secretariat, were he alive and given voice, would surely testify that he loved his Shorty as much as any horse can love a human. Ask any girl in your local Pony Club about the horse–human bond; ask the mounted exercise riders grinning at first light on the tracks at Keeneland and Woodbine. Ask me. But love can be, and is, exploited.

I am trying in these pages to understand Secretariat's world—the world of the racetrack. And it strikes me that it's a lot like the world of the writer—at heart, a solitary pursuit.

The handicapper bent over his *Daily Racing Form* is almost always alone, as gamblers always are. The trainer, with binoculars and stopwatch, nervously guards the flock like a rooster with hawks circling overhead. The jockey (or the jockey's agent) goes trainer door to trainer door, pleading and cajoling, scrambling for mounts. The exercise rider gets a leg up on that first colt or filly in the cold dawn. The groom, bolstered by strong coffee, leads a lathered horse. The horse stands alone in a stall for twenty-two hours a day. And the race, of course, which pits one horse against a dozen or so others, is a cruel sorting out.

The backstretch is Darwinism played out daily. There do exist helping organizations—the Jockey Club Foundation ("a charitable trust created to assist needy persons connected with the turf and racing"), for example, and the Winners Foundation (which helps backside workers overcome drug addiction). There are kind racetrackers, and many were generous to me as I researched this book. But horse racing is not about collegiality or sharing. It's about winning. (Somehow it seems significant that the Horsemen's Benevolent and Protective Association—which sounds like an organization that helps dispossessed track workers, and it does—actually represents owners, breeders, and trainers.)

A cruel fate often awaits those in track society—human and equine—who do not win, or do not win enough. Raymond Woolfe remembers all too well the day that a powerful and prominent owner called his trainer to the owner's private box at Saratoga. "He fired him on the spot," says Woolfe. "He used the worst kind of language, every kind of insult. I heard it myself. People turned away, they were so embarrassed for that trainer."

Raymond Woolfe has lived his whole life on and around the racetrack. "Fortunes can turn around quickly on the track," he says. "Reputations, lives. The track will break your heart in a minute; it'll make you a king in a minute."

A woman I know—well connected in racing—recalled, with fresh shock and disgust, watching as her then husband leaned on a pillar at a racetrack and bawled his eyes out. His mare, his favorite, had come in second in a famous race.

What about me? the young woman asked herself that day.

The man had pursued her, set aside his passion for horses while the courtship ensued, and the woman swooned at his attentions. She was too young to know the fervor would not last, that the other fervor would soon reassert itself.

The woman hated being left behind—left behind emotionally, spiritually, literally. Her husband was up at dawn watching those long-legged-beauties—the bays and the grays, the roans and the chestnuts—gallop in the morning mist.

~

When Go for Wand shattered her leg in the 1990 Breeders' Cup, trainer Ron McAnally struck a note that managed to blend sympathy, acceptance, and disgust. "It's part of racing," he said. "They give their lives for our pleasure." The filly went down only sixty yards from the spot where Ruffian was buried fifteen years before after shattering her right foreleg in a match race with Foolish Pleasure.

Tim Tam broke his leg during the 1958 Belmont and somehow finished second. Cool Reception finished second to Damascus in the 1967 Belmont—despite running on a broken leg for the last eighth of a mile. Why do so many horses break down on the track? Are injured horses—on painkillers like bute and Banamine—running when they should not? Are they too young, at the age of two, to be running at all? Are the track surfaces too hard? Is the breeding of Thoroughbreds too intense, the gene pool too shallow? Is racing year-round the problem?

Given the extraordinary value of these animals, the surprise is that we seem not to know the precise answer, but the numbers tell a tale. A University of Minnesota study done in 1993 revealed that 840 horses were fatally injured on American tracks the year before. One horse in every twenty-two races—3,566 horses in all—was so severely injured that he pulled up short of the finish line. Not included in this tally were all the horses suffering fatal injuries during morning workouts. Bill Nack, writing in *Sports Illustrated,* called the figures "appalling and unacceptable by any humane standard." A more recent Australian study, done at the University of Melbourne in 2003, noted that while less than 1 percent of racing Thoroughbreds suffer catastrophic injuries, more than 50 percent experience "career-ending or career-delaying musculoskeletal problems."

Nack had quoted a vet who had given up a lucrative twenty-one-year career working at Southern California tracks after he became disillusioned with what he called the "rampant" use of drugs at racetracks.

The vet lamented that drugs aimed at healing and pain control were now being used so an animal could run through pain and injury—"to force the animal, like some punch-drunk fighter, to make just one more round."

In his little classic on life at the racetrack (*Laughing in the Hills,* first published in 1981), Bill Barich says he was told by one trainer, "You can't get too attached to the horses." The author describes seeing a horse call Ruling Don die before his eyes during a morning work-out after shattering his right front leg. "It always gets to me when that happens," an exercise rider told him through tears. "Don't matter how often I see it, it always gets to me." Barich heard trainers curse the hard turf and the fact that "too goddam many sore horses running." One trainer just spat on the ground and said, "So what else is new."

What Barich describes seems a far cry from "the love of the horse" and the glory that surrounds a horse like Secretariat. Maybe the *company* of horses is what sustains the people of shed row. Best not to have favorites, for a horse—in the time it takes to change your mind—can be claimed, sold, injured, traded, shipped for meat, put out to stud, die. If Shorty Sweat knew that wisdom, it seems he ignored it. Maybe Secretariat was beyond resisting, so that when Eddie every day touched that Adonis of a horse and breathed in the colt's essence, when this supreme creature responded and bestowed on a humble man all his affection, the hook was well and truly set.

I told friends, as I wrote this book over the course of three years, that I was writing about a racehorse and his groom, a man called Eddie Sweat.

"Is that really his name?" some asked. As if the name Sweat were simply too apt to be believed; as if mucking out stalls and attending to a horse could only constitute hard labor. Some could not imagine that anyone would see such work as privilege, that contact with a great horse could make a man happy and proud and fulfilled. Eddie *Sweet,* more like it. But neither could my friends imagine the sordidness of the racetrack.

Some trainers inclined to drug a horse before a race are too cheap to deploy the same drugs when it comes time to ship even an injured horse to slaughter. A horse is worth more when shipped live (I imagine this is because they can squeeze more bodies into the truck and because horses meant for human consumption must arrive alive at the abattoir), and I pity any horse forced to make that journey. What kind of person would put an already-suffering horse on such a truck and deny that horse a painkiller?

There are no laws against hardheartedness. A horse is private property, and private property is a sacred notion. And so it is that some Thoroughbreds must literally run for their lives. There is glory on the racetrack, glory writ large. But there are shameful acts, too, and callousness.

The track has many names for trainers. Anthony J. Schefstad listed them in his thesis on the backstretch: A *horseman* is a respected trainer; a *class* trainer is a true professional; a *star* is a media hound; a *good guy* is naïve and easily taken advantage of. Then there are the *gyps,* whose cost cutting threatens even quality horses, never mind the claimers, the *barbers* without experience or education, and the *butchers,* who will drug an injured horse and run him.

Every year, Charles Hatton wrote "Profiles of Best Horses" for the *American Racing Manual,* and in 1972, he wrote, of course, about Secretariat. But in that first of his series on Secretariat, there is a line, understated as always, about horses breaking down. "Literally hundreds of horses suffer broken bones with each season," Hatton wrote then. "The adamant surfaces, together with the tax structure and stable costs, impel many racing men to make extensive use of horses." This man, who would die three years later, loved racing. But some of its practices apparently distressed him.

The Thoroughbred Retirement Foundation, one of several organizations that tries to accommodate retired racehorses, endeavors to place about eight hundred horses every year. It's a goodly number, but consider that some nine thousand Thoroughbred racehorses are sent to slaughter every year in the United States (the total number of horses killed for meat annually is eighty thousand, with twenty thousand of that number shipped north of the border). And since there are only three slaughterhouses for horses in the entire country (two in Texas, one in Illinois), it means a long trip for many horses. In Canada, some sixty thousand horses are killed for meat each year (including the twenty thousand exported from below the border). I got these figures from Dr. Nat Messer, associate professor of equine medicine and surgery at the University of Missouri.

The racehorse industry is adamantly opposed to sending racehorses to abattoirs, says Dr. Messer, and the Thoroughbred Charities of America has set up a trust fund to look after at least some retired racehorses. In 2005, $2.2 million went to 158 organizations that retire, rescue, rehabilitate, and adopt out former racehorses. At the American Horse Council convention in Washington, D.C., in April 2005, the American Association of Equine Practitioners hosted an "Unwanted Horse Summit," where Dr. Messer moderated. He is encouraged by what he sees but bothered by the number of horses going to slaughter. Maybe the simple answer is to breed fewer horses.

"I'm a practicing vet," Dr. Messer told me. "I used to work for Penny Chenery in Colorado, I grew up in the Thoroughbred industry, and my dad had racehorses. But there has to be a better plan. We have to establish a definition of responsible breeding. Research may help us answer this question, but maybe you don't have to breed, say, one hundred mares to produce a winner. Maybe the number is sixty." The breeders would then be spared the expense of raising all those foals, and fewer horses would board meat trucks. But tell that to Joe Riggs, Jr., who sees every foal as another crack at the lottery.

A friend of mine, Robert Danielis, sculpts wood for a living in Picton, Ontario, and one of his set folk art pieces is a miniature rocking horse with real horsehair as its mane. A rider in his youth, he recently made a trip to an abattoir and was given the massive eight-foot-long tail of a Percheron—enough material for a great herd of rocking horses. "I will never forget the smell of that place," Robert told me.

I imagine it's more than blood and bone, shit, piss, and body gases that conspire to make that stink. Into the mix must go despair and betrayal, fear and anguish and shock, all that a horse must feel in the last few seconds.

Michael O'Sullivan, executive director of the Humane Society of Canada, describes his own visit to a horse slaughterhouse a decade ago as a shattering experience. "The slaughterhouse is a numbers game," he says. "It's an assembly line, with rewards for volume, and the rush makes people sloppy. Everyone who sends a horse to slaughter should be made to go there and see for themselves. And I would say to them, 'This is what you did to your horse.'"

The Scottish author and adventurer R. B. Cunninghame Graham (1852–1936) once wrote, "God forbid that I should go to any heaven in which there are no horses."

If there is eternal heaven, may it be graced by horses, especially those who arrived there via hard passage. And if there is eternal hell, may the gyps and barbers and butchers enjoy their stay.

There were a few thousand horses at Woodbine when I was there in August of 2005, and most of the horses there lose most of the time. Losing is a constant, and, win or lose, so is work.

If you want to reach trainer Sherrie-Lee Hawley, it's best to call her between 4:00 and 7:00 P.M., just before she retires to bed. Her alarm clock goes off every morning at 2:45. After a lifetime of show jumping (she jumped at the elite World Cup level) and exercise riding (including thirty-two years at Woodbine), and all the falls and fractures that go with such a résumé, Hawley endures more or less constant pain in her back and knees. The role of owner, trainer, exercise rider, groom, and hot walker all converge in her lean, muscled frame. The only thing she doesn't do is put on the silks and race her three horses (though she was once married to a jockey, Sandy Hawley).

Just watching her work is tiring. Clean the feed tubs daily, or these fussy Thoroughbreds won't eat. Feed the horses—hay, grain, hydroponic grass. Make up their meds. Do the stalls. Pick the horses' feet, bandage their legs, put the tack on, gallop them, take the tack off, hot-walk them, graze them, talk to them. Grease the palm of the assistant starter, humor the vet, wait for the farrier, hope against hope. Hawley is a pepper pot of a woman, with biceps I'd be happy to call my own. But when I lament that there is no downtime in her endless string of twelve-hour days, when I offer a shoulder to cry on, she passes.

"Yeah, but it's nice," she says, emphasizing that last word. "The weather is nice, the birds are chirping, and you're working with animals. I could never work in an office." Some years, Hawley has earned $100,000 at the track, but she has endured some bad luck lately: One of her horses, a four-year-old filly called Aces Are Wild, almost died from a throat infection, another is off with an injury, and wins have been rare. Someone even stole her old wheelbarrow. She sometimes wishes she had other options, and yet the track at dawn, for all its flaws and dangers, tugs at her. I can see it in her eyes when she launches her defense of her grueling up-before-dawn regimen, and in that moment I understand why Eddie Sweat kept faith with the track all those years.

An old guy who has a stall next door to Hawley's three tells me he retired from the track and tried golfing for a year. "Nearly drove me crazy," he says, so he bought another horse, went back to predawn wake-ups, got back in the game. (*The Game,* by the way, is the name of a monthly publication read by racetrackers across Canada, including those at Woodbine.)

Leaning on the rail at Woodbine, a red ball of a sun rising in the east and the night cool already surrendering to the heat of the day, I watch riders by the dozen walk their horses up the ramp and onto the track—chatty girls in threesomes, a lone grim Japanese, pairs of men in cloth-covered riding helmets the black, green, and yellow of the Jamaican flag. And here she comes, in her brown jacket and battered helmet, a woman pushing sixty, galloping her filly Fancy Wish tight by the rail. I do not envy Sherrie-Lee Hawley, for there is little life left in the day when her horses are finished with her. But right then, as she flies past, what I feel most is envy. Creaky bones and all, Hawley's got zip, and not many—of any age—can keep pace with her.

They say there is no sentimentality at the track, but Fancy Wish wouldn't be here were that so. A friend of Hawley's had shipped the three-year-old dark bay to Kentucky for fall sale, but the filly failed to meet the reserve bid, and the owner threw up her hands when some cowboy from Nebraska offered to buy the horse and a truckload of others for a pittance. It was either that or pay to have the horse shipped all the way back to Canada. The promise of a newborn filly had given way to a hard business decision. But then Hawley's pal, a jockey's wife, had regrets, tearful ones. As a favor to a friend, Sherrie-Lee came on board as a partner, and they called the cowboy and paid a premium—financial and emotional—for this change of mind and heart.

Fancy Wish is as sweet as Aces Are Wild is sour. In a perfect world, the charming filly—doglike, she loves to be stroked and has the kindest of eyes—would reward Hawley with victory, Snowman-style. So far, that has not happened. The filly keeps "hitting the board"—achieving top-four finishes but nevertheless out of the money. "Horses," says Hawley, "know when they're in over their heads and they know when they're better than the competition." I am reminded of another track adage: Surround yourself with the best of company and your horses with the worst.

In mid-September 2005, I call Hawley back, wanting to know how Fancy Wish is faring, for I have taken a shine to her. Not as hoped is the answer. The vet found a big chip in her ankle and she has been retired. Hawley is also looking for a good home for Aces Are Wild, maybe as a broodmare. But so far, there are no takers, and giving her away is the next step. But even then, Hawley will see that strings are attached in order to spare the filly that trip on the abattoir truck.

When she was young and show jumping, Hawley bought and sold horses all the time and gave it little thought. Now, "the love of the horse" actually means something.

Hawley tells me she has taken on one lone prospect, a two-year-old, and a job in a tack shop. She is still in the game but is starting to pull back. On the phone, she sounds almost relieved.

In December 2005, just days before Christmas, we reconnect again. Aces Are Wild, I learn, has had surgery and is now moving nicely. Sherrie-Lee Hawley will try her in a new five-year-old maiden class next summer.

Hawley knows what Joe Riggs, Jr., knows, and what Eddie Sweat knew: that bad luck can turn to good; that one horse can change everything.

I had found a profile of Bill Nack, one of Secretariat's biographers, in a magazine published in Louisville to mark the 1998 running of the Kentucky Derby. The journalist, Josh Pons, observed that Nack had written in his book about Secretariat's unique way of accelerating. But Pons much preferred (and so do I) Nack's whole-body explanation to capture that moment in a race when Secretariat found his other gear. Here, in part, is what Nack said about Secretariat's action, with Pons offering color commentary:

> He would raise his shoulders and his forelegs would come up (Nack's chest swells and his arms fold at his throat) and he would *snap* them out like this (his elbows smartly spring his arms out to full extension) so that his forelegs were parallel to the ground for a split second. He would scoot his hind legs way under him . . . and *drive* down with the front, then come back up and repeat the motion. It was extraordinary to watch.

If you go to page 111 of Raymond Woolfe's book on Secretariat, you will see what Nack was talking about. Woolfe has a more succinct phrase for it—"his sensational looping rush"—but he is surely describing the same moment Nack was. Secretariat is actually angled upward, as if about to vault a fence. Nack marveled at the economy of his action, how his form lost nothing of its grace even at the end of long races.

And, as brilliant as the horse was in afternoon races, it is his work in the morning that continued to astonish his chronicler: "No horse on the planet," Nack wrote in his preface, "has ever hung up faster morning workouts than Secretariat."

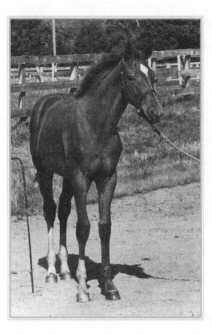

~ 3 ~

"YOUR MIRACLE HAS ARRIVED"

IT'S 12:10 A.M., MARCH 30, 1970. The temperature near Doswell, Virginia, has plummeted almost to freezing, the day marked by drizzle, fog, and blustery winds. In a two-stall foaling shed, number 17A at the Meadow Stud, just by the North Anna River in Caroline County, a strikingly handsome chestnut foal takes his first breath.

Howard Gentry, then sixty-two years old and the longtime manager of the farm, had been playing pool at home with a friend when the night watchman called to say that Somethingroyal was showing signs in the foaling stall on the western edge of this sprawling 2,600-acre farm: The mare's udder was swollen with milk and secreting a waxlike substance that dried on her teats like water on a just-buffed car. And, as advertised, the foal arrived that night. With white feet (save the left front), and a star and a stripe on his forehead, he looked ready for the world. In twenty minutes, he was on his feet; in forty-five minutes, he was nursing at Somethingroyal's teats.

In his alertness, his poise and manner, he seemed unlike any foal this illustrious farm had ever seen. "Big, strong-made foal with plenty of bone," Howard Gentry pronounced him.

Elizabeth Ham, the farm secretary and a knowledgeable horse-woman, remarked in her log on the arrival of the well-made colt: "good straight hind leg—good shoulders—good quarters. You just have to like him." Ham once worked for an American diplomat and delegate to a disarmament conference in Geneva, Switzerland, home to the old League of Nations secretariat, forerunner of the United Nations. She suggested the name Secretariat. (The name, though, was her *sixth* choice. Ham had submitted five other names to the Jockey Club, in this order: Scepter, Royal Line, Something Special, Games of Chance, and Deo Volente (a Latin phrase meaning "God willing"). But all five names were rejected, since they had already been used.)

Penny Chenery's own notebook entry was terse but keen: "Wow!"

The little twenty-four-by-fourteen-foot shed featured two doors and a wood railing on one side, and a little nubbed awning at the front. But this humble box housed a foal with royal blood coursing through him.

The colt's sire, Bold Ruler, was one of the finest Thoroughbred stallions of his time. His get, or offspring, tended to be fast as two-year-olds. And, contrary to a commonly held belief (as Raymond Woolfe, Jr., points out in *Secretariat*), they could also go the distance as three-year-olds. On the other hand, Bold Ruler horses often suffered from unsoundness and went lame early in their racing careers.

Bold Ruler himself seemed accident-prone in his early years: He once almost lost his tongue in a barn accident, and on another occasion, he came close to breaking his leg at a water trough. And though he could be hot and unmanageable, he could be a sweet horse for the right person.

The writer Charles Hatton was at Belmont the day in 1956 that Bold Ruler won the Futurity. Gladys Phipps, wife of Ogden Phipps, the owner of the horse, had taken a shine to Bold Ruler and fussed over him. After the race, this tiny woman, who could not have weighed more than ninety pounds, went down to walk Bold Ruler to the winner's circle. Hatton called it a most amazing sight: the big colt lowering his head to her and walking beside her amiably—"like an old cow."

The dark bay colt impressed as both runner and sire, though he was as plain in his looks as his sire, Nasrullah, was flashy. Bold Ruler earned $764,204 for his owner over the course of three racing seasons and he was named leading sire in the United States a stunning eight times. Remarkably, he sometimes carried punishing weights (up to 136 pounds) and still managed to win—twenty-three times in thirty-three starts. But by the time Secretariat came around, Bold Ruler was arthritic and suffering from cancer. By 1971, when Secretariat was just a yearling, his sire—only seventeen—would be dead.

Somethingroyal, the colt's dam, was by Princequillo, and his get tended to the rough-and-tumble. "The Princequillos will run all day," one breeder told Penny Chenery. Better yet, Princequillo himself—a small bay horse born in Ireland in 1940 and brought to the United States as a yearling—produced astonishingly good broodmares. He was leading broodmare sire in America for seven years, so Something-royal was a proven mare from a proven line.

Would Secretariat be that rare kind of racehorse, both a sprinter, with the speed to win at a mile or less, and a stayer, with the toughness to win at distances of more than a mile?

It seemed there was cause for great hope, but there always is when a leggy foal comes into the world, and especially a foal with such classic lines. But worry over the Bold Ruler flaw was not the only one in the air that night. For all its size and tradition, the Meadow Stud was tottering. Christopher T. Chenery, the farm's eighty-three-year-old patriarch and founder, was in failing health, and his daughter Penny had taken over (her older brother and sister having declined). In 1970, when Secretariat was born, she was a capable rider and possessed a master's degree in business, but neither of those qualifications really equipped her to run the farm. Her learning curve would be steep, her education on matters of breeding and racing just beginning.

Her father, an engineer who had made his millions in utilities, had bought the family homestead—which had passed out of his ancestors' hands after the Civil War—in 1936. A polo player and huntsman who rode daily, he dreamed of transforming his ancestral home into a fine horse farm. Against all advice (he was told the land was too wet, the fields too poor), he drained the swamps, reclaimed the pastures, then replanted them.

Christopher Chenery also bought horses shrewdly, sometimes on the advice of his horse-wise friend Arthur Boyd "Bull" Hancock, whose wife had inherited, in 1910, thirteen hundred acres of prime land in Kentucky's Bourbon County—the start of the illustrious Claiborne Farm. Princequillo was a Hancock horse, and so was Nasrullah, Bold Ruler's sire. The Hancocks and the Chenerys, Claiborne Farm and the Meadow Stud—all would figure in the Secretariat saga.

But those august Virginia and Kentucky bloodlines, human and equine, appeared not to count for much when Secretariat was born. The Meadow's greatest success seemed behind it, and the grand breeding and racing operation was high on expenses, low on income. "We need a miracle," said Penny Chenery. On the morning of March 31, Howard Gentry told her over the telephone, "Miss Penny, I think your miracle has arrived."

Lucien Laurin was born in St. Paul, near Joliette, some twenty miles north of Montreal. He, like jockey Ron Turcotte, was a Francophone who had spent time in his youth working in lumber camps. *"Use ton propre jugement,"* Laurin would sometimes say to Turcotte before a big race, meaning "Use your own judgment." Laurin likely would have said the same thing to the horse if he'd thought the horse could understand him.

"I never believed in fighting horses, trying to change the way they want to run," Laurin would say. "I lost a lot of races when I was a jock by taking too many orders from people who didn't know enough about horses." You might think he was a loose and easy man, one inclined to prepare horse and rider as best he could before letting the fates decide once the starting gates clanged open.

My sense, though, from poring over the literature on this trainer, is of a worrywart, but a funny one, someone who always had time for the press. He was universally well liked. His barn foreman, Ted McClain, thought him a tough taskmaster but a fair boss, though often a tempestuous one. "He was hot and cold. He'd go ballistic one minute," McClain told me, "and the next minute you would never know anything had happened."

Lucien Laurin died in 2000. He had fallen at his home in Key Largo, Florida, but subsequent surgery on his hip led to complications, from which he never recovered. He was eighty-eight years old, and for seventy-one of those years, he had lived the racetrack life.

Like Eddie Sweat, the man he would later employ, Laurin quit school early and fell into a life with horses. He got a job at Montreal's Delorimier Downs hot-walking horses and then as an exercise rider. By 1929, he was a jockey. By his own admission, he enjoyed only middling success. (Though he did, in 1935, ride a horse called Sir Michael to victory in the King's Plate. Now called the Queen's Plate, the race has the same stature north of the border that the Derby has south of the border.) But three years later, at one of the small East Coast American tracks where Laurin was then plying his trade, someone found in the pocket of his jacket—which he had hung up during a card game—a battery-powered device used to shock horses in hopes they'll go faster. Such devices were then illegal, and they still are, although they continue to be found. Laurin insisted he had been framed, and perhaps he was. Several years later, he was reinstated and went back to riding, but only for a time. During his expulsion from riding, he had turned to training, and he seemed to have a knack.

Eventually, he was hired on by a businessman named Reginald Webster, and a champion filly named Quill fortuitously came his way. The champion filly of 1958 was a daughter of Princequillo (the sire, remember, of Secretariat's dam, Somethingroyal), so the Secretariat-Laurin connection seemed to have been ordained by the fates. Years before that, Laurin had bought into a training facility in Holly Hill, South Carolina, which was where he crossed paths with groom Edward "Shorty" Sweat and exercise rider Charlie Davis. Both men would play key roles in the racing life of Secretariat.

Laurin had even worked as a trainer for Bull Hancock, father of Seth Hancock, who would later run Claiborne Farm—the stud where Secretariat would spend the last sixteen years of his life. You would think someone had planned this whole Secretariat thing—decided that this or that person would be touched by an almost mythical creature, and that others would miss contact by a hair's breadth. If, for example, coming to train the horse of the century was like winning the grand lottery, Lucien Laurin had managed to win without buying a ticket—his own son had handed him the winning number just before the draw.

Roger Laurin, Lucien's son, would have trained Secretariat, but in

1971, Roger accepted a job training horses for Ogden Phipps, one of the great names in Thoroughbred racing. When Phipps died in 2002 at the age of ninety-three, he was the longest serving member of the Jockey Club and its former president. A World War II naval commander and seven-time American tennis champion in the 1930s and 1940s, he had enjoyed great success breeding such horses as Personal Ensign, Easy Goer, and Buckpasser—a horse who won twenty-five of thirty-one starts and earned Phipps some $1.5 million. Both Buckpasser and Easy Goer would stand at stud at Claiborne Farm in Kentucky, and the latter horse, ironically, would occupy the same stall that Secretariat would when he came along. In signing on with the Phipps operation, Roger Laurin was sure he was heading to greener pastures.

Before he left, Roger urged his fifty-nine-year-old father to come out of retirement and take his old job at the Meadow Stable, working for Penny Chenery.

Ogden Phipps owned Bold Ruler, the sire of Secretariat. And he would have owned Secretariat, too, had he called "heads" and not "tails" during a small ceremony in 1969. Under a complicated agreement he had with Penny Chenery, they flipped a coin to decide first choice of the progeny from two Meadow mares bred that year and the following one to Bold Ruler. I use the word *complicated* because one mare produced a foal, then proved barren, so there would be three horses to choose from, not four. The parties thus agreed on this arrangement: The winner of the coin toss would get one foal of his or her choice, and the loser would get the other two foals, which prompted both horse owners to joke about hoping to lose the toss. This was in the fall that year at Belmont Park, inside the offices of the New York Racing Association's board of trustees. Phipps called "tails" when that fifty-cent piece rose in the air. Tails it was.

Phipps took into his stable a filly (out of Somethingroyal) called

The Bride, a dud at the racetrack, never finishing better than sixth in four races. Of the two young horses whom Penny Chenery won that day, a colt (out of Hasty Matelda) called Rising River appeared unsound and was later sold for fifty thousand dollars on the strength of his bloodlines. And when Somethingroyal was bred again to Bold Ruler, the foal was Secretariat. Winning a horse like that on a lost coin toss is like finding a priceless gem in a birthday-party surprise bag.

Many people—Penny Chenery among them—are firmly convinced that the planets aligned in Secretariat's favor from the day that coin was tossed. Ron Turcotte may have been the perfect jockey for that horse, for he knew how smart and capable the horse was and, for the most part, quietly guided him to the finish line. Lucien Laurin was perhaps the perfect trainer for a horse who thrived on fast, blistering workouts. Track wisdom has it that a trainer inclined to coddle a horse would never have suited the big chestnut, with his immense appetite for work and food. (In fact, two years before he died, Lucien Laurin told *Thoroughbred Daily News* that maybe he should have pushed Secretariat even harder than he did. "He was a tough horse," he said. "A really tough horse.") Finally—and who can say where this ranks in the Secretariat saga?—the right groom came along to rub the great horse into legend.

⌒

Another Meadow employee, Howard Gregory, was around Secretariat from the time of his birth, and he remembers the colt as something special. "We knew from the get-go he was different," he would later tell *The Blood-Horse* magazine for an article that gathered the recollections of old Meadow grooms. Just walking the young Secretariat to the paddock, he said, was an exercise in maintaining focus, because the instant a handler lost his, that horse knew it—"he was gone."

Whenever the farm won a big race, the grooms got a week's extra pay. Now Penny Chenery wondered if she had anything like her father's touch, or his luck, as she struggled to restore the balance sheets and the winning tradition—all this while some family members considered the wisdom of selling the farm and playing the stock market with the proceeds. On Bull Hancock's advice, Chenery brought in a new trainer, Roger Laurin. Some horses were sold, and some were bought. In 1971, the Meadow's future was still precarious, and Penny Chenery patiently waited for the "miracle" horse to take shape.

Tattooed inside the colt's upper lip was a number (all registered horses have one, for identification purposes). Secretariat's was Z20669.

⌒

In the paddock, he was, by all accounts, a bruiser. Bigger than other foals his age, he would cuff his playmates, bite and kick them, and try to outrun them. In her book *A Year at the Races,* the Pulitzer Prize–winning author Jane Smiley considers the theory that the relationship between dam and foal is critical to the young horse's formation and future happiness. There is some evidence that the happy, well-grounded, and nurtured horse is more successful at the track than one with a lackluster upbringing. The horse, Smiley seems to be saying, is more like us humans than perhaps we imagine. No matter the genus, upbringing matters. And the picture I have of the young Secretariat is of a horse secure in his place. Somethingroyal apparently licked her young foal not just at birth but long after, and her affection for him may well have helped make him even and brave. And the Meadow staff, too, may have played a role in all this: They made a point of handling every foal, driving home the point that humans posed no threat.

Even so, the rambunctious young Secretariat had a mind of his own when being led from barn to paddock. He would bolt for the grass in a heartbeat, and staff had to loop a chain through his halter and over his nose to keep him in check. Howard Gentry called him "a very aggressive type of colt," especially in his paddock, where he soon became the dominant foal. The colt was precocious and bold and very competitive. He was as healthy as his appetite—a "good doer," as some call a horse who loves his feed bucket.

Meadow staff had a habit of putting the three best weanlings in adjoining stalls, with the best of the bunch getting the first, stall number 11. Secretariat got that stall, so there must have been some agreement that he looked to be the finest prospect. Staff who worked with him remember how easygoing he was, but some also recall his temper.

The young Secretariat was groomed by several men at the Meadow, and all remember him fondly. One, Louis Tillman, is dead now. A photograph in Woolfe's book shows Tillman holding the horse for his Jockey Club ID photo, and you can see the whites of the colt's left eye as he worries about the photographer and that rod in the ground with the number 9 hanging on a hook. You can also see Secretariat's ribs, so the colt had yet to put on the fleshiness that marked his youth.

What is remarkable about the photograph is just how muscled the horse appears, even as a foal—long before any serious exercise or training. "He was muscle-bound from the beginning," Raymond Woolfe told me. "I remember walking behind Secretariat with Lucien Laurin, and Lucien would wonder aloud if the horse would ever run—he was that muscled. He didn't walk, that horse; he waddled. I know there was talk later on that Secretariat was on steroids, but Lucien never messed with that stuff." Secretariat on steroids, said Woolfe, would have created a true freak.

Woolfe likened the foal grooms at the Meadow to mother hens, but

Tillman, especially, he wrote in his book, had a feeling about Secretariat. Tillman had remarked on the colt's presence.

After the colt was weaned from his dam—with the usual dashing round the paddock and plaintive calling—other grooms took on the task of caring for Secretariat. There was Bannie Mines, now in his late sixties and still living near the Meadow. "He gave you an idea even then," Mines later said, "that he might turn into something." Mines remembers him as easy to work with, but also a horse with a temper.

There was the aforementioned Howard Gregory, of course. And Charlie Ross (also now in his late sixties, and a brother-in-law to Bannie Mines), who these days works at a nearby truck stop. Ross spent nearly a year grooming Secretariat when the horse was a yearling. He told *The Blood-Horse* magazine how proud the Meadow was then, how they would repaint the training barn every year. Outside the young Secretariat's stall, Ross hung a plaque that announced the horse's name, sire, and dam. And he remembered how Secretariat's size worked against him when he was young, how only slowly did he learn to run with any grace.

In August of 1971, Secretariat moved from his virtual nursery to the compound of stables inside the oval of the Meadow's training track. It was a kind of kindergarten, where young colts and fillies were introduced to horse realities, such as saddle and bit and rider.

Secretariat had good and capable men in his corner, and you have to think that this, too, contributed to his later success. Patiently and by degrees, the young horse experienced a saddle on his back, then a bit in his mouth, and the weight of a rider across his back. Charlie Ross would hold the young horse while Meredith Bailes—son of the Meadow's former trainer and, like his father, a fine and sensitive horseman—sat astride the horse in a stall. Later, they did the same things in the indoor exercise shed, and the rider taught Secretariat about pressure from the legs and the reins and what this all meant. Then Charlie Ross let horse and rider walk and trot by themselves. Finally, they went out on the track.

For all his dashing good looks and promising bloodlines, Secretariat was so oafish on the track that "Ol' Hopalong" became his nickname. On January 20, 1972, the big colt left the Meadow and rode in the van to Hialeah, in Florida, where almost everyone agreed that Secretariat was plump and pretty, clumsy and slow. Laurin paired the chestnut with a horse of his own, one named Gold Bag. The latter would become a good racehorse (and later a stakes winner), and he left Secretariat eating his dust.

It seemed the colt could not take the racing game seriously. What he did learn in Florida was how to dump his exercise rider by slamming on the brakes and veering hard to the left. After the colt tossed off Paul Feliciano one morning, Jimmy Gaffney suggested a different bit—and that seemed to curtail the dumping. But the young Secretariat continued to record unimpressive morning workouts, even after he was taken back north to what would become his "home barn"— Barn 5 (stall number 7) at Belmont Park, on Long Island. One morning in June, however, he caught Lucien Laurin's attention by going five furlongs in 57⅗ seconds. Secretariat was like a teenager who had finally grown accustomed to his new body, to his suddenly acquired height and weight. In the early days of that summer in 1972, the flashy two-year-old chestnut began to show what he was made of.

He had put the Ol' Hopalong character behind him for good, and his workouts continued not just to impress Lucien Laurin but to astonish him. "We have a racehorse on our hands," he told Penny Chenery.

In his brief but starring role as racehorse, Secretariat would enter twenty-one races. Given the way he won some of them, several observers—Ron Turcotte, Charles Hatton, Raymond Woolfe among them—would later wonder how it was that he had ever lost even one.

Lucien Laurin, Secretariat's trainer, was reminiscing in 1981 about the Triple Crown victories.

The Derby: "Most people don't know this about Secretariat," he told Joe Hirsch at the *Daily Racing Form,* "but his best game was around turns. He could fly around turns: faster than any horse I've ever seen, before or since. I never saw a horse run as fast as he did that day, from a point leaving the backstretch to the head of the stretch."

The Preakness: "He was fourth going into the first turn. But then he caught sight of the two horses on the lead, Ecole Etage and Torsion. As competitive as he was, Secretariat wanted to run with them, and once he picked them up he was in high gear. Ronnie [Turcotte] couldn't hold him, and rather than strangle him, he just let him run his own race. Pincay, on Sham, was in front of Secretariat on the first turn. Suddenly he looked over to see the Red Horse alongside and he must have gotten the shock of his life. You can see his reaction in the films."

The Belmont: "I couldn't believe the fractions . . . [Penny Chenery] kept looking at me and saying, 'He's going pretty fast, isn't he?' Fast? If I'd had had a gun I'd have shot myself."

After the race, Laurin asked Turcotte, "Ronnie, he wasn't short, was he? Was he out of wind?"

The jockey replied, "He could have gone faster."

Laurin told him, "Ronnie, don't tell that to anybody else."

After the Belmont, the late Holly Hughes—a Hall of Fame

trainer—told Laurin that he had seen Man o'War, Citation, and Count Fleet race, and none could compare with Secretariat, especially in that Triple Crown campaign. "You have," Hughes told Laurin, "the greatest horse in the history of racing."

~ 4 ~

"Eddie Was a Prince"

Racing literature tends to focus on the owner/trainer/jockey triumvirate, a hot mix of ego, blame, praise, and meddlesomeness. Every winner's circle photograph masks the small wars among them that have invariably preceded victory. But the fourth character in those photographs, the groom, tends to be nameless.

And when the photograph has been taken, the owner goes back to his or her fancy box, the trainer and jock move on to the next race, and the lowly groom, horse in tow, does his or her duty—walk, bathe, feed and water the horse, muck out his stall, pick his feet, blanket him, rub him down, load him on the van. No one understands that horse better than an astute and caring groom, and no one gets less credit.

Here is Susan Nusser, author of *In Service to the Horse: Chronicles of a Labor of Love,* talking about the relationship between Samantha Burton and an accomplished event horse named Tailor. (Three-day eventing, the most challenging equestrian discipline, requires horses to master conventional show jumping, cross-country courses, and dressage.) At the time Nusser was writing this book (2004), Sam and Tailor had spent almost every day of the past four years together. "Before he knows he's hungry, she is feeding him. Before he knows he's frightened, her voice is calming his fears, and before he knows he's hurt, her hand is soothing his pain. She knows his quiet emotional side better than anyone else in the world. . . . [Tailor] quietly follows the groom he trusts, and, in his own horsey way, loves."

Another book, *The Event Groom's Handbook: Care of Horse and Rider,* likewise focuses on eventing, a discipline quite different from that of racing. But I like its wisdom on the relationship between groom and horse, a way of seeing that surely also applies to the track.

Early in the book, authors Jeanne Kane and Lisa Waltman offer this message to would-be grooms. "One of the most desirable traits in a groom—and one of the reasons for having the job in the first place—is the ability to get under the skin of the horse that you are caring for and to notice and understand all the tiny idiosyncracies of each individual animal. You must realize that is why you have been employed—this is your gift and your contribution towards a successful team."

This is your gift.

The more I learned about Eddie Sweat and his extraordinary gift, the more I was drawn to the man. Everyone who ever knew him or saw him with a horse described his way with horses in terms of its exceptional nature. Bill Nack, for example, wrote of Eddie's "lyrical" touch with horses.

Raymond Woolfe's book *Secretariat* is a remarkable assemblage from someone with impeccable credentials: lifelong horseman and steeplechase jockey, horse trainer, horse-farm manager and, for eleven years, chief photographer for the *Daily Racing Form*. Woolfe, seventy years old when I spoke with him, lives at Hawk's Nest Farm, near Charlottesville, Virginia.

"Eddie Sweat really loved Secretariat," Woolfe told me. I said I was writing about Secretariat and his groom, and that the book owed a great deal to a photograph Woolfe took of Eddie Sweat with his back to the photographer, an image that captured all the emotion of the day he surrendered his horse at Claiborne Farm.

"I just caught him sitting there," said Woolfe. "He had been crying but when I asked him what was wrong, Eddie said, 'I just got a cold.'"

"Eddie was very special," Woolfe went on. "He was the only one who could handle Secretariat. The horse wasn't mean; he was just powerful. Eddie was as strong as an ox. But Riva Ridge and Secretariat, they respected him. Damn right they did. Eddie called the tune; they listened."

What was Eddie like? "He was sweet," said Woolfe. "As kind a guy as you'd ever want to meet."

Eddie Sweat's image is peppered throughout Woolfe's book, though most times you see just a piece of him. He is behind the horse, or just out of the frame, but if you follow the chain-and-leather lead, it invariably ends in the big hands of Eddie Sweat. He is almost always holding Secretariat via that lead and, at the same time, looking directly at Secretariat to see what he might be up to; or he is holding Secretariat and looking away to see what the photographers, videographers, and onlookers are up to. Eddie looks more relaxed in photos taken during dawn workouts, when crowds were infinitely more sparse and more distant. But on race days, there is about him a measured vigilance.

Years later, he talked about both his fondness for the horse and the constant worry. He told the *Thoroughbred Record* in 1979, "Secretariat was special. I had to work that much harder with him. I had to keep my mind on business and be more serious. There was a lot of pressure when grooming a Triple Crown winner. You can't make any mistakes and you have to keep your eye on other people."

On special occasions such as big races, Eddie would trot out his best duds—wild stripes and checks in pants, spats for shoes, florid shirts, loud hats. Some of Woolfe's photographs are in black and white, so I've had to imagine the color of those hats. Goldfinch yellow, I'm thinking, or willow green. Dean Eagle, the sports editor at the *Courier-Journal* in Louisville, said that Eddie Sweat looked "more like a flamboyant golfer than a stable hand." Red Smith in the *New York Times* once remarked—in a column about Secretariat Day at Aqueduct late in 1973, to mark the horse's retirement from racing—on Eddie's puffy new cap, his mod jacket, burgundy slacks, and two-toned shoes.

A cartoon in the *Daily Racing Form* of November 6, 1973—just when Secretariat was making his final appearances at the track—depicts the horse at the center of a mock scene from *Othello*. Below the art is a line uttered in the play by the noble and brooding Moor: "Farewell the tranquil mind! farewell content! . . . Farewell the neighing steed . . ." The characters are all dressed in Shakespearean costume on a proscenium stage, and Secretariat (up on his two hind legs) holds forth while a grieving Penny Chenery clings to his neck as Lucien Laurin, Ron Turcotte, and Elizabeth Ham all blow into their hankies, and Eddie Sweat, with his eyes closed, plays a flute stage right. The cartoonist has him in plaid pants, so Eddie's sartorial splendor must have been widely appreciated. What is off about the cartoon is that Eddie seems to be the only one *not* crying, and no one shed more tears on Secretariat's retirement than Eddie Sweat.

Raymond Woolfe's photographs are closer to the mark. In one of my favorite shots, Woolfe has caught Eddie at leisure: He is looking off into the distance, leaning on a stall board with his right hand, and his left arm is cocked and fisted into his waist. He is wearing a peaked cap and short-sleeved shirt, exposing his bulging forearms. The man looks youthful and vibrant and very much at home.

In another black-and-white photograph, which bears the caption "A serene Secretariat with Eddie Sweat," groom and horse stand in a grassy area behind the track. I am not sure the horse is all that serene. (But neither do I question Raymond Woolfe's horsemanship; perhaps for Secretariat, this *was* serene.) The horse looks suspiciously at the photographer, who has snapped him from the side, so the viewer can admire the horse's biceps and triceps, the muscle on muscle. It is Eddie who looks serene, though even now he has *two* hands on the lead—a relaxed right hand, and the left hand as a backup, just in case.

But the most telling of Woolfe's photographs, for me, are the ones taken the day that Secretariat moved to Claiborne: Eddie leading him up the ramp to the plane; Eddie crouching low in front of the high wooden box stall inside the plane and, as always, watching Secretariat; the horse gripping Eddie's jacket as the plane takes off and the jet engines' roar begins to unnerve the big chestnut. In the latter photograph, Eddie is leaning into him, his eyes are closed, and I imagine him saying something like "It's okay, Red, I'm here. I'm here." And I read into Secretariat's eyes gratitude and a little fear. I'm *so* glad you are, the eyes say.

Raymond Woolfe has been around horses and horsemen all his life and he had never seen a connection quite like that between Eddie Sweat and both Secretariat and Riva Ridge. "Never did this author," he wrote in his book, "ever see horses and their groom more devoted to one another. . . . It was nothing less than profound."

A year later, Eddie happened to be back at Claiborne to pick up a foal for Lucien Laurin. "And don't you know they remembered me," he told a reporter. "Secretariat, he came over and pulled on my shirt, just like he always did. And when I made a noise at Riva, he came up to that fence so fast he almost slid down."

Remember him? They *adored* him.

⁓

Edward "Shorty" Sweat had far more contact with the racing Secretariat than anyone, and no one could claim a fuller understanding of that horse. No one felt that horse's defeats as he did, no one reveled more in his victories, and no one suffered more when it all came to an end than Eddie Sweat.

A black man had bonded with a racehorse. And while much about the man, the horse, and their relationship was extraordinary, the track has seen the like before. Many black grooms who worked at the farm in Virginia where Secretariat was born once lived at nearby Duval Town—built after emancipation to house freed slaves.

The tie between Thoroughbred horses, on the one hand, and black riders and grooms, on the other, goes back a long way. In his book *The Great Black Jockeys,* Edward Hotaling points out that in the first Kentucky Derby, held in 1875, thirteen of the fifteen jockeys, including the winning rider, were black. Before the Civil War, slave owners had used slaves as riders and had given them cause to ride hard and fast: A losing jockey could see his family sold as punishment. Consequently, the best riders in the South, long before and long after the war, were black. And though racetracks were segregated until well into the 1960s—with "colored" people forced to use separate entrances, washrooms, and seating—the track's best and most devoted grooms, for all of the nineteenth century and most of the twentieth, were black.

Hotaling describes raids by British cavalry on South Carolina Thoroughbred farms in 1780, during the American Revolution.

Lt. Col. Banastre Tarleton had set his sights, in particular, on an imported English racer and sire named Flimnap, but each time the Brits got close to him, his black grooms hid him in the swamps. The raiders captured one such groom and offered him a huge reward to reveal the horse's whereabouts, but the man refused. Even after being threatened with death, he would not betray the horse. The troops strung the man up on a tree and left him to die. (Servants at the manor later rescued him.) I thought of Eddie Sweat when I heard that story of loyalty to a horse.

And I thought of him again when I read, in *The Great Black Jockeys,* the obituary of Austin Curtis published on January 5, 1809: "A colored man, aged about fifty years—well known for many years past, as keeper of race horses; in the management of which useful animals, he particularly excelled.—His character was unblemished; his disposition mild and obliging—his deportment uniformly correct and complaisant—he possessed the esteem of *many*—the respect and confidence of all who knew him."

In his book *Secretariat: The Making of a Champion,* Bill Nack points out that Charles Hatton—the great racing writer of the twentieth century, who never tired of extolling Secretariat's virtues—owed much of his expertise to the tutelage of Billy Walker, a former slave and retired jockey. The old black man had taught a young white man the secrets of horse conformation, how a horse's assemblage can presage his speed and endurance. Here was a refrain I would hear often on my travels and in my reading: "An old black man taught me all I know. . . ."

In the winter of 2005, I traveled to Eddie Sweat's birthplace and grave near Vance, South Carolina (as I had the previous summer gone to Secretariat's birthplace in Virginia and his grave in Kentucky). I talked to Eddie's siblings, his son, nephews, and nieces, his closest friends and fellows, all the while marveling at this extraordinarily humble man and his connection with perhaps the greatest racehorse who ever lived. Every person had a slightly different take on Eddie, each had stories to tell, until a kind of mosaic of the man began to form.

As I learned more about him, the huge affection that his comrades and relations felt for him became genuine for me, too. I began to fathom how the love of a great horse could sustain a man, and how such a love lost might break a man.

Often on the scene when Eddie Sweat groomed Secretariat was Ted McClain, then barn foreman for Lucien Laurin, the horse's trainer. I had heard that he lived in Paris, Kentucky, and that he had left the track and gone into his father's insurance business.

Ted McClain was not, at first, welcoming of my inquiries. "How did you get my name?" he asked. "And my telephone number?" This, I thought, is going to be a very short telephone conversation, and my hopes of an in-the-flesh interview had about the same chance as a forty-to-one long shot in a claiming race.

I told him I knew about his association with Secretariat and had found his name in the phone book. The truth was a little more complicated than that. In the late 1980s, I had made several trips into outback Wyoming, riding a horse on weeklong treks as part of research for a book called *Wild About Horses*—a book about the horse–human connection through time. On those rides, I met several New Englanders, one of them a former equine nutritionist in Lexington, Kentucky. When, years later, I wrote her and pressed her for Kentucky contacts as I researched this book, she gave me the name of another equine nutritionist, Amy Gill, who, in turn, introduced me to several useful contacts and gave me an insider's view at a yearling sale.

"You know," Gill said on the phone one day when I was still in

Lexington, "I used to be married to Lucien Laurin's assistant. He worked with Secretariat. He was there. You should talk to him. Just don't tell him I gave you his number." It seemed great good luck—one of those "six degrees of separation" stories—to have found him in this way. Finding him and getting him to talk, though, appeared to be two different things.

But when I told Ted McClain that I was especially interested in the relationship between Secretariat and his groom, Eddie Sweat, everything changed. There was a long pause, clearly an emotional pause, on the other end of the telephone line.

When McClain had gathered himself, he simply said, "Eddie was a prince. . . ." We chatted a little more, and it was apparent that the icy line had dramatically thawed. Suddenly, I was welcome to see him in his office (I would interview him there twice), and he later lent me a cardboard box full of articles and clippings. All because I had uttered two words. Eddie Sweat.

When we did talk in person, in the summer of 2004, McClain admitted that my mere mention of Eddie's name had almost brought him to tears. For months afterward, I could not think of Eddie Sweat's name without hearing in my head Ted McClain's words, like something you would include in a eulogy or etch onto a gravestone: "Eddie was a prince. . . ."

In the flesh, Ted McClain is warm, with a dry, self-deprecating humor. He was then a youthful fifty-five, a Kentuckian born and bred, and so the words come slowly, each syllable stretched out like dough under a hot summer sun. We chatted at first in his office, with its view of Main Street, Paris, Kentucky. Behind McClain's desk is a massive framed painting of the great red horse, so clearly the ex-horseman remains proud of his connection. Who would not be? No doubt clients think better of their broker upon seeing that horse looking over his shoulder, as if blessing their business.

Ted McClain dresses the part of insurance salesman—long-sleeved white shirt, red tie with elegant blue stripes, gray suit, and—the kicker—a pen stuck behind his right ear. But the body of this imposing man—six two, solid frame, a square, handsome face, a full head of hair tinged with gray—says middle linebacker, but a gentle sort of one. Later, poring over old newspaper clippings at the Keeneland Library, I would spot him. Photos showed him always wearing a cloth cap as he walked Secretariat, as he looked up from a bucket, as he smiled at the camera. Big horn-rimmed glasses gave him a slightly geeky look then, and whenever he was lined up with Eddie Sweat or Lucien Laurin, he towered over them: a giant cast among the little people.

McClain described what an indifferent student he had been at the University of Kentucky—"I wasn't hittin' the ball real hard," he drawled—before setting out for Long Island's Belmont racetrack with little more than a love of horses in his pocket. "I was just going to land wherever I landed," he said, but a client of his father's had lined up a job for him—at the barn, as it turned out, of Lucien Laurin. (It was a name he pronounced as Kentuckians do: *Lush*-en *Lore*-en.) McClain started, as they all do, as a hot walker, then became a groom, then barn manager.

I asked him what relations were like among Secretariat's owner, trainer, jockey, and groom. Was it a happy family or a dysfunctional one? McClain corrected me. "It was owner, trainer, jockey. And everybody else was . . . a grunt." Though McClain would go on to become a trainer, he put himself squarely on the side of the grunts. Everything he learned about horses, he learned from Eddie Sweat and other black grooms from Holly Hill, South Carolina. "The Holly Hill gang," he called them.

This man was seemingly a bit player in the Secretariat story, but he got close to the horse and close to his groom. "Other than the night watchman and Eddie," he said, "I spent more time with that horse than anybody in the organization for the twenty months that he was in the stable at Belmont. I was around him a lot."

McClain has had three decades to think about why this horse still matters to so many. He observed that more recent horses, such as Funny Cide and Smarty Jones, were "feel-good stories" that naturally appealed. Funny Cide was a New York–bred horse, bought as a lark by longtime pals in the small town of Sackets Harbor. He was the little horse that could. Then his jockey—trying for a comeback—was falsely accused of cheating, which only made him, and the horse, more friends when he was cleared. Smarty Jones, meanwhile, overcame a horrific starting-gate accident en route to his success, and the horse's jockey had battled back from alcohol addiction. Everyone in racing wanted these horses to win the Triple Crown. Neither did. The horses became footnotes.

Secretariat, on the other hand, will *always* be remembered. "He was," said McClain, "the biggest, strongest, most attractive and powerful animal you could ever lay your eyes on. He was a heartthrob. What he did in the Belmont, to this day every time I see a replay of that stretch run—I'm sure it's the same for everybody—I get chills. The country was in rough shape then and he just took our breath away. He was a *man*. He was John Wayne and all the movie stars rolled into one, the toughest athlete around. He had presence and he commanded respect and attention. That's my thought on why he's endured the way he has."

Ted McClain has a vivid memory of Charles Hatton, the grand old man of racing journalism, coming around to see Secretariat in the fall of 1972. McClain had grown up reading the *Daily Racing Form,* in which Hatton had a column. A visit from Hatton—"a wordsmith of the highest order," McClain called him—was like a visit from Hemingway. Hatton, back in the 1930s, had coined the name Triple

Crown to denote the three grand races of Thoroughbred racing in America.

On that day, Hatton walked down the shed row at Belmont Park, Barn 5, stall number 7, then home to the young Secretariat. "He just stood there," said McClain. "I guess he looked at Secretariat for five minutes and never said a word. He was in awe of him. He had already written enough about him. To Charlie Hatton, they need not make another racehorse. He was *it*." Someone later told McClain that Hatton never visited the backside, which may or may not have been the case, but what impressed McClain was that this esteemed writer had gone to see the young chestnut horse who was making such a splash. And the horse had stunned Charles Hatton into silence, though not for long, because Hatton wrote about him constantly and always found new ways to praise him.

Hatton was among the first to recognize Secretariat's potential greatness. The "dean of American racing writers" loved his coloration—"a scarlet colt, star and narrow stripe, and three white stockings . . . He looked to be coming up the stretch with flags flying." Hatton loved, too, how Secretariat won so many of his races with come-from-behind surges: "He swooped down on his hapless foes with a paralyzing burst, like a hawk scattering a barnyard of chickens, and pandemonium rocked the stands."

Hatton had clearly been watching the horse carefully, and he even spotted what he took to be minor flaws—the neck a little too straight and heavy, the knees not set perfectly. But he loved the way this horse moved ("his extended action had floating power"), he loved his conformation (the particular way his body parts were assembled and conformed to the ideal), he loved the horse's legs ("simply perfection"). Hatton would die in 1975, and maybe he realized as he scrutinized Secretariat that day at Belmont that this was the horse he had waited all his life to see. Secretariat is, wrote Hatton, "the most capable horse we ever saw, and geriatrics [Hatton's own] defeat any thought of seeing his like again."

McClain remembers, too, the day that Secretariat arrived at Barn 5 from training at Florida's Hialeah Park. It was April 3, 1972. For Lucien Laurin's staff, this was their first glimpse of him. The horse, some opined, was too fat, but he was also the most stunning horse they had ever seen. "The fella in the barn next to us," McClain said, "an old-time hardboot trainer named Henry Forrest"—he had won the Kentucky Derby twice, with Kauai King in 1966 and Forward Pass in 1968—"I'll never forget it. He took one look at him and said, 'My God, that looks like a big old shiny red apple. He is absolutely gorgeous.'"

But the wisdom in the barn, once they learned that his sire was Bold Ruler, held that he was a sprinter at best, not a stayer. He would not go the distance, and besides, he was a chestnut, and Bold Ruler had never sired a decent chestnut.

One thing I was curious about was Secretariat's temperament. In all that has been written about him, there are as many stories of his testiness as there are of his kindness.

It was only when he was being groomed, McClain remembers, that he might bite or kick. "Eddie," he said, "had a way of talking to him, not necessarily to calm him down, because he was always on the muscle and ready to do something. But they had a mutual respect for each other. Eddie wouldn't have had it any other way. He liked it that Secretariat was tough."

But there must have been another side to Secretariat that writers either knew nothing about or chose not to report. McClain had just finished telling me that "there was no meanness in the horse," when a story came to him, a story contradicting what he had just said.

"I'll never forget this as long as I live," he began, smiling as he settled into his tale. "I think Secretariat had already gone to the Derby and the Preakness, and while he was gone, we cleaned out his stall and aired it out. And a cat had had a litter of kittens in his stall, maybe four or five. As cute as they could be. And they were underfoot, you know. And one day, Eddie was leading Secretariat outside and the horse saw one of those little kittens out of the corner of his eye and he did that." McClain brought a closed fist down hard on the table in front of him. "He sure did. That was the only bad thing I ever saw him do." As for Scooter, the six-toed kitten that found his way into the record on Secretariat, McClain was laughing when he said, "Secretariat spared him." The cat would enjoy a brief sojourn as the Derby cat, Secretariat's good-luck charm, before someone stole him.

When Ted McClain left the stable two weeks after the Belmont— I had the impression he didn't much like Penny Chenery, the horse's owner, and felt about to be caught in the continuing cross fire between owner and trainer—he knew he would miss everyone there. But the man he would miss most was Eddie Sweat.

"He taught me so much about horses," McClain said, "about how to keep on an even keel, how to be on time, how to be dependable. He taught me the importance of regimentation, that there's an order in the way we do things to get ready for the day, to get through the day. In the fifteen years I trained horses, I had only two people working for me who were similar to Eddie. If he had a philosophy about working with horses, it was his own. You didn't have to tell him anything; he knew what to do. I don't think you learn to be a horseman. Either you are or you're not, and Eddie just was. I never saw him upset or what you could call mad. He just took fantastic care of his horses."

I knew that Eddie had grown up with horses and mules on the farm in South Carolina, but surely he had to learn the groom's craft. I asked McClain about that "Yeah," he replied. "He had to learn which brush to use and how to pick a horse's feet; we all have to do that. But his identification with them—you don't teach that. You don't give this guy a shank and say, 'Go walk that horse.' Either he's going to have a comfort level and the horse is going to have a comfort level with him or he isn't. I'm not saying I'm any great horseman, 'cause I'm not, but you can tell who belongs and who doesn't. With Eddie, it was like putting a hand in a glove." (One trainer later told me that McClain was, in fact, a very fine horseman, with a deft sense for pairing stallions and mares.)

Kind but firm is how Eddie Sweat was with horses. "His temperature gauge," said McClain, "stayed more level than mine would have. And he talked to the horses constantly. It was a personal thing for him. He was their protector. And he was very important to Secretariat's success. I don't think there's any question. Secretariat was just a tuned-up machine, and the harder he worked, the better he felt. He reared up on me several times, just 'cause he was feeling good. But Eddie kept him level-headed, if that's possible in an animal."

What especially endeared Eddie to McClain was the respect that Eddie paid to horses and humans alike. This was why, in McClain's mind, Eddie was a prince. "It didn't matter who he was talking to, whether it was the owner of the horse or the groom down on his luck from the barn next door or the hot walker; he treated everybody with dignity, whether they were above him or below him. He sort of took me under his wing, some dumb kid from Kentucky who didn't know squat. He put up with me; he tolerated me. He was a snappy dresser, always neat and clean, and he made sure his horses were neat and clean. And though he wasn't educated, he was smart."

For the good of the barn, Eddie, as senior groom, would put other grooms in their place. "Let's face it," said McClain, "some of those grooms were screwups, and they were never going to do right." But whatever Eddie Sweat did to set them straight, according to McClain, "he did it the right way."

As for his love for Secretariat, offered McClain, "Eddie and that horse were like brothers. Eddie lived with him; he traveled with him. They were kin, joined at the hip."

I thought out loud of all the people who had bought Secretariat posters and videos, and how they loved and admired this horse—but always from a distance. They had crowned a horse their king and they were his willing subjects. Eddie Sweat was the pauper in this tale, but he actually lived with the king.

"You think about it," McClain responded. "It's like having a child. You have to feed him, take care of him, bathe him. He's yours. In a lot of ways, he didn't belong to anybody else *but* Eddie. You would feel that way, too, if you were the constant companion. You'd either hate each other or love each other, one of the two. You'd be so damn glad to see him go, or it would kill you."

After his time with Secretariat, McClain stayed in racing for another thirteen years. He went from Lucien Laurin's barn to work for Woody Stephens. (The latter died in 1998 at the age of eighty-four.) "By then," said McClain, looking bemusedly back on his own youthful arrogance, "I was *real* smart." For three years in succession, he had been employed by barns whose horses had won the Kentucky Derby: Riva Ridge in 1972, Secretariat in 1973, Cannonade in 1974. "I thought that was the way it was supposed to be, but it ain't never that way." And the travel, which had seemed so exciting in the beginning—Kentucky in the spring and fall, Chicago in the summer, New Orleans in the winter—began to wear on him, never mind its effect on his marriage to Amy Gill. That partnership would end in less than two years.

McClain discovered that training horses was hard work, that expenses—vet and farrier bills, transportation costs, stable hands' wages—could be overwhelming, and that horses like Secretariat and grooms like Eddie Sweat were as rare as blue moons. As McClain put it, "I finally waved the white flag."

But all those years of rising before dawn left him with a longing for first light. Later, when I told him what a thrill it had been for me to see the riders at dawn on the Keeneland track, he nodded. "It's still my favorite time of the day," he said. "I still get up with the sun. The regimen has stuck."

Ted McClain and I chatted one more time when I returned his box of clippings, and he showed me a painting that Penny Chenery had commissioned. She had prints made, framed three of them, and gave one to Ted. The painting's foreground shows Eddie Sweat leading Riva Ridge, then the star of the stable, while the white-haired Lucien Laurin looks on approvingly, his arms folded. Very much in the background, exercise rider Charlie Davis is leading away a chestnut wearing a blue blanket with white trim. The horse, of course, is Secretariat.

~

Sometimes Marvin Moorer, Eddie Sweat's firstborn son, will catch himself in this pose: standing with his weight on his back leg, his left hand in the back pocket of his jeans, the thumb of his right hand tucked into the front pocket. If Eddie ever stopped moving, that was the stance he would sometimes adopt. And his son, without thinking, does the same.

The last time I spoke with Marvin, late in 2006, he was living in Arizona and studying for a new career as a computer technician. In the 1980s, he had worked at the racetrack as a groom alongside his father, who had taught him many of the finer elements of the craft, but only after helping his son overcome a rather large hurdle: fear of horses. It seems, in retrospect, almost amusing—the father a natural horseman, the son a reluctant practitioner.

"My dad taught me how to love animals," says Marvin, forty-seven when we spoke in 2006. "I never understood how they'd obey him. He showed me that horses had more sense than most humans, and that you didn't have to be mean. Carrots and sugar work better. I was a pretty good groom, but he was the best. He had a charm with horses and he spent a lot of time working on legs and feet. I'd go away and come back to the barn and I'd say, 'You still on that one leg?' He would use liniment or warm alcohol, just his hand on that leg, giving a massage. But you could see the result. His horses always looked good."

At the end of those long days, father and son would sometimes take a drink, or two. Eddie liked Smirnoff's vodka; Marvin liked Budweiser. "We were more like best friends," says Marvin. "We'd talk each other to sleep. When I was a teenager growing up in the Bronx, there were gangs, and he kept me away from that. He would never touch me, but he'd threaten. We had a pretty good bond. 'Boy,' he'd say—he always called me 'boy'—'you gotta slow down.' I miss him. And I dream about him all the time."

It seems like everyone in Eddie's circle had a nickname. Eddie used to call his son "Chesterhead," for his square head—shaped, said Eddie, like a chest of drawers.

The only keepsake Marvin has of his father is a Seiko watch, once given to Eddie for a stakes race victory and passed on to Marvin when he won his first stakes race as a groom. The son, though, has his memories, complete with soundscape. When Marvin calls up Eddie, he imagines him grooming the horse he adored and talking to him in the Creole language called Geechee.

Marvin paints a picture of a gentle man with Popeye arms—his forearms were the size of his son's calf. Eddie's father, David, was tall and slim, a sharecropper who worked land—his own fifteen-acre plot and that of others—between Vance and Holly Hill in Orangeburg County, South Carolina. David Sweat had a beat-up old car and an old mule (later replaced by an aged tractor), a dog, a few pigs, and some chickens. "He was gentle with the grandkids," says Marvin. "He'd give us what we wanted, if he could. I never saw him angry. He was always under control. My father was just like him."

Eddie's mother, Mary, was short in stature and generous in spirit, but she brooked no nonsense. Growing up, Eddie would have been "whupped" for disobedience. But the Sweat homestead—a tiny one-story cinder-block house with a wooden porch and three bedrooms, the nine kids stacked inside like kindling, with no running water and just a woodstove for warmth in winter—was as good a home as the times would allow. As late as the 1960s, water to the place still came from a hand pump atop a well, with a privy as toilet. "There was a lot of love in that house," Marvin told me. "Sometimes it was hectic, especially after my father left. He kept the family together. He promised he'd send them things, and he did."

By the age of fourteen, young Eddie had found steady work with horses. He was a country kid with a sixth-grade education and a burning desire to leave the place he was born in. Lucien Laurin's Thoroughbred training center, Holly Hill Farm, was a springboard to a job at the track and a new life in the big city.

"When he lived in New York," Marvin says, "his fridge was always overflowing with food. He never wanted us to lack for anything—clothing, shoes, but *especially* food. He would invite new guys at the track back to the house for a meal." It was as if Eddie saw hunger as an old enemy that might return at any moment. Friends from the New York days say he seldom got angry, but one thing could make him irritable: if dinner wasn't ready when he got home.

Shorty Sweat would never forget the hardships of his childhood, working in the fields for pennies under a boiling summer sun, the constant dearth of food and clothing, money and living space. School was a building that also served as a general store and, on the weekends, a bar. "I'll never go back," Eddie would say. He would visit all right, make his rounds, dish out money or gifts where he thought those were needed most, then hightail it back north to Belmont.

Even in New York, young Eddie—still a teenager—would work out in a boxing gym with his friend and fellow racetracker Fred Davis. This wasn't about becoming a prizefighter; it was about keeping in shape and learning the art of self-defense. Eddie was a black man in a white man's world, and there were always fights. Later in life, Marvin would ask his father about the racism he had encountered in his life. Marvin himself had been spared that scourge: His best friend growing up in New York was a white kid. "He said he had stories to tell, but he wasn't going to tell me," says Marvin. Maybe they were too awful to tell, and the father wanted to spare his son.

In 1939, the year Eddie came into the world, Mississippi senator Theodore Bilbo introduced a Back to Africa bill that would have "repatriated" (read deported) American blacks. When Eddie was eight years old, Jackie Robinson became the first black man to play on a major-league baseball team. Although ballplayers from the two races had played together after the Civil War, segregation had the same impact on both the diamond and the racetrack: Black jockeys and black ballplayers were ousted. Many black jockeys went to Europe. Black baseball players formed their own Negro League and the so-called color barrier ruled for many decades—until Jackie Robinson came along. An army private from Cairo, Georgia, Robinson had once been court-martialed for refusing to sit at the back of an army bus. With the Brooklyn Dodgers, he had to abide the taunts and racial slurs of fans, opponents, even players on his own team, who at first launched a petition against him.

Growing up in rural South Carolina, Eddie would have endured the same, or worse. Segregation was deeply entrenched in a state that ranked among America's poorest, with income levels half the national average, and high rates of illiteracy and disease. (The slave ships had brought people from Africa and the Caribbean who were adept at growing rice and tolerant of the heat, but the ships also brought mosquitoes and malaria. A German doctor visiting Carolina in the eighteenth century said it was "a paradise in spring, in the summer a hell, and in the autumn a hospital.")

To help ease the transition from slavery to freedom, black families living near the coasts of South Carolina, Florida, and Georgia had been famously promised "forty acres and a mule" by a Union general in 1865. Some families did get land, only to see it given back a year later to its original white owners. The words *poor* and *black* have been partners a long time. Though much has changed in South Carolina, Vance continues to struggle. In a town where 85 percent of the people are African-American, the annual per capita income, according to the latest census data, is under nine thousand dollars. Small wonder that Eddie fled. He was part of an exodus that had begun in the 1920s, when black men and women headed north in search of jobs and a measure of freedom.

In New York, Shorty Sweat had his own house in Queens, about ten miles from the track. It was a beautiful home, Marvin remembers, a one-story brick house with three bedrooms, a large dining room, a sunporch, and a big backyard. Eddie also had a car. For a time, it was a 1969 brown Mustang. In 1972, no doubt feeling flush with Secretariat on his list of horses to groom, Eddie bought a brand-new black Dodge, which he was very proud of. His brother Morris was a mechanic, and Eddie, too, knew his way around an engine and would tinker with the car. At home, he would cook his favorites—stewed chicken, catfish stew, fried pork chops, grits and tomatoes and fatback bacon. He followed the New York Mets, his chosen team. He would play pickup basketball, "or try to," Marvin says with a laugh. His dance was the boogaloo, a style of music that blended rhythm and blues, rock and roll, soul, and mambo. Eddie didn't read much—just the *Daily Racing Form* and the racing section of the *New York Daily News*. He smoked cigarettes, Salems, and a pack might last him three days.

Edward "Shorty" Sweat was shy in the company of white folks, especially those he would have seen as above his station—such as owners and trainers. All that changed in the company of family and close friends. Marvin called his father a smooth talker, a snappy dresser, a ladies' man. In his lifetime, Eddie would father four children by three different women.

When I asked Blondella Davis—Eddie's friend for thirty years—what she remembered about him, she said, "His mouth. He had a very big mouth. He'd say what he wanted to say. He was very straightforward. I used to call him 'Big Giant.' I'd say to him, 'You are a very short man with a very forceful voice.'"

Eddie's greatest fear, his son told me, was of losing his job. Grooming horses was all he knew, and it was fear of unemployment—as much as respect for his bosses—that made him shy and quiet in the company of his white superiors. But in the company of black friends and black family, everything changed. "Around us," Marvin says, "he was the man of the house. We all went to him for advice. When he said something, we all stopped and listened. And he could make us laugh. He was the life of the party." New guys on the track would be ripe targets for his darts, but he always did it in such a way that even the butt of the joke laughed along.

Blondella's husband, Fred, worked with Eddie on the track for many years and they were fast friends all their lives. Eddie and Linda Sweat, Fred and Blondella Davis got together often—for Christmas parties and cookouts at the Sweat home, for trips to the track. "My memories of Shorty are good ones," Blondella said from her home in South Carolina, just steps from the cemetery where both Eddie and Fred are buried. "Shorty was a lot of fun when he was having fun and he liked to make us laugh. He would call me 'Miss Blond.' A sincere family man, a good family man. He loved his horses to death, especially Secretariat. That was his baby."

No doubt about it: The big red horse was family. Marvin has seen the photo of his father crying the day he surrendered Secretariat at Claiborne Farm. "Secretariat was like a brother to him," says Marvin. "My father loved him as much as he loved me or my sisters. It hurt my father a lot when Secretariat died. He said he'd never have another horse like that." And he was right. He never did.

⌒

I found trainer John Veitch to be a sympathetic and insightful voice on the subject of racetrack grooms. We met briefly at a Thoroughbred horse sale in Lexington in the summer of 2004. He was by himself and leaning on a rail outside the auction barn, watching the slow parade of gorgeous colts and fillies. He seemed immediately friendly to my project: The name Eddie Sweat was still working its magic for me, like a diplomatic passport. I was reminded yet again of the high esteem in which Eddie was held in track circles. I did not want to disturb Veitch that day, so we talked later on the telephone, just days before the 2005 Kentucky Derby.

I was trying to make sense of Eddie. The stories I was hearing of his drinking in his later days, for example, seemed to give off a whiff of self-pity. But that may be too harsh a judgment, and I wondered if a prominent trainer who knew and liked Eddie Sweat would have a clue.

"Being a Thoroughbred groom," Veitch told me, "is not a living. It's your life. It's seven days a week and it's a life with tremendous disappointment, because horses are fragile. Eddie rubbed a horse who was the second-best who ever lived." (Veitch ranked Man o'War first.)

"And after that experience, after hitting that pinnacle, he realized it wasn't coming back."

The sad fact is that racetrack grooms are not paid what they should be, but then, said Veitch, two-thirds of trainers are not making a living, either. "It's just the game," he said; then he added a bittersweet note. "This used to be a great sport."

For Veitch, the loss of black grooms like Eddie Sweat—accomplished, learned, and devoted horsemen—is almost impossible to measure. What these men gave to horses was their time, and just about every second of it. Now, said Veitch, there are "instant trainers" and "megatrainers," some of whom never even see the horse they are supposed to be training. By Veitch's estimation, some 95 percent of the best-bred horses in America are controlled by ten trainers. Some of them, he said, care little for their stable help, and turnover is absurdly high. The loyalty, the sense of craft, the high standards that defined Eddie Sweat's approach to the job are harder to find.

In Secretariat's time, the grooms had revealing nicknames, names as colorful as those of the horses they tended. Veitch knew, or knew of, many of them: Liquor Ben, Never Sweat Hays, Hard Times, Slow 'n' Easy, Lyin' Lefty Daub, Kitchen Sittin' Smitty, Frank 'n' Beans, Radio Joe, Easy Money, Can't Talk, Sweet Potato, Gate Mouth, Snow Fields, Sloan "Duck Butter" Price. Bill Nack compiled the list in a piece he wrote on grooms and their plight for *Sports Illustrated* in 1991. These men were members of a black fraternity, and they all hailed from South Carolina, Kentucky, Georgia, and Alabama.

None of them hit the high that Eddie did, but some came close. Some enjoyed their moment in the sun, then went back to what they had been doing before. Some never got over their loss, and Veitch wondered if that described Eddie Sweat. "But I don't know," he said. "I'm in deeper waters here. I can only speculate." This much-lauded trainer knew only that a good groom is his eyes and ears, and that no one listened or watched more attentively than Shorty Sweat.

Veitch—the son of Hall of Fame trainer Sylvester Veitch and himself a notable trainer of Alydar, among others—told me that the old black grooms like Eddie Sweat brought something special to the racetrack. He lamented their loss.

He cited the example of Clyde Sparks, who galloped horses in Lexington before World War II and then worked as a groom for Veitch's father. "Clyde," he said, "was born and bred in Lexington and he worked his entire life with horses. He became a groom for my father in the forties, worked through the fifties and sixties, and then, in 1974, came to me. He never missed a day, except for two months after he got kicked by a horse." In 1977, Clyde Sparks started grooming Alydar.

Alydar ran second to Affirmed in all three Triple Crown races in 1978, a keen rivalry that many racetrackers remember fondly. Alydar, a chestnut, won fourteen times, earning close to one million dollars. And in the breeding shed, he—not Affirmed—was the star and America's leading sire in 1990, when he broke a hind leg in his stall at Calumet Farm, where he is buried.

"Clyde Sparks knew Alydar better than any person in the world," said Veitch. "Good grooms develop a bond with their horse. It's stronger than marriage, stronger than any religious devotion. It's almost mystical."

John Veitch knew Eddie Sweat and the skill and dedication he brought to his task. "At one point," said Veitch, "the best job in the world for a man of color was to be a racehorse groom or a porter for the railroad." (Veitch might have added jazz musician to his list.) Imagine how grateful Eddie would have felt. Imagine his pride and sense of good fortune. His wages, though likely low (Veitch said it was well known that Lucien Laurin ran a stingy barn), would still have far surpassed what farmworkers—black or white—could hope to earn. Eddie had escaped the sharecropper's fate and found a world where he mattered mightily.

"The groom is the life of the horse," Veitch said. "A good groom will make your horse; a bad groom will ruin him." A skilled, caring groom will report to the trainer the slightest heat or swelling in the leg. Catch it early and you can fix it. Fail to catch it and the horse's potential may be lost forever.

Epidemiologists talk about something similar in the world of medicine. If you can come to know a baseline in the health of a given population, get a fix on what is "normal," you are much better equipped to sniff out the abnormal and deal with it. A good groom has the same intimate knowledge of a horse, and any deviation from the norm sets off alarm bells. Thus alerted, a good trainer will put out the fire before it's even a fire. But preventive medicine—whether on the racetrack or in human health care—is seldom practiced or valued.

The good black grooms from the American South, said Veitch, spent all their lives around horses. The best arrived at the track as young but fully fledged horsemen, and they worked for the same stable until they dropped. They would notice if the horse ate or drank less, quicker or slower, if the horse was lying down more, any change in the color, amount, smell, or frequency of the horse's urine or feces. Today, Veitch said, many grooms are Hispanic and they don't possess enough command of English to report such subtleties to the trainer— even assuming their skill. (On the other hand, many California trainers today swear by their Mexican grooms.)

Veitch remembers that some stables used to give their grooms sweaters of that stable's racing colors. The black men wore the sweaters with pride, as soldiers wear their dress uniforms in a parade.

~

Roger Laurin, son of Lucien, was sixty-nine when I interviewed him for this book. He lives in Miami Beach, Florida, and owns a few horses, but my sense now is of a dabbler, not a player.

"What do you miss about the track?" I asked him.

"I miss winning," he said, showing some of his father's wit. "Getting beat was no fun."

Roger Laurin hired on Eddie Sweat in the early 1980s, after his father retired. Eddie's time with Laurin senior went back decades, to the time that Lucien owned a training operation in Holly Hill, South Carolina. Father and son both knew that when it came time to hire a groom, the best was Eddie Sweat.

"What did he have?" I asked Roger.

"If I knew that," he replied, "I'd bottle it and go back into business. Every generation, someone like him comes along. He was just in the right place at the right time. My first memory of him is back at my father's farm in South Carolina. Eddie had the biggest forearms I'd ever seen. He was very strong, though he wasn't a big man. But he didn't muscle horses; he didn't use that strength of his. He had no problems with horses. He was a very steady guy, a good and likable man."

It bothered Roger Laurin that I knew he had helped out with expenses at the time of Eddie's death, that Roger had paid the airfare when the groom's wife and family flew from New York to Eddie's funeral in South Carolina. Maybe Roger was protecting his own privacy, like some philanthropists who insist on discretion. Or maybe he was protecting Eddie Sweat's memory, or the Sweat family's dignity. Maybe he felt that the Laurin family was in Eddie's debt.

In any case, everyone would agree that Eddie had no problem with horses. It was money, said Roger Laurin, he had a problem with. "Eddie and money," he said, "didn't stay together very long. It didn't matter what you paid him. A friend would ask him for money and he would give it to him." I have the sense that loans on the backside are seldom, if ever, repaid.

Eddie Sweat was not like so many who drift to the track, where the wages are slim but so are the prerequisites—no education, references, or résumé required. A stable may try you, and if you show up on time, do a decent job, and remain sober (or sober enough), you stay on for as long as your punctuality, work ethic, and sobriety last. When they go, you go.

"You have to like the horses," said Roger Laurin. "You have to have a feeling for them. Too many times, the first questions asked are, 'How much do you pay?' and 'How much can I borrow?'" Even if Eddie Sweat did have money, Laurin speculated, he would have worked with horses until he dropped.

A few years ago, I was in Cleveland and spent an afternoon at Thistledown, a B track featuring cheap, spent, and sometimes rank (obstreperous) horses. For the riders, it was risky business just mounting some of them. I watched the grooms intently, eyed the hovels they lived in as I entered the grounds, heard their banter before and after races. What I took from the day was their light and easy manner: Whatever their circumstances, they did, indeed, seem to love the game. They were, as many are, drawn to the beauty of the horse.

Bill Barich captured that sense of the grooms' loyalty to their horses in his book *Laughing in the Hills*. Grooms, he wrote, "lived the most rigorous and honest lives on the backstretch and seemed to have fewer illusions than anybody else." Barich said that grooms were as suspicious of owners as they were of trainers, and one groom told him in confidence that he had left his former employer after being instructed to mistreat the horses. Barich painted a picture of grooms as gypsies, drifting from this track to that one, from one trainer to another, for good reason or bad reason or no reason at all, and if the booze in their bottles did not last long, neither did their marriages and relationships. "But through it all," Barich wrote, the grooms "remained faithful to some inner model of goodness, an eccentric and singular moral code, and always to the horses."

⌒

Tom Wade was to Seattle Slew what Eddie Sweat was to Secretariat. In the mid-1980s, when Eddie was grooming a horse called Chief's Crown for Lucien Laurin, the two grooms spent about a week together when that horse was sent to Three Chimneys Farm in Kentucky.

I spotted a picture of Chief's Crown in Lucy Zeh's book, *Etched in Stone.* The photograph shows a bruising dark bay, winner in 1984 of the Eclipse Award as champion two-year-old male and, later, twelve races, which netted his owner $2.2 million. Chief's Crown would also sire Chief Bearheart, twice Canadian Horse of the Year in the late 1990s. Chief's Crown died in 1997, the year before Eddie did, and as I stared at the horse's photograph, I wondered if the person holding the lead shank, but not visible in the picture, was Shorty Sweat.

Wade and Sweat shared common interests, of course, and common friends, and at Three Chimneys Farm, they spent every moment they could in each other's company. Tom Wade had grown up in small-town Kentucky, the son of a painter father and a hairdresser mother, and at the age of fifteen he left home to work on a horse farm in South Carolina. His brother, a groom who would later gallop horses for Lucien Laurin at Holly Hill, had known Eddie in those days. This was the 1970s, and the Wade brothers were among the few grooms who were white.

"I was a white man in a black man's world dealing with horses," Tom Wade told me. "I respect them for the way they gave their souls to the horse. In their era, if they had a good horse, they had it all. There wasn't much else to have in their day."

Tom Wade sat at his kitchen table, welcoming but cautious. A heavyset man in his early forties, he was wearing a black T-shirt and blue jeans. He had placed his hands and arms on the table and sometimes he would lean back and squint at me or display a lopsided grin.

The bond that forms between a groom and a champion horse is one that few ever experience firsthand. I had a hunch that Tom Wade could help me make sense of Eddie Sweat's life-altering connection with Secretariat. For twenty years, starting in 1982, Wade was Seattle Slew's one and only groom, and for those twenty years he had mostly declined to be interviewed about what that had meant to him. During that time, he did not want the added burden of having to explain or justify something he had said to the press.

When Slew died on May 7, 2002, Wade said, he felt an obligation, and perhaps a freedom, to speak freely. He had determined that if a writer approached him, he would be candid and open. And so he was with me.

"What," I asked, "separates an ordinary groom from a great one like Eddie Sweat?"

"The good groom," Wade replied, "has focus. He doesn't allow outside interference. You put the horse first, above all else. It's pretty basic, pretty simple. You see, I think you're blessed to be around a good horse, and once you're given that opportunity—it's more of a huge responsibility, really—the focus, the dedication have to be there." His list of "outside interferences" included wine, women, song, business, and family.

"A lot of these grooms," Wade explained, "are in for life. You're married to the horse. It's like marrying your spouse. Humans generally outlive horses, so Kathy always knew her time would come. But in Slew's life, he came first. Kathy and I were married fifteen of the twenty years I took care of the horse, but I wouldn't have married her if I'd thought it was going to be a distraction. We did this as a team."

Some would argue that a horse owner has no right to inflict on a groom—especially given their generally poor pay—that kind of total dedication to a horse. But if grooming Seattle Slew constituted a supreme sacrifice, Wade willingly made it. Two days into caring for the dark bay horse, he realized the degree of his commitment. "I knew that I would be with Slew till death do us part. I didn't see it any other way."

Nor was Tom Wade bothered that grooms get little credit for what they do to secure a horse's comfort and confidence. He harbored no bitterness about hours worked or vacations missed. Eddie Sweat likewise never whined about his hours, his wages, the sacrifices he made as father, husband, brother, son. On the contrary, he seemed, by most accounts, a happy man made more so by the company of a special horse. "A pauper," as Horace wrote, "in the midst of wealth."

The odd thing about Wade's grooming Slew all those years is that the horse *hated* to be groomed, hated what most horses love—the brushing of skin and mane and tail. Tom Wade did not much groom the one horse he was paid to groom.

What he did do was this: "Manage, or manipulate—and I don't mind using the word"—the stud-farm manager, the barn foreman, the exercise rider (Slew was ridden at the stud farm for years), the blacksmith, the veterinarian, the farm owner, the owners of the horse. "I felt I had to manage all those people in a way that they would respect the horse and the needs of the horse. Because if you have ten people involved with the horse—and these are important and, some of them, powerful people—everybody can't have his own way. This is probably the first time I've used the word, to *manage* a horse, but there's a lot that a groom can do."

"So you saw yourself," I asked Wade, "as speaking for the horse?"

"I saw myself," he replied without hesitation, and even raising his voice, "I saw myself as standing up on a stump and screaming and hollering for the horse. That's exactly right." But Wade is as careful with words as he is, no doubt, with horses. He adds that keeping all those vested interests on the same page with Seattle Slew was not always difficult.

Slew himself could be difficult, and he bit Wade "a few times," as he put it. Always, said Wade, because the groom "provoked" him. One time, a visitor to the farm stood alongside groom and horse while some photos were taken, and the visitor was rattling keys. The key rattler herself did not bear the brunt of the stallion's annoyance; Tom Wade did—apparently for permitting the nuisance. Another time, Wade, perhaps feeling pressure to rush the daily routine, entered Slew's stall to take him outside. The great horse, who preferred his groom to wait at the entrance, showed his anger by biting him on the chest.

"I knew better," Wade told me. If he needed medical treatment because of Slew's teeth, he kept quiet about it. No need to malign the horse when the groom was the one at fault. "He was a horse who had his limits," said Wade. "Early in the morning, you could do anything in the world with him. In the afternoons, he'd get tired of the heat and the humidity." Then he could be cranky and one had to be careful with him.

Wade remembers Slew as an honest horse (if he took a chunk out of you, it was always straight on, never from behind) and an extraordinarily smart one. The eyes said it all. They were amber, as if some alchemist blending golds had added a tincture of silver to make an amulet for a king. Seattle Slew's eyes, said many who saw them, pinned you with their brilliance and intelligence.

Above all, he was a horse in love with run. Wade would release him in his paddock, and any frustration in that horse would immediately reveal itself, for he would explode into motion. Secretariat had the same penchant and need. Speed was his friend, his brother, his tonic.

And despite their two-decade-long relationship, Tom Wade said, "I never took for granted that Slew knew me personally. I didn't treat him like no dog. I didn't treat him like a pet. I treated him like he was a *serious* horse." Wade saw himself as Slew's caretaker—the one who fed him, bathed him, took him in out of the storm, and solved his problems. Let's get through that part, Wade took Slew to be saying, before we get into anything else.

Wade was making a critical distinction: Slew loved the service, not necessarily its provider. I had never heard a longtime horse–human relationship put in quite those terms. The groom as British butler—loyal to his master, professional to the core, discreet, cool, and aboveboard.

"It sounds," I told Wade, "as if you don't belong to the mystical school of horsemanship."

He couldn't agree quickly enough. "I don't whisper," he said (as in "horse whisperer"). When it comes to humans and horses, Wade believes, it is the horse's world the human enters, not the other way around.

If you give your life to being around a horse, said this lifelong groom, you literally ask that horse's permission to be included in his world. "You don't drag that horse into your world. My time around Seattle Slew, I followed him; he didn't follow me. He taught me; I didn't teach him. That's *honestly* how I saw it. That's not just blowin' smoke."

But whatever transpired in the groom's life between 1982 and 2002—losing both parents, getting remarried, becoming a stepfather—the horse was somehow part of it.

"I don't worship no horse," the groom said as he tried to explain a point that I took to be fundamental for him. "But I wanted to live my life for Slew to be proud of me. That's how I looked at Seattle Slew." Later, when the groom rediscovered his Christian faith, he would often ask himself if that's what the horse would have wanted. Wade believes the horse did.

⌒

It is tempting to put a simple spin on Tom Wade's profound sense of his own good fortune. What groom—and a high-school dropout at that—would not be grateful to be living as he does? His house outside Lexington is part of a new subdivision carved out of a Thoroughbred farm, so home is a rather splendid place, and the aquamarine pickup truck in the driveway looks new. The tangible benefits of "doing right by the horse," as Wade puts it, are all around him, and he admits quite frankly that he has been well looked after by the owners of Seattle Slew (who, in turn, insist that this largesse comes from Slew and not from them). I'll wager that no groom in all of horsedom has what Tom Wade has. In his heart of hearts, Tom Wade must look at the fate of Eddie Sweat, lying in his humble grave in South Carolina, and say to himself, There but for the grace of God go I.

I talked with Wade about Sweat's visit to Three Chimneys. "In that week you two spent together in November of 1985," I asked Tom Wade, "what did you talk about?" I wondered if the two esteemed grooms might have shared some horse philosophy or traded tips and stories. But no, they talked about money.

"He had a family," said Wade, "and he didn't get home much and he didn't get much money. He talked to me about whether it was worth it. We had a serious conversation once about—I think he had bought a car, and I don't know that he always had a car when he worked. With Lucien, I doubt it. And he talked to me about buying a car and taking a few weeks' vacation and being right back where you started. I don't think he had a big nest egg and I think there was a lot of doubts at the time.

"Chief's Crown's people," Wade went on, "were a little bit more in tune to Eddie and Eddie's needs and things than in Secretariat times. So times had changed. Lucien Laurin had trained Secretariat, and Lucien's son Roger had trained Chief's Crown. Roger was a classy guy." It was Roger who flew Eddie's family south for the burial.

Before I left Tom Wade, I asked him if he had a photograph of himself and Slew—maybe like the one I had seen showing Will Harbut and Man o'War cheek-to-cheek on the cover of *The Saturday Evening Post*. He knew just what I was talking about and tried, but failed, to find in another room the photograph he had in mind. Maybe it was the one I found in the Seattle Slew file in the Keeneland Library: That photograph shows Wade to the front and left of the horse, with the halter loose in his left hand while the index finger of his right hand rests on the horse's nose and may be lightly rubbing the nose. Slew's eyes are soft, his ears are forward, and his mouth is a little open in pleasure.

It says a lot that Tom Wade did not choose to describe that shot, or one like it, as his favorite. He offered, instead, this image: "He's standing in the middle of his paddock. There's yellow dandelions on the ground. He's standing there . . . no *distractions*." The groom wanted only what the horse wanted. Seattle Slew was a horse who loved mornings, winter snow and cold, and, above all else, his quiet time.

I deeply regretted that Eddie Sweat was not around to offer the image of Secretariat he most treasured. I suspected his choice would have mirrored Wade's. We on the periphery gravitate to the classic images of victory: the great horse coming down the stretch, in the winner's circle, the jockey's hand raised in victory. The groom treasures the quieter moments, when the charger is at peace.

For twenty years, Tom Wade was at Slew's beck and call, and I know he counts it a privilege. But if things had gone differently, if there had been no pot of gold at the end of the rainbow, would he be as content now? The groom just shook his head and said, "That's new ground," and we left it at that.

⁓

"I think, therefore I am" was Descartes's line. "I ride, therefore I groom" might as well be mine, and thus I feel a small kinship with Eddie Sweat and his work on the ground with horses. I own a horse and typically ride him up to four times a week—always grooming him beforehand and afterward. Grooming can seem ritualistic, and sometimes riders forget *why* they groom and simply do it out of habit. But the habit, as Eddie well knew, is rooted in the safety and comfort of the horse.

Grooming means brushing away mud and dirt, which, if pressed under saddle or girth, could discomfit the horse and, worse, land the rider in trouble—hence the expression "You got a burr under your saddle?" The action of the brush enhances blood circulation, and cleaning out the hoof is a wise precaution—especially if there is a stone jammed in beside the shoe or in the frog (the V-shaped underside of the hoof). Not to clean hooves before and after the ride is to risk lameness. "No foot, no horse," another saying goes. The ritual of grooming also helps forge a bond, and a trusting horse soon abides his rider cleaning sleep from his eyes and even attending his private parts with sponge and soap and water.

My horse is a burly Canadian, a handsome dark bay born in the spring of 1994 and named, in full, Saroma Dark Fox Dali. Sometimes I will be riding Dal on the trail and feel a powerful sense of harmony and equilibrium with him. The feeling comes most readily when we're moving over snow, which can be like riding on air. I can imagine that I have found the sweet spot in the tension on the reins, that the barrier between the flesh of my arms and the leather of the reins has disappeared: I *am* directly connected, or so it feels, to my horse's mouth. He will make a little chuffing sound with his nose as he goes, and I take him to be humming. His stride is strong and even and effortless, and I can tell by the position of his head and ears that all is well in his world. I know without really thinking about it when he is about to drop a load of manure, and I rise in the saddle as a courtesy. I think I know my horse, and then I think of Eddie Sweat and what he knew about Secretariat, and a little humility sets in.

Whatever transpired between Eddie Sweat and Secretariat operated at some other level, with each bringing to the table far more than I bring to my stable or my horse offers to me. But the more I care for my horse and feel for my horse, the more Eddie-like I am around him, the closer Dal and I seem to get to the kind of communion that Sweat and Secretariat enjoyed.

Someone who was there that cold, drizzly day (October 28, 1973) at Woodbine in Toronto remembers Eddie leading Secretariat around the clubhouse turn and back to the race barn. Eddie, the observer noticed, kept patting the big red horse on the withers as they walked in the gathering darkness.

What, I wonder, was the groom thinking at that moment as he led the horse, *his* horse, still warm from the last race he would ever run? Eddie, almost surely, would have been talking as they walked. He was always addressing Secretariat, who always seemed keen to listen. This moment marked the virtual end of their remarkable partnership, so perhaps Shorty Sweat was looking back at its beginning, when he tacked Secretariat up before his maiden race on July 4, 1972. It seemed like only yesterday, yet they had come a long way.

On that day, Ol' Hopalong was up against Herbull and Master

Achiever, Fleet 'N Royal and Big Burn, Burgeon and Count Successor, Rove and Knightly Dawn, Strike the Line, Quebec, and Jacques Who. Who indeed. All those horses, and all the other horses Secretariat raced and defeated in the sixteen months that followed, are pretty much forgotten now. The name Secretariat lives on.

A Parade of Stallions

One time in Ocala, Florida, a friend took me to a celebrated Thoroughbred farm nearby for a free and lavish lunch—soup in silver tureens, breaded chicken on skewers, fancy cakes, all under a massive white tent. The only requirement for the hundreds gathered was that we sit in lawn chairs and watch as each of the farm's several dozen studs were paraded before us, maybe ten feet away, and their records read, their virtues extolled, their beauty taken in.

I remember how haughty these horses looked, how they taxed their handlers, how they danced on their toes and floated over the grass. The term *blood horse* perfectly describes a Thoroughbred stallion.

Many of us, myself included, had bought a raffle ticket. If your name was one of the dozen or so drawn, you got one free "cover": You could bring the mare of your choice to the farm, and the sire of your choice would be bred with her. My friend, it turned out, was among the winners. What was shocking to me was how much *I* wanted to win. I had managed to put aside all the logistics that winning would have entailed, feeling some primal urge to own a Thoroughbred racehorse.

Everything about this sport—the romance of dawn workouts, the thrill and danger of racing, the little high that comes with owning even one of these stunning horses—is addictive.

~ 5 ~

"Full of Run"

LUCIEN LAURIN WANTED the horse's owner to be there when Secretariat ran his first race, and he even delayed the occasion to accommodate her schedule. The trainer was sending a signal: This horse is going to be something. The owner should be on hand to watch his journey begin.

But preparation for racing had gone slower than anticipated, and though the colt was starting to turn heads with his morning workouts, there were still doubters in the Meadow camp. Some harbored suspicions against chestnuts, especially Bold Ruler chestnuts. Some, like jockey Ron Turcotte, complained that the mischievous young horse thought it a lark to bump other horses walking out to the track

in the morning. And both the jockey and the head groom still struggled with their first impressions of the horse.

Too pretty, Eddie had said. "Too big an' fat."

Turcotte called the new horse "Pretty Boy," and the rider, too, remarked on his fleshiness. "Kinda fat, ain't he?" he said to Lucien.

The trainer had to agree, and he tailored the clumsy colt's workouts to avoid stressing him while he worked the pounds off and
found his stride. At last, Secretariat did lose weight, and his morning numbers likewise tumbled. Eddie Sweat agreed to take him on,
though Riva Ridge remained his favorite and another Meadow groom,
Mordecai Williams, would sometimes fill in for him and groom the
new horse. Time would tell. They would see what the summer would
bring.

July 4, 1972, Aqueduct. Secretariat's first race (every race is a
"maiden" race until the horse wins) starts badly when he is bumped
hard by a horse called Quebec. Jockey Paul Feliciano will later report
that only Secretariat's great strength stopped the horse from going
down. The chestnut seems out of the running—he is tenth of twelve
horses—but he soon begins to gather himself. Feliciano finally finds
a hole in the wall of horses in front of him, takes Secretariat to the
rail, and the horse finishes fourth—just a length and a quarter behind
the winner.

After the race, Secretariat attacks his food, unlike most horses,
whose appetite suffers in the wake of competition. Neither does he
exhibit any of the classic signs of exertion: a tightening of the muscles, rapid breathing, lather on his chest and loins. It is as if he had
gone for a jog and the little run had drawn off only a bit of his go.

The *Daily Racing Form* gushes over him, says he finished "full of
run." The race was only five and a half furlongs. Despite the horrific

start, he was charging at the end and doubtless would have won a longer race. All in all, a fine debut.

July 15, 1972, Aqueduct. Six furlongs this time, and in this race Secretariat goes off as a six-to-five favorite (that late charge in his first race has not gone unnoticed by the handicappers). He is slow to start, but Feliciano will later report that once the horse found his gear, he "went past everybody else like they were walking." He wins by six lengths.

Secretariat, says the *Daily Racing Form,* "drew off with authority."

Eddie Sweat, meanwhile, has warmed to the horse in their five months together, warmed to him in a major way.

July 31, 1972, Saratoga. Another six-furlong race, featuring horses who have yet to win two races. Another slow start, with Secretariat last at the quarter turn. He has a new jockey now, Ron Turcotte, who follows precisely Lucien Laurin's advice not to rush the colt but to let him "feel his way, then come on with him." And feel his way he does, taking command down the stretch and winning by a length and a half. Once again, he had been the favorite.

Turcotte likes how the new horse keeps his ears back as he runs, not from anger, but because he's attentive to his rider. The jockey echoes what Feliciano had said, that the big colt's speed is deceptive, his stride easy and seemingly effortless. "He just floats," says Turcotte.

Racing writer Charles Hatton would later observe that in Secretariat's first year of racing, he was inclined "to pound his forefeet when extended," leading to fears that he would ruin his legs. But in his second year on the track, Hatton wrote, Secretariat ironed out that kink. Or nature did. Secretariat's conformation softened and grew refined by the time he was three. All the pieces now fit perfectly, divinely, and, as Hatton so gracefully put it, "his action was a buoyant, kinetic plea-sure, and it was remarked, 'He wouldn't break an egg.'"

August 16, 1972, Saratoga. Up another notch, this time to his first stakes race, the Sanford. The favorite in the race is Linda's Chief, who has won five straight.

It seems that Secretariat has learned from previous races. He hangs back at the start, avoids traffic, and makes his move heading into the turn before the homestretch.

Linda's Chief, the *Daily Racing Form* reports, "loomed boldly . . . but was no match for the winner." The winner's purse is $16,650, the margin of victory three lengths.

August 26, 1972, Saratoga. The winner of the Hopeful Stakes will earn for his stable $51,930. Bigger money, but the strategy is becoming old hat for Secretariat: Let the other horses blast out of the gate, then attack from the rear. He once again turns on the jets, goes wide and takes the lead by the halfway point, and surges ahead to win by five lengths. And despite covering more ground by using an outside lane, he still manages the six and a half furlongs in 1:16⅕—three-fifths of a second off the track record.

Before the Hopeful Stakes, Secretariat had dumped exercise rider Jimmy Gaffney following a workout. Henceforth, Eddie would *al-ways* come out and lead the horse from the track after his morning ex-ercise. (That was highly unusual. Most horses inclined to act up after a workout would have been given the company of a well-behaved track pony. Not Secretariat.) To illustrate the point, Gaffney sent me a black-and-white photograph taken at Belmont of himself, Eddie, and Secretariat. They're all walking back to the barn after a workout. The rider's gaze is toward something beyond the camera's frame, but he's attentive in the saddle. Eddie, in porkpie hat and jacket, looks a little sleepy as he leads Secretariat, but he is also watching the horse. Secretariat is wide-eyed and is looking off in the same direction as Gaffney, so there must have been a commotion over there. I would say the horse was scheming, but if he was, Eddie was set—right hand on the chain, left hand on the leather end of the lead.

"Secretariat was just so full of himself," Gaffney said, "and always felt so good that he would raise hell at the gap. The day he dropped me at Saratoga before the Hopeful was the last time he ever came out the gap without someone meeting him."

September 16, 1972, Belmont. Many people have now taken note of this huge chestnut horse, not least among them other trainers. Prior to the Belmont Futurity, with an $82,320 purse going to the winner, several trainers scratch their entries.

Frank "Pancho" Martin withdraws his horse and jokes that he does not want his colt to be in the way when the big horse makes his late charge. "I've never seen a more perfectly balanced colt," he says, "so large and with such a perfect way of going." Another trainer, George Poole, says that Secretariat's late dramatic rushes remind him of Native Dancer.

Woody Stephens, a Hall of Fame trainer, keeps his horses right next to Lucien Laurin's at Belmont, so he has ample chance to watch the horse that everyone is talking about. "The thing I'll remember about him," he will say later, "is his disposition. You never had to worry about him causing any trouble. Calmest horse I ever saw. You could let him stand by the rail and graze while the races were going on, and he wouldn't even turn his head. That's how calm he was. Nothing bothered him. He knew he was a champion."

The Belmont Futurity, a six-and-a-half-furlong race against just six other horses, unfolds much like the others. The *Daily Racing Form* remarks that Secretariat was "unhurried following the start." He is still fifth at the halfway point in the race; then he draws away and wins by almost two lengths.

In his book, Ray Woolfe reports that an unusual thing happened after the race. As Ron Turcotte and Secretariat neared the winner's circle, a woman in the crowd (and New York crowds can be tough) started clapping and urged everyone to do the same. And they did, until the whole place was cheering for the tall red horse.

October 14, 1972, Belmont. Another step up in class, the fattest purse to date ($87,900 to the winner) and, in every way but one, the same outcome as the previous six races. Secretariat enters the one-mile Champagne Stakes as a seven-to-ten favorite. True to form, he is slow off the mark ("void of early foot," as the poets at the *Daily Racing Form* put it), then charges home on the outside and wins by two lengths.

But the cheering soon fades as INQUIRY goes up on the tote board. Stewards rule that Secretariat brushed Stop the Music near the 3/16 pole, and the latter horse is given the win. Secretariat—to the dismay of many—is disqualified and officially places second.

Ask Ron Turcotte and Bill Nack about that ruling now and both will shake their heads. They have watched the films and say that the brush was a dubious judgment and would never be called today.

October 28, 1972, Laurel. During a downpour, Ron Turcotte guides Secretariat to victory in a manner that is becoming almost formulaic. A Raymond Woolfe photo taken after the race suggests that both horse and rider have been to the mud baths, so how did the horse—despite the gumbo, despite his wide route to the wire—manage to come within a fifth of a second of the stakes record time?

Stop the Music is in this race, too, but four lengths back. He was, says the *Daily Racing Form*, "easily second best." This year, almost every horse is just that when Secretariat is in the running.

November 18, 1972, Garden State. The distance: a mile and a sixteenth. The purse heavy: $179,199 to the winner. The result: same old, same old. A three-and-a-half-length victory, with the horse only truly accelerating in the homestretch.

Secretariat will winter in Florida, where Lucien Laurin gets the news that his sprightly colt has been voted Horse of the Year, the first time a two-year-old has won the honor. Laurin himself is named Trainer of the Year.

After nine starts, Secretariat has finished the year with seven wins, one second, and one fourth and he has contributed $456,404 to the Meadow's coffers. Riva Ridge, meanwhile, has brought home almost $400,000 and is being syndicated, his breeding rights sold to shareholders—for $5,120,000. That winter, Secretariat is also syndicated, for $6,080,000, then a record. What a difference a year, and a horse or two, can make in a farm's fortunes.

March 17, 1973, Aqueduct. His first race after a relaxing winter in Florida. In the Bay Shore, a short (seven furlongs) race, there is no late charge on the outside. Secretariat and Turcotte come up behind a wall of horses but somehow cut through, winning by four and a half lengths.

April 7, 1973, Aqueduct. The Gotham Mile is like the Bay Shore in that the imposing red horse departs from his usual come-from-behind tactic. In this race, he takes the lead from the start, winning by three lengths and equaling a track record that has stood since 1968.

Charles Hatton remarks on how "frightfully keen" the horse

is—*after* the race. It takes two lead ponies and an outrider to break the Secretariat express. Says Hatton, "He constantly overran his finishes and wags were fond of saying, 'He pulls up going faster than former champions ran.'"

April 21, 1973, Aqueduct. The Wood Memorial is supposed to be just one more prep race in Secretariat's run for the Triple Crown. The Kentucky Derby is only two weeks away.

The mile-and-an-eighth race starts like so many others, with Secretariat sitting in the reeds. But when Ron Turcotte chirps to his horse in the late going, the rocket thrusters don't kick in. Whether due to an abscess in the horse's upper lip, his jockey's working him slowly in a prerace workout (a riderless horse on the track provoked the caution), or some other mysterious circumstance, Secretariat is not himself today.

Eddie Sweat will later blame the abscess, caused by a burr in the horse's hay. "It bothered him a lot," Eddie will tell the *Thoroughbred Record* six years later. "On the day of the Wood, I went to get him for the race and when I put the bridle on, he wouldn't let me put it in his mouth. It took me a long time before I finally got it on." In fact, it took him a full five minutes.

The horse was saying, I don't want to work. I can't. He was not listened to. Exercise rider Jimmy Gaffney told me he had taken note of Secretariat's prerace sluggishness and passed on that information to Lucien Laurin's assistant, Henry Hoeffner. But the jockey, Ron Turcotte, is apparently kept in the dark. "I had no idea Secretariat wasn't right," he told me. "Charlie Davis and Eddie Sweat both knew about the abscess, but they later told me that Lucien had instructed them not to tell me. I wish I'd known about the abscess because I would have run him differently. I would have turned him loose and hoped for the best."

Was the trainer—amid the confusion and turmoil that followed a death in his family—fully aware of the major change in Secretariat's condition? Was Laurin convinced that other horses were no match for even a weakened Secretariat? Did the trainer worry that word of the abscess would unnerve his jockey? Without Lucien Laurin's testimony, it's anybody's guess.

A stablemate, Angle Light, wins the Wood Memorial, with Sham—a Claiborne Farm horse who has turned in some sensational results on the California circuit—coming in second and Secretariat a shocking four lengths back of the winner. A "sure thing" suddenly looks beatable.

On April 23, a plane takes Angle Light, Secretariat, Eddie Sweat, and Charlie Davis to Louisville for the Kentucky Derby—that most famous of races. The press corps that has been tagging Secretariat for months has become an almost unbearable distraction for the horse's owner and trainer, jockey, groom, and exercise rider.

The doubters in the press corps disinter the old Bold Ruler rap, that his get will not go the distance. A few see Secretariat as the moody son of a moody sire, and prone to sulking.

Drawn by the charismatic Secretariat, the media horde is unusually large and includes a great many scribes and broadcasters who know precious little about horses and who are easy prey for backside pranksters. Derby entrants are given a numbered cloth to be worn under the saddle to help journalists pick them out during morning workouts (Secretariat's is yellow, with black numbers). But the mischievous on shed row attach a similar cloth to the sorriest-looking nag in their barn, just to watch the note takers chase him.

Eddie Sweat has a dream one night just before the Derby. He tells his nephew, David Walker, about it on the phone. "Looka here, I had a dream about the Triple Crown. We're going to win the Derby, we're going to win the Preakness, and we're gonna do something never seen in the Belmont. It will be totally unbelievable."

The day before the Derby, the post positions for the thirteen horses entered are chosen according to a time-honored ritual. Into a leather-covered bottle are placed numbered ivory balls, 1 to 13. Secretariat draws number 10, farther to the outside than Lucien Laurin would have liked.

For a man inclined to worry, it is one more item for his fret list. A six-million-dollar price tag on a racehorse can rattle even the calmest horseman, and the fiery little Quebecois trainer is far from calm these days. Will he be able to keep Secretariat focused and fit in the days leading up to and throughout the thirty-five-day Triple Crown campaign? If the trainer begins to unravel, how might it affect others in the Secretariat camp? And even assuming the trainer's even keel, how will the Meadow staff respond to the unrelenting pressure? Will the much-second-guessed jockey get rattled by the great expectations placed on him? Can the groom spare the horse the crackling tension that now runs through the barn and that will only get worse? Will all the travel in the coming weeks, the press of journalists, the crush of adoring race fans (not to mention all the attention from nervous members of the Secretariat syndicate wondering how their precious investment is faring) wear the horse and his team down? Or will Secretariat, as the nation is hoping and track wise men are predicting, be the first horse to win the Derby, the Preakness, and the Belmont in twenty-five years?

May 5, 1973, Churchill Downs. On race day, a record crowd of 134,476 packs the track, and most have come to see one horse. Some of the other entries are familiar to Secretariat. There is Angle Light, the neighbor on shed row who beat him just two weeks before. There is Gold Bag, who used to outrun Secretariat during that first sojourn at Hialeah. And there is Sham, whose trainer, Frank "Pancho" Martin, is noisily predicting victory. The band begins playing "My

Old Kentucky Home" and thousands of people are drinking mint juleps—that blend of sugar, fresh mint, crushed ice, and bourbon that seems to go only with the Derby, in the way that Greek food calls out for retsina. Alone, such drinks are best avoided.

The start is delayed five minutes when Twice a Prince, in the number 6 slot, rears in the starting gate and falls backward. Ron Turcotte smartly stays clear while the dust settles. Secretariat is thus among the last to load and is spared the stress of sitting in the gate all that time.

At a mile and a quarter, the Derby marks the longest race these three-year-old horses have run in their lives. Lucien Laurin has pulled out the stops to prepare for it—mixed up slow gallops with breezes and blowouts. He wanted the horse in peak condition before the Derby, but a trainer can wear a horse out by working him too hard or leave him unprepared by exercising too lightly. It's a fine line, and this trainer can only hope he's gotten close to the line without crossing it.

The log shows that Secretariat was walked on April 24, galloped on April 25 and 26, and did three-quarters of a mile on April 27 in 1:12 ⅗. He was walked again on the twenty-eighth, and galloped on the twenty-ninth and thirtieth. May 1 saw him gallop again, and on May 2 he ran five-eighths of a mile in :58 ⅗. Any time between fifty-five and sixty seconds for that five-furlong distance is considered fast. But Secretariat's rider was not pressing, just letting him out, and Turcotte came back from that ride with a smile on his face. On Thursday, May 3, the chestnut was walked, followed by a gallop the day before the race.

After every workout, Eddie Sweat is always there to orchestrate the bath, the blanketing, the cooling out, the feeding, the almost clinical examination of Secretariat's body to look for heat in the legs or any sign of chill or discomfort or distress. By the time of the Derby, Eddie has been a groom for more than two decades. He had already seen Riva Ridge win the Derby the year before, but the preamble to that race was nothing like this one. This time, it seems the entire world is watching. Eddie stays in the barn around the clock. Night watchman is now added to his long list of duties.

There are those, like Eddie, who quietly know a great deal about horses. And there are others with precious little experience in equestrian matters who nonetheless speak into a megaphone. A Las Vegas oddsmaker named Jimmy "the Greek" Snyder incenses the Meadow camp when he tells an Associated Press reporter that track insiders are telling him an awful secret: Those on Laurin's team are routinely icing one of Secretariat's knees. This is just one of many wild rumors that fly around the track in the days leading up to the Derby (another story has it on good authority that Secretariat will be scratched just before the race). The trainer offers to fly Snyder to Kentucky and to look on as the vet of his choosing examines Secretariat. Laurin is willing to bet a thousand dollars the horse is sound. Jimmy the Greek wisely declines. (Ray Woolfe reported in his book that Snyder, who died in 1988, admitted—during a dinner with Ron Turcotte seven years after the race—that he had invented the rumor so he could win a bet on Secretariat.)

The Derby goes off as planned at 5:37 P.M. The track is fast, Secretariat has not been scratched, and his knees look just fine.

In this race, Secretariat neither makes a late charge nor grabs the lead, but adopts a middle strategy. Turcotte has him a relaxed fifth at the halfway point, then uses the whip, once at the midpoint of the race—"just enough to let him know I was serious," as he will later put it—and again as they turn for home. The race is like a two-minute opera, the tempo steadily rising for Secretariat as the piece unfolds.

Down the stretch, the jockey simply shows the whip, and this, too, yields yet another surge. Another jockey in the race, Laffit Pincay, Jr., will later win the Kentucky Derby and three consecutive Belmonts in the early 1980s. He will retire in April 2003 as the most successful jockey in horse-racing history, with 9,530 victories. But on this day, his mount, the noble Sham, cannot match Secretariat down the stretch. The two horses run together for some one hundred yards, Pincay turning in vain to his whip, Turcotte sailing past, his whip silent.

The red horse "willingly drew away in record-breaking time" in the words of the *Daily Racing Form.* Jockey Larry Adams, aboard Shecky Greene—who has led for the first half of the race—will later remember looking back as Secretariat made his charge: "I glanced back and saw him coming and thought, If I get in his way, I'll get killed. He looked like the Red Ball Express!"

Turcotte feels underneath him some new sense of stride and purpose in the young horse, as if the ten victories leading up to this one were mere rehearsals. Secretariat is picking off horses one and two at a time, but there is nothing surgical about the process. He's moving along with surreal and apparently effortless grace, switching leads to fuel the drive. "It was the first time," his jockey will say later, "he ever put everything together." As for the other horses: "They were rolling. I was flying."

Just before Secretariat makes that final thrust to gain the lead, Eddie Sweat looks on, screaming and waving his white hat, the one with the purple headband. The horses are nose-to-nose, but Eddie is convinced the duel is over, and he shouts out words to that effect. He is, of course, right.

The victory is by two and a half lengths. The time is 1:59⅖, beating the record set in 1964 by a Canadian horse, Northern Dancer, by three-fifths of a second (the equivalent of three lengths). Even more astonishing is that Secretariat—even though he took an outside, and therefore longer, path—actually *increased* his speed as the race progressed. The quarters went like this: :25 ⅕, :24, :23 ⅕, :23 ⅖, and :23.

As for Angle Light, there would be no repeat of his win in the Wood over Secretariat. He finished well back, in tenth. And Gold Bag, winner of those little schoolyard sprints in the paddocks of Hialeah? He was eleventh. Twice a Prince, meanwhile, paid a price for rearing and dumping his jockey in the starting gate: He was second to last, ahead of only Warbucks. On this day, there is only one horse, and all the rest follow in ragtag succession.

Eddie Sweat is wearing for Derby day a pair of wild candy-colored pants: black, white, and yellow. Near the winner's circle, someone hastily hangs a garland of red roses over Secretariat's withers, while someone else reaches out and touches the horse on the flank. Hard to say which causes the horse to recoil, but recoil he does, and Eddie is tossed into a retaining rope and suffers rope burns to his neck. But he's back on his feet in seconds and seeing, as always, to the horse. If there is pain, Eddie feels none of it, only exultation.

When Secretariat is cooled out back in stall number 21, Barn 42, at Churchill Downs, Eddie makes him an enormous feast—six quarts of oats, a quart of sweet feed, two quarts of bran, and several carrots. The champion tears into his feed tub. Next morning, he is so wired that Charlie Davis is unable to hand-walk him and instead saddles him up and rides him around shed row to exercise him. It was Lucien Laurin's idea to tack him up, make him think he was going to the track as a way of settling him down.

Secretariat is a horse who loves to work. Any stress, any worry, any tension in him seems to get ironed out by a pure and simple run—the longer and quicker, the better. The horse knows it, and so, it seems, does his trainer.

"I never trained a horse in my life as hard as I trained Secretariat," Lucien Laurin will later tell the *Thoroughbred Record*. The horse is eating fourteen quarts of grain daily and twenty-five pounds of hay. "A horse that does that well, you have to work him," says Laurin, "otherwise he's going to get fat." He gallops the horse farther than any other in his stable, often a couple of miles a day. And no matter how hard Secretariat works, he never backs off his feed.

Lucien Laurin is astonished that the horse continues to grow—both in stature and in the flesh. Despite precautions, the saddle slipped a little during the Derby. Now a new girth—measuring an enormous fifty-three inches—is fashioned to accommodate him.

As Eddie Sweat leads the untacked Secretariat away for the usual postrace saliva and urine tests after the Derby, his right hand is on the lead, his left fist raised in a victory salute. The crowd in each section cheers horse and groom as they pass, the sound rippling through the stands like a slow, rolling wave.

May 19, 1973, Pimlico. I have often wondered whether racehorses sock away in their memory banks horses they have faced in previous encounters. Does one horse remember besting another? Or losing to that horse? Does victory embolden them? Does a loss shake their confidence?

Sham, for instance, beat Secretariat in the Wood Memorial but lost to him in the Derby. A lot of hearts went out to Sham on Derby day: The horse had to steam in the starting gate for a full five minutes while Twice a Prince was being sorted out. So unruly was Twice a Prince that one of the assistant starters had left Sham's side and gone to the aid of his colleague. When the gates clanged open, Sham hit the gate with his head and knocked out two front teeth. Even so, Sham finished second in the Derby and he, too, broke Northern Dancer's record—in his case, by about one-fifth of a second. The *Racing Form* noted his hand ride down the stretch to the finish and how, though clearly beaten by Secretariat, Sham "continued resolutely to dominate the remainder of the field." Will this classy horse now dig a little deeper for the rubber match that is the Preakness? Or will the bloody business in the starting gate unravel him?

With Jimmy Gaffney dispatched from the Meadow barn after a dispute with Lucien Laurin, Charlie Davis is exercising Secretariat at dawn these days. Charlie had ridden him in Florida, but the horse was in his clown phase then. The new Secretariat astonishes and delights his rider. "Like ridin' on air," Charlie says, or driving a Rolls-Royce.

Another record crowd—61,657 people—comes out for the Preakness, most of them there to see the one horse who's been making such a fuss. Traffic in Baltimore is utter chaos, the worst in the city's history. The race has drawn a good many young people, some of them seeing a racetrack for the first time in their lives. They toss Frisbees, gather around the rock bands there to entertain them, and use backpacks for pillows as they lie tangled like snakes in the sun. The longhairs are not the usual Preakness patrons, but the copper horse's star appeal has clearly crossed the generational line.

Secretariat's convincing victory in the Derby has brought some measure of ease to the Meadow camp, but the tension builds anew as post time for the Preakness approaches. Only six horses will leave the gate at 5:40 P.M.: Secretariat, Sham, Our Native, Ecole Etage, Deadly Dream, and Torsion. The wisdom is that only Sham is game enough to challenge Secretariat. Both horses have the same grandsire on the dam's side—Princequillo—and both have run record times in the Derby.

Sham is indeed up for this race, but he is still no match for the red horse. Turcotte lets Secretariat ease into the pace in a manner so casual, you would think he was a race-car driver wanting to listen to the engine rev for a few seconds before stepping on the gas. There is no whip this time, just a small message with his hands that tells Secretariat it is time to go. And go he does.

Turcotte passes Our Native on the outside, then Deadly Dream and Torsion, before sprinting past the leader, Ecole Etage. All this in a quarter of a mile.

The jockey takes Secretariat wide at the clubhouse turn and then makes what the *Daily Racing Form* will call "a spectacular run" approaching the backstretch. He leaves Sham two and a half lengths back. Jockey George Cusimano, on Ecole Etage, will later describe what it was like to get passed by Secretariat: "I got to hearing this noise beside me—them big nostrils goin'—and I knew what it was. When he came by, it felt like a freight train passing—blew the number right off my sleeve."

Before the race, there was speculation that Secretariat's long, easy stride was the longest of any horse in history. So they measured it, and at first there was disappointment. His longest stride was just shy of twenty-five feet, but well shy of Native Dancer's twenty-nine feet. But, as Dr. Manuel Gilman of the New York Racing Association later explained, Secretariat uses both a long and a short stride, and it was the short one they had measured at the Maryland racetrack.

Secretariat, said Gilman, "is a most unusual horse. He's very heavily muscled and looks like a sprinter . . . but he also has the body length of the long striding horse. He's an all-purpose horse, a sprinter and stayer—and he uses the typical stride of each at different points in a race . . . and the way he accelerates is fantastic."

Sham did get within a few lengths of Secretariat down the stretch, but Laffit Pincay, Jr., was lashing his mount to get even that close. Ron Turcotte, meanwhile, simply let out his horse a little more. There was plenty of power left to be called upon if need be. But there was no need for the whip or any chirping. The jockey, as racetrackers say, sat chilly.

Despite a gutsy effort, Sham again finishes second, two and a half lengths back, as he did in the Derby. Our Native likewise finishes as he did in the Derby, coming in third. No horse in the small five-horse field posed any real threat. "Won handily" was how the *Racing Form* summed up both the Derby win and Secretariat's victory in the Preakness.

A pigeon feather was making Secretariat's whiskers itch back in the stables the night before the Preakness. Eddie Sweat blew it away and the feather floated into the hand of Bill Nack, Secretariat's vigilant scribe. Nack would keep in his wallet that feather and the two-dollar pari-mutuel ticket he had on Secretariat to win the Preakness. (Feather, ticket, and wallet, sadly, were lost to a pickpocket in 1983, when Nack was at Madison Square Garden to watch a prizefight between Roberto Duran and Davey Moore.)

June 9, 1973, Belmont. Secretariat will go for the last leg of the Triple Crown, the punishing mile-and-a-half Belmont Stakes, on his home track. On Friday night, Eddie Sweat has a dream—nightmare, more like it. Big Red has a huge lead when he goes down, is passed by the field, somehow regains his feet with Turcotte still in the irons, and desperately chases the leaders, to no avail. Eddie does not sleep. He agonizes.

Others do not lack for confidence in the red horse. The Associated Press will report after the race that one man at an offtrack betting joint plunked down $35,000 on Secretariat to win.

The press corps has by now swollen. Raymond Woolfe will later liken it to "an invasion of ants," and some on the shed row begin to resent Meadow Stable for drawing all these insects that are making their own work impossible and even dangerous. Secretariat's image graces the covers of magazines and the front pages of newspapers. Bill Nack, in his book, will later report that 28 million people had watched the Derby on television, and that a like number had watched the Preakness. When Eddie and Secretariat returned to their home barn at Belmont, some sixty reporters, photographers, and film crew members were gathered at shed row to greet them—until new rules were laid down and the hordes were banished to the perimeter.

And though Secretariat is the overwhelming favorite in the 105th running of the Belmont Stakes, and surely the sentimental favorite, he still faces the stiffest test of all. So many horses before him, and after him, have won the Derby and the Preakness, only to falter in the Belmont. Some horses lack stamina for the epic race; some have been weakened by the two races preceding it. Injury, fatigue, rider error, the horse gods: Any or all can prick a balloon.

The jockey and trainer are both confident going into the race, and they say so to the press. But everyone on the Meadow side just wants the Belmont Stakes to be over.

At 5:38 P.M. on that muggy day in New York, just five horses leave the starting gate: Secretariat, Twice a Prince, My Gallant, Pvt. Smiles, and, back for his third Triple Crown race, Sham. Lucien Laurin's instructions to Ron Turcotte before the race were much like the others. Neither send the horse nor hold him back. Just let him roll. *Use ton propre jugement.* "Use your own judgment," Laurin was saying, "and let your horse use his."

Secretariat breaks sharply. It seems there will be no lazy beginning this time, no stalking from behind, no leisurely acceleration. By the first turn, two horses are in the lead, sprinting. Secretariat's on the rail, Sham on the outside. They are embarked on a viritual marathon, and yet they are running as if the finish line were a hundred yards away.

After one furlong, Sham actually has a lead—a head, a neck, even a half length. But Secretariat stays with him, and then passes him. This is not a move meant to take a lead and try to hold it, but something else.

The copper horse leads Sham by a head at the half-mile point, and by seven lengths at a mile. A half mile to go, and Secretariat—unhurried by his jockey—continues to pull steadily away from the field. There is no field, just one horse and one rider operating in some other dimension, beyond gravity and the usual forces of nature.

Somewhere behind is Sham. The early dash and the attempt to stay with Secretariat have left him with nothing. He's coasting now, Pincay all too aware that this fine horse is done. Three times Sham has valiantly faced his nemesis, and three times he has tasted defeat. This one is crushing. For three-quarters of the race, Sham has been right there with Secretariat and then, perhaps demoralized and completely out of gas, "stops badly" (in *Daily Racing Form* parlance). He will finish last, forty-five lengths behind Secretariat. Sham's racing career is over. Several days after the race, a hairline fracture will be discovered in one of his cannon bones and he will be retired to stud.

Twice a Prince will grab second, thirty-one lengths back of Secretariat.

The miracle in this race is that Secretariat never lets up, even when the other four horses are several dozen lengths behind, with no chance of overtaking him—unless Eddie Sweat's dream was prescient. Victory is by a stunning, almost unimaginable margin: thirty-one lengths.

A horse length, nose to tail, is about eight feet. Secretariat, then, is some 248 feet ahead of the horse behind him as he crosses the finish line. In baseball, this would be almost the distance from first base to third. In football, imagine running almost three-quarters the length of the field. That's how far ahead Secretariat was.

Turcotte never touched him with the whip, just hand-rode him home. Throughout the race, this son of Bold Ruler did not once lose form or slow or give any indication at all that the mile and a half race was cutting into his extraordinary reserves of power and grace. Among the almost 68,000 fans in the stands, there is bedlam.

You might think that one horse racing alone lacks drama, that a rout in any sport is dull and lifeless. But those who looked on that day knew they were witnessing one of the greatest moments in horse-racing history. Secretariat was putting on a show. I'm guessing that he ran so long and so fast simply because he felt like it. Humans have names for such a feeling: joy, elation, glee. Whatever its equivalent in the equine world, it was now coursing through him. His blood was up, way up. He had never been more fit in his life: The Derby and the Preakness and all those workouts before and after had sharpened him as never before. Whenever talk turns to the greatest racehorse of all time, this is the one race that Secretariat backers offer as evidence in debate. The Belmont displayed a magnificent horse at a pinnacle moment, doing what he was bred to do as only he could.

One newspaper ran a photograph showing the turn for home and Ron Turcotte looking back, way back, over his left shoulder at the trailing field of horses. The playful caption read "Hey! You guys comin' or not?"

Sports Illustrated used an astonishing close-up photo from the race in its June 18 issue. In it, Secretariat is fifty feet from the finish line; his mouth is slightly open, his ears are back, and you can see the lather at his neck. Turcotte has turned to face the photographer (he's actually peeking at the infield Teletimer) and his eyes are wide, his mouth pursed to form a small *o*. His is a "holy cow" look of shock and awe.

The article, by Whitney Tower, tried to set the 105th running of the Belmont in some sort of context. He likened it to Joe Namath tossing ten touchdown passes in a football game, or golfer Jack Nicklaus shooting a 55 in the U.S. Open.

"If there was one moment I would want him remembered for," Penny Chenery later declared, "it would be the Belmont Stakes. The fact that he was able to outrun what people considered the limitations of his pedigree. And really, he was running that fast just out of the joy of running. Not from the whip, not from competition. He was running because he loved it. Glorying in his own ability."

Dave Anderson wrote in the *New York Times* about what he had seen and heard at Belmont. The writer took note of Eddie Sweat's red undershirt the morning of that sweltering day, Secretariat's blue reins, how a crowd of a hundred or so followed groom and horse from barn to tunnel to paddock. "You see," wrote Anderson, "why everybody has fallen in love with this horse. He's beautiful, he's just beautiful." A man told his child to stop crying: "While you're crying, you can't see the horse." As the horse circled under the trees of the paddock, applause followed Secretariat. "Bravo," said someone. "Bravo." After the race, some fans ran after Secretariat. One reached out and touched him. As officials swabbed saliva from his mouth into a basin, one woman said, "To think that they're treating him like any other horse."

Penny Chenery told someone after the race that she loved Riva Ridge for his gentleness. "It isn't that I don't love Secretariat," she explained. "I love him, but at the same time I am in awe of him. I am in awe of his bigness, his good looks, his power." Before the race, she talked about how Secretariat loved to run and came back wanting to play after a workout—"as if he thinks racing is a game we thought up for his amusement."

June 30, 1973, Arlington. The Arlington crowd of 41,223 is the largest in three decades. The applause for Secretariat is constant from the moment he appears on the track. In a rare move, the infield has been opened. A band plays.

Secretariat is so fit, so raring to go all the time, that any notions of resting before the race have gone out the window. When Charlie Davis tries to hand-walk him as exercise, the horse drags him around like a pull toy. On the track, Ron Turcotte has the same problem when he tries to give the horse just light exercise. The powerful rider's arms are sore from holding Secretariat back. Finally, the horse gets his wish—some fast workouts in the morning.

Sacrificial lambs are hard to come by, and Secretariat takes on just three other horses in the Arlington Invitational. He goes wide at the clubhouse turn, then ducks inside. No horse challenges him, and My Gallant, the second horse, is nine lengths back at the finish. College kids have propped a beer keg on a wheelchair, and as Secretariat turns down the homestretch, hundreds of them shoot up their arms in the power salute. There is brisk business for a man selling pennants that read SECRETARIAT 1973 TRIPLE CROWN WINNER AND SUPER HORSE.

Before the Arlington, trainer William J. Resseguet, Jr.—who had a horse in that race, Our Native (he came in third, as he had in the Derby and the Preakness)—instructed his groom to take a photo of Secretariat's head.

"Why just the head?" asked the groom.

"Because all I've seen all summer," the trainer replied, "is his rear end."

August 4, 1973, Saratoga. Man o'War's lone loss was to a horse called Upset. Secretariat has lost to several horses, but today's loss in the Whitney to one called Onion will be the most memorable.

The town of Saratoga Springs welcomes Secretariat as if he were an emperor home from a great conquest. Blue-and-white-checkered flags, the Meadow's colors, hang from lampposts, and hawkers at souvenir stands are selling everything from Secretariat T-shirts to bags of the horse's droppings. People throng to the track to pay homage, to see the great horse cruise to another victory. Some five thousand faithful go to the track three days before the race just to watch him gallop, and thirty thousand come on race day.

The race starts badly for the red horse: He bangs his head on the starting gate when he lunges forward. Some observers thought he had lost weight before the race, and it is perhaps also significant that he is up against older, four-year-old horses. Later, it will be discovered that he is running a fever. For whatever reason, Secretariat does not have his usual dramatic acceleration at the end. "He didn't fire up" is how the winning jockey Jacinto Vasquez puts it. Secretariat loses by a length and stuns the crowd into silence.

Ron Turcotte told me he had pleaded with Lucien Laurin before the race not to run the horse—for everyone in the barn knew that Secretariat was sick—but Laurin apparently warned his jockey that if he chose not to ride him, another jockey would be found. The trainer John Veitch includes himself among those who believe that Secretariat should never have lost a race. Veitch believes that a horse of Secretariat's stature can dupe a trainer into thinking that his horse, even when he's not firing on all cylinders, can still beat any other horse, that malady and lack of conditioning can be overcome. "That's human frailty," says Veitch, and should not be held against the horse. After the loss, Secretariat stood facing the back of his stall and ignored all attempts at communication or condolence.

September 15, 1973, Belmont. The first running of the one-and-one-eighth-mile Marlboro Cup Handicap gathers a classy field of seven horses, including Riva Ridge, the aforementioned Onion, and a quick Canadian horse called Kennedy Road. And for a while it is Riva Ridge (with Eddie Maple up) and Secretariat in a battle before the red horse pulls away. He wins by three and a half lengths, setting a world record along the way.

Track sage Charles Hatton is dumbfounded that the horse—who looked "distressingly ill" and "bloody awful" from a coughing virus picked up the day before the Whitney—has rebounded so mightily. The horse has gained weight and he seems to be thriving on punishing workouts, setting track records in his dawn runs. Lucien Laurin, writes Hatton, "never got to the bottom of him actually." And Laurin will later say the same thing.

September 29, 1973, Belmont. Secretariat has never run on grass before, but he seems to like it when Turcotte takes him for his first training on grass. "He loved it!" the jockey will enthusiastically report afterward. "I could ride this horse over broken bottles or a plowed field if we had to! He adapts to anything."

However, even great horses need time to adjust to new surfaces. But there is no time. Wet weather means that Secretariat, not Riva Ridge, will run in the mile-and-a-half Woodward, which has always been plan B. Plan A was to run the red colt in the Man o'War Stakes on October 8, giving him nine more days to work on grass.

Lack of conditioning, then, may explain why he comes up flat in a stretch duel with Prove Out in the Woodward. Prove Out wins by four and a half lengths.

October 8, 1973, Belmont. Now the Man o'War Stakes looms, and so does Tentam, widely seen as the best grass horse in America. His trainer originally decided against entering the Man o'War Stakes, but seeing Secretariat falter on the grass at Belmont gave him hope. When the trainer, MacKenzie "Mac" Miller, starts taking note of Secretariat's training times on the grass (one is the quickest five furlongs ever recorded on grass), he has grave second thoughts. "At times he is frightening," the trainer says. "I've never seen a colt with more fluid, marvelous action."

In this race, the copper horse simply takes the lead and never relinquishes it. Without seeming to strain, and running against the wind down the backstretch, Secretariat covers the mile and a half in 2:24 ⅕, matching the world record for that distance on *any* surface.

October 28, 1973, Woodbine. Penny Chenery is intent on retiring Secretariat to stud at Claiborne Farm on November 15, so there is time for just one final race. Among her options are the Washington International and the Jockey Club Gold Cup at Aqueduct. There is also the Canadian International on the grass in Toronto, and that choice prevails for obvious reasons.

"I favor the Canadian race," the owner says, reminding reporters that the horse's trainer and jockey are both Canadian. "This brings a degree of sentiment into the decision." She is also well aware of what E. P. Taylor, the owner of Northern Dancer, and others in Toronto have done for North American racing: "I believe it would be nice to reciprocate."

The stars, though, do not align. For one thing, Ron Turcotte is suspended for five days for a racing infraction just days before the Woodbine race. So Eddie Maple is chosen to ride the red horse, though Maple is dispirited after riding Riva Ridge to an ignoble last place in the Jockey Club Gold Cup. It marks a cruel end to the horse's long and sterling career. (Riva Ridge will then stand at stud at Claiborne Farm, where he will die in 1985. Secretariat was buried next to him.)

Eddie Sweat notes Secretariat's mood the day of the Canadian International Championship (now called the Rothmans International). "The morning of the race felt real good," he will tell the *Daily Racing Form.* "We took him out and he just bounced around the shed row. He was kicking at the tubs, he was kicking at the wall boxes; anything that got in his way he was kicking at it."

Bruce Walker, then working in publicity for the Ontario Jockey Club, has vivid memories of the week before the race. "Eddie," he told me, "would lead Secretariat to the walking ring under the trees. And the owners and trainers and grooms would line the fence to watch them and admire the horse. The horse always looked magnificent. He was rubbed to glistening. And what struck me was that Eddie was always talking to Secretariat and the horse would cock his head, as if he understood every word. On the morning of October twenty-fifth, there was heavy fog, and I remember hearing his hooves on the track; then I heard that huge *whoosh* from his nostrils. Then, finally, I saw him. He came flying out of the fog. It was just amazing, almost magical. I couldn't believe the power, and his stride was immense." Secretariat did five-eighths of a mile in a scorching fifty-seven seconds "and change," as racetrackers like to say.

And as Secretariat left the track each day, he passed a kind of honor guard of grooms. They would all line the roadway. Bruce Walker is convinced they were there to pay homage to the horse: "People on the backstretch knew they were in the presence of royalty." But the grooms, said Walker, were also paying respect to a great colleague. "There was admiration for Eddie, too."

On race day, more than 35,000 fans brave cold, wet weather to watch a great horse run for the last time. Some ten thousand fans came earlier to watch his morning workout on the grass. My brother, Wayne Scanlan, now a sports columnist with the *Ottawa Citizen,* had gone to the race with a friend and they were waiting interminably to buy a pari-mutuel ticket. "We all wanted the same thing," he said, "a souvenir of Secretariat's last race. Finally, my friend said, 'I'd rather see the horse.' So we walked down to the paddock and we got within fifteen to twenty feet of Secretariat. It was such a thrill to see him. And I'll never forget his size and his beauty. That memory means a lot more to me than a ticket stub I would have stuck in a drawer." (Track officials later estimated that more than $100,000 in uncashed pari-mutuel tickets remain from Secretariat's races.)

The Woodbine crowd cheers the star horse from the time he comes out on the track until he enters the starting gate, and they keep on cheering. Secretariat wins convincingly, by six and a half lengths, but only after enduring two hard bumps from Kennedy Road, with Avelino Gomez up. After that, Secretariat takes the lead—a decision he apparently makes himself. Maple will later surmise that the horse was angry, that he took off in a huff.

Secretariat, along with his francophone jockey and trainer, struck a chord in Canada. In late 2003, an unidentified Thoroughbred breeder in Canada paid $21,600 for the blanket worn by Secretariat after his last race at Woodbine. Penny Chenery sold the cooler to benefit the Secretariat Foundation, which funds equine research.

⌒

Secretariat never races again, but he does go to the track one final time—for Secretariat Day at Aqueduct on November 6, 1973. Some 33,000 people show up to say good-bye and to hear from a tearful Penny Chenery. "The most memorable thing we do have," she says into the microphone, "is the memory of Secretariat in his moments of triumph. We have also been proud of him in his moments of defeat."

His record for twenty-one races would stand at sixteen wins, three second-place finishes (including a disqualification), one third-place finish, and one fourth-place result.

Ron Turcotte jogs Secretariat—whom he calls "the smartest and boldest horse I ever rode"—out onto the track and then into the winner's circle. But the muscled horse appears angry that there will be no racing that day, and he tries to eat the bouquet of roses that Penny

Chenery holds in her hands. And then, four friends make their way down the track and off into the sunset: Charlie Davis on Billy Silver, Eddie Sweat leading the blanketed Secretariat.

Someone asked Eddie what Secretariat would miss most in his retirement. "He's going to miss running," he replied. "Every morning he would wait for someone to put the tack on so he could get out and run. He loved it."

On another occasion, Eddie observed of Secretariat, "The only thing he knows is eat, relax and run. He never acts up. He's always loose. Lots of times he'll look around at the crowd while we're going to the post, like he's saying, 'What's them people doing here?'"

And when, that day at Claiborne, he was asked what he would miss most about Secretariat and Riva Ridge, Eddie answered without hesitation, as if he had already carefully considered the matter. "Early in the mornings," he said. "Every morning at five thirty Secretariat would be sitting there waiting for me. Both of them would be waiting, looking down the shed row. . . ."

For the next sixteen years, Secretariat would stand at stud at Claiborne Farm. It was indeed a place fit for a king. Today, the farm encompasses three thousand acres (it was once bigger, but a Saudi sheikh bought six hundred acres), with 55 barns, 650 stalls, 45 employee houses, 90 miles of fencing, and 27 miles of paved road. Secretariat's own paddock at Claiborne was 1.9 acres. Seabiscuit was born here, as were Forego and Kelso, but the most frequently asked question in all the time that Secretariat lived there was, of course, "Where's Secretariat?" During Derby week, six hundred people a day would pour in to Claiborne. In the spring of 1974, the farm was forced to close its doors to visitors after so many came that traffic derailed normal operations at the farm. Every visitor wanted to see the horse and, more, to touch him. As the years passed and the pilgrims to Claiborne continued to come, more people saw him up close at the stud farm than got close to him at the track. This may explain why he never lost stature, even decades after he ran.

When Secretariat first went to Claiborne, he would race the stud in the next paddock (Round Table in the early days), but he eventually chose to ignore the other studs. He knew he was the star attraction, the horse visitors approached first. His dam, Somethingroyal, had the same imperiousness and may have passed it on.

Lawrence Robinson was the head caretaker of stallions at Claiborne. "He's kind, a very kind horse," he said in 1977. "I really think he's the most kindest horse I ever groomed. He's perfect in every way.

"I've seen this son of a gun some cool mornings circle around this paddock and I mean really cut loose. It looks like he's almost lying down around those turns. But he never slips."

Robinson worked at Claiborne Farm for forty years. He suffered a stroke in 1981. He told *Time* magazine in 1988, not long before he died, "The stroke made me forget some things. But I'll never forget the day that beautiful horse stepped out of that trailer." As he spoke of his eight years with Secretariat, Robinson was sitting in a lawn chair near his home on a hill, which overlooked Claiborne, and his eyes teared up. "I sit up here every day and think about that horse," he said then. "That horse loved me. I could see it in his eyes." The aged groom had cared for hundreds of horses, including Bold Ruler, Nasrullah, and Princequillo, but he had fallen in love with only one horse.

Secretariat's routine at Claiborne rarely varied; out to pasture at 7:45 A.M., then back to the barn at 2:00 P.M. He would get two quarts of grain in the morning and twenty-five pounds of hay in his stall. During his six hours in the paddock, he never stopped eating grass. Robinson guessed he ate twenty-five pounds of grass a day.

A reporter for a newspaper in Hamilton, Ohio, wrote in 1974 of going to visit Secretariat at Claiborne. The horse apparently liked to play pickup sticks: He would have a stick in his mouth and you were supposed to take it from him and then give it back.

Bobby Anderson, Secretariat's groom for the horse's last six years at Claiborne, talked about Secretariat in the spring of 1989, only months before the horse died. "He's really a smart horse," said Anderson. "He listens to your voice a lot. Most of them, you've got to kind of discipline them and make them mind, but if you raise your voice to him, you've hurt his feelings."

Anderson said that visitors would take as a keepsake straw from Secretariat's stall, his droppings, filaments of his mane if they could get them. They would take home photographs, and memories, too, of how he walked, how he stared at them, how he ignored them, how he grazed. He was a lord in his manor, self-aware and proud.

Ron Turcotte gave an interview to the *Louisville Courier-Journal* in 1998, on the twenty-fifth anniversary of the Triple Crown win. "He was something special," his old jockey said, "like God decided to make the perfect horse. There is no word I can find to explain what it was like being on him. It was just like, instead of pushing the accelerator, I was pulling the throttle, because I'd pull on the reins to make him run faster."

I later asked Turcotte the obvious question: "How did you stop him, given that the usual method of stopping a horse—applying the brakes—only made him go faster? "I'd drop his head," the rider replied. "That put him into idling mode. He learned that at Hialeah."

"The only thing I can tell you," Turcotte told the *Courier-Journal,* "is that nobody has seen the true Secretariat. A horse reaches his peak at five, and this horse was barely a baby when he was retiring. He was just learning how to run."

As a stud, he was very, very good, though some were disappointed that he did not sire a horse to equal his own stature. His first "cover" of a mare was a test, since there was some concern that his sperm count was low. Of two test mares sent to him, one took—an eight-year-old Appaloosa called Leola. They picked her because she was gentle, more so than high-strung Thoroughbred mares. The result was a hefty colt called First Secretary—he had markings much like his sire's, and he would grow to 17 hands.

Gus Koch, who is now the farm manager at Claiborne but was the stud manager in Secretariat's day, saw the stallion every day for seventeen years. "He made my job easy," said Koch. "He was up in one jump; he never took longer in the shed than three or four minutes; he was fertile, an easy keeper. I can still see him coming to the breeding shed. Poetry in motion. He sure had a personality, and he was so smart. You could tell by the way he carried himself. Other stallions would be jumping around and showing off. With him, there was no wasted motion."

Secretariat would sire 663 foals, including fifty-nine stakes winners, and they would win some $29 million on tracks all over North America. Risen Star, who won the Preakness and the Belmont (by fifteen lengths) in 1988, was voted champion three-year-old colt. Lady's Secret, a filly and Horse of the Year in 1986, retired as all-time leading female winner with $3,021,425 in earnings. General Assembly was a fine horse, as was Kingston Rule, a tall chestnut, who won Australia's famous Melbourne Cup.

Secretariat's great-grandson Charismatic won the Derby and Preakness in 1999 and was in the lead to win the Belmont when he tragically fractured a front leg and was pulled up by jockey Chris Antley.

Secreto, a grandson on the dam's side, won the Epsom Derby in 1984. Tabasco Cat, another grandson, won the Preakness and Belmont in 1994. Erhaab, whose sire, Chief's Crown, is out of Secretariat's daughter Six Crowns, won the Epsom Derby. Secretariat's daughter Terlingua won seven stakes races and earned $423,896. Pancho Villa, a full brother to Terlingua, won $596,734 from 1985 to 1986. Secretariat's daughters were good, and so were the sires out of his daughters—like Storm Cat and Gone West and A. P. Indy. The latter horse was by Seattle Slew out of Weekend Surprise, a daughter of Secretariat's. How's that for bloodlines?

On the other hand, the $1.5-million Canadian Bound and the $550,000 Grey Legion—among Secretariat's first draft of sales yearlings—were duds on the track. Yet a great-grandson of his sold at auction for $5.5 million. So much for no faith in his bloodlines.

"What is certain," noted *The Blood-Horse* magazine, "is that Secretariat's daughters already have assured their sire a lasting mark on the breed." Runners from his daughters earned $33.8 million.

The debate continues about Secretariat's mark as sire, but there is no doubting his enduring legacy. Think back to 1973: student protests against the war in Vietnam; White House lies and cover-up. And out of that dark and charged time stepped a hero: a stunning horse with a coat of copper and red that turned a burnished gold in bright sun. Handsome and smart, strong and playful, he was an athlete we could cheer for when it seemed there was little to cheer about.

While Secretariat was running for the roses, Vice President Spiro Agnew was resigning in the wake of charges of income tax evasion. This was the year of Woodstock and Wounded Knee, when the hit movies were *The Godfather, The Exorcist,* and *Last Tango in Paris.* Pete Rose was named the National League's Most Valued Player in 1973 and O. J. Simpson set an NFL rushing record, but both athletes would later fall from grace. Secretariat was, and remains, the unsullied hero of that era.

Looking back on that time, Penny Chenery remembers that "horse racing was in a down period. The country was in a blue mood. It was the time of Watergate and the Nixon scandals, and people wanted something to make them feel good. This red horse with the blue-and-white blinkers and silks seemed to epitomize an American hero." Secretariat was everything the Watergate crooks were not: an elegant creature without vice or motive, and beyond corruption.

George Plimpton called Secretariat "the only honest thing in the country at the time. . . . Where the public so often looks for the metaphor of simple, uncomplicated excellence, the big red horse has come along and provided it, and made the air seem a little cleaner and nicer to breathe."

The former general manager at Pimlico Race Course, Chick Lang, once said of Secretariat: "It is as if God decided to create the perfect horse!" (Lang had another good line about Secretariat: "He even grazed better than any horse I ever saw.")

Secretariat was famous, but, of course, he did not seek fame, nor was he moved by fame. He simply was—perhaps the best ever at what he did. Secretariat ran, as track wise men say, a hole in the wind.

In the same week in 1973, he graced the covers of *Time, Newsweek,* and *Sports Illustrated.* 'AT LAST, AN HONEST FACE' was the small headline over the various letters that later appeared in *Time* by way of response. Corruption in Washington was then clearly on everyone's mind, as one reader asked, "Who can question the honesty of Secretariat's face?" Another slyly wondered, "How many readers wrote in to remark that it was refreshing to see the front end of a horse on the cover of *Time*?" Underneath the letter was the number—sixty-five—and editor's world-weary comment: "so far."

A Las Vegas nightclub offered Penny Chenery $25,000 if her horse would appear twice a day—prance onto a stage, stand fifteen minutes, then walk off again. The offer was rejected, as was a plan to market Secretariat's droppings. A hotel, also in Las Vegas, created the Secretariat Suite: a four-thousand-square-foot spread, with two parlors, four bars, a game room, an eighteen-by-thirty-five-foot pool, a sauna, and four bedrooms.

Today, Secretariat remains the source of intense hero worship. At the elaborate Web site Secretariat.com, dedicated to his legacy, fans can pitch questions to Penny Chenery or buy bobble-head dolls and snow globes, T-shirts and ball caps. In 1999, Secretariat became the first Thoroughbred to be honored with his own U.S. postage stamp. The state of Virginia plans to offer Secretariat license plates to raise funds for a horse museum in Caroline County, where he was born. The plate will show Secretariat on the left, staring out from his white-and-blue blinkers, with his name and "Triple Crown Champion" below. A stable for retired racehorses near Lexington, opened in 2004, was named the Secretariat Center. The $400,000 Secretariat Stakes in Arlington Heights, Illinois, helps keep his name alive. There is even a chocolate bar ("the official fine chocolate bar of America's horse") named after Secretariat and made by Kentucky's venerable Ruth Hunt Candy Company. Claiborne Farm still gets flowers meant for his grave. He was no mere horse; he was, and remains, a legend.

In the spring of 2000, a letter appeared in *Newsweek* in response to a column by Anna Quindlen on how professional athletes had earned irrelevance by their often awful behavior. The correspondent, one Jerry Redmond from Huntington, New York, lamented the "egotistical louts" whose lawyers finagle them counseling programs in lieu of jail time. "For every gentlemanly Wayne Gretzky or Nolan Ryan," Redmond wrote, "we have a platoon of John Rockers and Mike Tysons"—both of whom were punished, the baseball player for racist comments, the boxer for rape. "For that reason, my favorite athlete of all time is Secretariat. At least he always knew how to behave in public."

Vogue magazine called Secretariat "the Clark Gable of horses." Secretariat won the Triple Crown—the Kentucky Derby, the Preakness, the Belmont—all in dramatic fashion. (In both the Derby and Preakness, he came from dead last.) His times in all three races still stand as the fastest in history (though it should be noted that the Preakness record is unofficial, owing to a fault in the Teletimer on race day). Secretariat shattered track records and world records, and he won the Belmont by a staggering and unprecedented thirty-one lengths—a feat witnessed by more than fifty million fans on television. That he lost a few races, to lesser horses and often when either his health or training was compromised, only endeared him all the more to his admirers. When Secretariat was three years old, three secretaries were employed at Claiborne Farm to answer the two hundred or so letters sent to the horse *every day.*

When, near the end of 1999, ESPN assembled its list of the top fifty athletes of the twentieth century, only one animal made the list. Secretariat was thirty-fifth, ahead of Mickey Mantle and Pete Sampras. In 1984, *The Blood-Horse* magazine asked its readers to rank the ten best Horses of the Years in the past half century; 89 percent included Secretariat on that list, but when turf writers were parceled off from the two thousand who sent in ballots, the figure was 100 percent. And when *The Blood-Horse* in 2000 asked seven experts to rank the top one hundred horses of the twentieth century, Secretariat was second only to the great Man o'War. (Seabiscuit, that game and storied horse, ranked twenty-fifth.) Charles Hatton, the dean of turf writers in America, would have scoffed at the survey. He saw both Man o'War and Secretariat run, and he called the latter horse "the greatest I have seen and the greatest anyone has ever seen."

In 1999, *Time* magazine ranked the ten most influential athletes

of the twentieth century, and there, again, was Secretariat, alongside
Babe Ruth and Michael Jordan. The Athlete of the Year in 1973 had
not been forgotten.

An MIT professor named George Pratt, an authority on the biomechanics of the equine gait, examined Secretariat at Claiborne Farm
in 1987 and pronounced his the most efficient ever measured. "He
looked," said Pratt, "like he would run through a stone wall. He is a
mountain of muscle, a mountain of dignity, a mountain of aristocratic
bearing—the most impressive live creature I have ever looked upon."

Professor Pratt uttered the comment in the course of a TV documentary made by the Canadian Broadcasting Corporation and first
aired on November 15, 1989—just six weeks after Secretariat's death.
Dr. Pratt's comment that Secretariat had "a magic way of going" gave
the documentary its title. In a note to me, the MIT professor emeritus
elaborated on what he saw at Claiborne Farm:

> Flying back to Boston with the program's producer, we were chatting
> about horses and I described my visit to Claiborne Farm in Kentucky
> where Secretariat was at stud. I was then and still am a great fan of that
> horse on whom I have done a detailed biomechanical analysis. I went
> down to his stall with the stallion manager who brought him out for
> me to see. Well, it was truly a religious experience. I was blown away
> by this god-like creature who simply paralyzed the shed row by his
> majestic presence. Nobody said a word. All the other stallions, all the
> workers, every living thing there froze at the sight of him.

No one who saw Secretariat up close will ever forget him. He had
presence, he had majesty, and he had a look about him—the look of eagles. It's a phrase that some may stumble over. How can a horse look like
an eagle? One day in Lexington, I went to the Hall of Champions at
Kentucky Horse Park, where some modern-day racing legends—John

Henry and Cigar among them—were being paraded around a small amphitheater while a park employee with a microphone told the audience their stories. I was up in the far reaches, maybe ten rows back in the bleachers, and fussing with my telephoto lens as Cigar was being circled by a groom. Cigar, for the record, was Horse of the Year in 1995, when he won ten races in a row, extending that to sixteen in a row the following year, after which he retired, having won some ten million dollars, more than any horse in history. He was about thirty feet away from me. I looked up to see him stop, look me square in the eye, and hold my gaze for about five seconds. This grandson of Seattle Slew was not looking *at* me, but *through* me, and I felt both honored and fixed by his imperial gaze.

Secretariat had that look, and then some. Raymond Woolfe loved his "clean, broad head with lovely bright eyes, which to horsemen signifies intelligence and good sense." Woolfe admired his short, strong back, his powerful shoulders, his deep chest, his fine balance, and his straight hind legs. And it seemed he loved to be looked at, especially if you had a camera in your hand. Woolfe, who took thousands of shots of Secretariat, said the horse would pose for him, arching his neck, flashing his eyes, flaring his nostrils, and pricking his ears.

He pinned you with his look, for it struck everyone who saw him that he was a glory of creation. The Pimlico track official who watched Secretariat run, the Texas sculptor who cast him in bronze, and the jockey who rode him for almost two years all had the same notion: that God had set out to make the perfect horse, and Secretariat was the result.

Eddie Sweat saw him from the ground, and he saw perfection in the horse's feet, which he proclaimed "one of the beautifullest set of feet of any horse I ever rubbed." There were no chips or cracks in Secretariat's hooves, Eddie told Raymond Woolfe: "His are *smooth,* just smooth all over. But you know, *he's* perfection all over."

In his book *Blood Horses: Notes of a Sportswriter's Son,* John Jeremiah Sullivan describes Secretariat "not as the greatest horse, nor as the greatest runner, nor even as the greatest athlete of the twentieth century, but as the greatest creature. The sight of him in motion is one of the things we can present to the aliens when they come in judgment asking why they should spare our world."

⟝ A GIFT ⟞

Roger Broomes is using a pitchfork to lift and drop straw in a just-vacated stall. His motion is practiced and circular as he deftly separates clean from sullied and forms small piles, the good stuff in one corner, the vile in another. The ammonialike whiff of horse urine comes in waves, and some grooms here wear surgical masks, but Broomes is not among them.

I've been on the backside at Woodbine racetrack in Toronto since 4:00 A.M., up with the keeners and the early early risers. Now it's eight o'clock: rush hour. Outside the stall flows a lively traffic of men, women, and horses. Everyone calls to one another amiably and warmly, like Shriners at a picnic.

The birds are yahooing over spilled grain, the stall fans droning, hooves clip-clopping on asphalt. On the grassy boulevards, sweaty horses are being soaped up and hosed off, and it's good to smell water and soaked earth during what has been a long, drought-plagued summer.

Broomes—the word *strapping* leaps to mind when I first see him—is wearing denim coveralls over his almost six-foot frame and a fashionable red pirate's kerchief over his long black dreadlocks. There is a palm-wide piece of white tape halfway down the handle of his fork. Offering comfort and grip for the lower hand, the tape has been worn almost black from use and the wood owns a fine sheen of dirt and sweat. Like an old bat in a glass case at Cooperstown.

Roger Broomes was born in Barbados. There's a singsong melody to his words, and his laughter is easy, his mouth wide, his manner calm. He knows full well what he brings to the table to keep a horse happy and healthy and eager, and he is not pleased that grooms get no credit. "Apart from Eddie Sweat, I don't think any grooms ever got it. Seabiscuit, Northern Dancer, Phar Lap. Nobody ever talk about the groom." I haven't the heart to tell him that even Eddie Sweat, "groom of grooms," got sparse credit.

Just then, a trainer and rider named Victor Ramos ("Famous Ramos," they call him; he is the nephew of jockey Avelino Gomez) walks past. He looks me in the eye, points at Broomes, and says, "He's the best." So Broomes's everyday professionalism is noticed, much as Eddie Sweat's professionalism was noticed, at least by some.

In 1990, in only his second year in Canada and still very much a rookie at the track, Broomes heard that Sweat was coming to Woodbine. Broomes hoped to meet him and could not believe his good fortune when he learned that Eddie and his outfit had set up shop in the stalls next door.

"It was like a gift for me," Broomes says of the pairing. "I saw him every day, from April to November, that year. I was so fortunate. To see him handle a horse, only then would you understand. The horses he had weren't great, not stakes winners or anything, but they were classy because of the way he handled them."

I wondered what he saw in Eddie. "What set him apart?" I ask.

"It was an honor to know him and watch him work," Broomes says. "Applying a bandage, for example—I'd look at what he had done and I'd say, 'Why doesn't my bandage look like that?' Or giving a horse a bath. His horses were so quiet. They would stand until he was finished. My horses would be playing around and I'd be soaking wet by the end."

Watching Eddie work around a horse, Broomes says, was like

watching a master carpenter build a cabinet. "He seemed a natural at what he did."

Eddie talked all the time about Secretariat. A small circle of shed-row workers would gather around him to hear these stories, sometimes over a beer or a cigarette. But somehow, Eddie was never seen to brag.

"Yeah man," says Broomes, "I really admired him. He was so down-to-earth, so full of goodwill. There were no airs about him. He was a humble man, laid-back and quiet. Always classy. He was legit. And you won't find anyone who says different. No one on the backside had a bad experience pertaining to him. He was confident and he knew he made a difference to any horse he looked after. He was one of a kind."

"Was he happy?" I ask.

"Always, always, always. I can't recall a moment when I didn't enjoy his company. He was always cheerful."

"Did he talk to his horses?"

"Always. And maybe it was what the trainer [Roger Laurin] called for, or maybe it was Eddie's idea. But every night he'd cook up his horses a warm mash of oats and corn. It was little things like that. He was a great man, a horse man. His work was his passion."

Eddie would talk about how relaxed Secretariat was, how confident. "Like the groom," Broomes says. "I credit Eddie's attention and good care. They both had each other."

Eddie spoke of Secretariat as a proud father would speak of his son. "And that's how a groom *should* feel," Broomes says. "I dream of that. That kind of fame. To be around a great horse. I don't begrudge Eddie, but I wish it was me."

~ 6 ~

Catching a Glimpse of Glory

Punch in "i saw secretariat" on an Internet search engine, visit Secretariat.com, or spend time at Keeneland Library reading its many thick files on Secretariat, and you will find myriad tales from individuals who were on the scene in the early 1970s, when the awesome chestnut ran—at Churchill Downs, Pimlico, Belmont, Saratoga, Aqueduct, Woodbine, Arlington—and, later, when he stood at stud at Claiborne.

Take Jean DellaRocco, for example. Her memories of Secretariat are intertwined with those of childhood and simpler times, when the track was a family gathering place. "It seems," DellaRocco wrote in a note to me, "like most of my childhood was filled with 'horse heroes.' Why this is I can't be sure. I've loved horses for as long as I can remember, and Secretariat was the first of my heroes. He was so beautiful and strong, and seemed so invincible, even to a young child of five." The horse struck the young girl then as almost mythological—"the real-life version of a storybook horse."

DellaRocco saw Secretariat in the flesh, but her memories are bittersweet. She spent summers as a child at Saratoga Springs, in the rolling horse country of upper New York State. The track at Saratoga is to Thoroughbred racing what Fenway Park is to baseball: sacred ground. DellaRocco's parents, her sister, her aunt, and her grandparents went every weekend to see the stakes races. Seeing the Whitney Stakes of August 4, 1973, is one of her earliest childhood memories, but if DellaRocco can truthfully say "I saw Secretariat," she must add one word: *lose.*

"I was so upset to see him lose that day," she wrote from her home in Latham, New York. "The fact that my grandfather had bet on the winner, Onion (and thus against the entire family) established this story as the kind you pass on for generations. I still remember my grandmother admonishing him for doing that and making me so upset."

A trainer (the appellation Triple Crown Chick forms part of her E-mail address) has posted a message at Secretariat.com calling Secretariat the pinnacle of beauty and grace, speed and heart. If she were to train a horse who had even one-quarter of his gift, she wrote, she would consider herself truly blessed. Other correspondents confessed to shedding tears—at seeing Secretariat's trophies and bridles on display at Kentucky Horse Park, at seeing him race, at visiting his birthplace or his grave, upon giving him mints one crisp fall day. This particular horse moved them, and *still* moves them, in a way that someone without affection for horses might find incomprehensible, even nonsensical. The word *hero* crops up a lot in the testimony of those smitten by Secretariat.

Then there is Cindy Tunstall, who reprised in *Equus* magazine her encounter with Secretariat at Claiborne Farm in 1985. Farm manager John Sosby had apparently given this clearly devoted fan one of the champion's horseshoes. "To this day," she wrote, "I don't know of anything that has moved me more." Then they went out to see the horse, who was grazing at one end of his paddock but galloped to the fence to meet them. Tunstall recalled that he was older "and more than a few pounds heavier than in his days of glory," but he still looked the part. She ran her hands over his neck and shoulders and chest—*strong* and *broad* and *muscular* were the adjectives she used to describe each. A wall in Tunstall's home has become a shrine to Secretariat. She has the horseshoe mounted on a plaque, and several photographs of the stallion (including one with Tunstall beside him, and one taken the day before he died) hang there. "He lives on that wall," she wrote. "And in my heart."

That same year, Bob Swisher of Paducah, Kentucky, was with his wife in Lexington for a ten-kilometer run—and a surprise encounter with Secretariat. (He would later tell the story in a letter to the *Louisville Courier-Journal* in 1998, when readers were asked to submit stories to mark the twenty-fifth anniversary of Secretariat's Triple Crown victory.) On a whim, the Swishers drove out to Claiborne. "Could a man who just drove two hundred and seventy-five miles see Secretariat?" he asked the foreman, stretching the truth a little.

The foreman obliged, and he took Swisher and his wife to Secretariat's stall for photos. Then the foreman asked him, "Would you like to walk him to his pasture?" Naturally, Swisher was thrilled, and when the foreman turned Secretariat loose in his paddock, the champ, wrote Swisher, "turned two laps at top speed around his playpen. What a spectacle! The world's greatest athlete 'doing his thing.' And I was there. That's how it was the day I walked Secretariat to his pasture."

After I put an ad in the *Daily Racing Form* requesting stories about

Secretariat, one woman wrote me to say that in 1973 she was fifteen years old and taking a course at school on the care and training of the Thoroughbred racehorse. The students gathered one morning at Belmont, and the closer they got to Barn 5, Lucien Laurin's barn, the louder was the banging. When they asked the trainer about all the commotion, he said, "'Oh, that's Secretariat wanting to go out.' Seemed Big Red demanded that he go for a jog at least every morning. He was the king in the barn."

Another woman called a National Public Radio program in 2002 when the subject was television's most unforgettable moments. For her, the most enduring moment was the first time she saw Secretariat run. She had been walking to her seat in a restaurant, she recalled, when "I saw this animal run and I realized I was seeing something I would probably never again see in my life, the way that animal moved and owned the racetrack."

When Secretariat went to Arlington in late June 1973, an elderly couple waited four hours at O'Hare Airport in order to catch a ten-second glimpse of him walking down the ramp from the turboprop to a horse van. Mrs. Ray Kling was asked by George Plimpton—who was on assignment that day for *Sports Illustrated*—if the long wait was worth it. "Yes, *heavens yes,*" she replied. "This is much more exciting than Lindbergh's landing. And I was *there.*"

Even the jockeys who lost to him that day in Chicago (Secretariat Day, as Mayor Richard Daley proclaimed it) seemed jocular after the event. There was joy in simply being close to this horse, even in eating his dust. George Getz, the trainer of Blue Chip Dan—last at the first turn, last at the finish—said cheerfully before the race that his horse was David to Secretariat's Goliath, except "my horse doesn't have a slingshot and a rock." There were only four horses in that Arlington Invitational, and yet some twenty jockeys in their silks were on hand in the saddling area to watch Ron Turcotte hop on board the people's horse. "There's not a pimple on him," said jockey Larry Melancon, staring at him as he spoke. "I've never seen anything like him."

A neighbor of mine is typical of another sort of fan. Never an aficionado of racing, he was nevertheless drawn to Woodbine that bitter day in Toronto to see Secretariat's final race. The neighbor put two bucks on him to win and never cashed in the ticket, but kept it as a memento—which he still has in a drawer.

Another friend, who worked one summer for the *Daily Racing Form* and who still bets the ponies, remembers being in a small-town bar in northern Ontario for the June 9, 1973, running of the Belmont. David Carpenter is a collegial sort, the type who will organize an impromptu and friendly draw in a bar full of strangers as post time nears. I have seen him at work, writing down the names of the entries on pieces of folded paper, dropping them into his blue Leafs ball cap, looking like a supplicant as he makes his rounds and the patrons drop a hand into the cap to see which horse is theirs. A teacher and a writer (of mystery novels), David sometimes plays the role of the barfly who always talks to the guy beside him. On that day in June, the man on the next stool was a now-belligerent, now-chummy drunk who insisted on betting against Secretariat.

My friend pleaded with him, tried to educate him on the folly of such a bet and the splendor of the favorite, but to no avail. Like oil and water, alcohol and logic do not mix. Each man put a dollar bill on the bar, with David taking Secretariat and offering the tinderbox beside him the rest of the field. And, after the race, when TV commentators prepared to show the replay of Secretariat's thirty-one-length victory, the silly drunk seized on the thought that Secretariat was about to race a *second* time, and insisted on another dollar bet (it was either that, David recalls, or step outside). My pal escaped with the two dollar bills and counted himself lucky to have seen a great race and kept all his teeth.

~

Some of Secretariat's admirers got close enough to photograph him, and some even touched him. Judy Jones did all of that and more. She was a young equine artist on a mission in the mid-1970s when she visited the champ in his paddock near Paris, Kentucky, with two female friends while a groom held the stallion for picture taking. The visit would end rather dramatically, as she eventually explained.

I had met Judy Jones in a happenstance sort of way. We were in line together at Kentucky Horse Park the day of the bronze unveiling in July 2004 and we started to chat. She is a native Chicagoan and has been an equine artist all her working life. Later, over coffee at the Springs Inn, she showed me two compelling prints: One was her pencil sketch of Affirmed, Seattle Slew, and Secretariat—Triple Crown winners in 1978, 1977, and 1973, respectively; the other was of John Henry, the irascible champion from the early 1980s. I bought both prints and am glad to have them and the stories Jones told me that day.

Horse crazies—a term Judy Jones used to describe herself and her friends—will go to great lengths to fuel their passion, which is, at heart, a girl's infatuation not dulled by time or age.

The woman in the red print dress and glasses sipping coffee opposite me seemed shy and tentative at first, but she warmed to her stories. She was like a child opening up her toy box for a stranger and plucking out items, slowly at first, then quickly and at random. "I saw Secretariat race," she said, "in the Arlington Invitational"—a race created specifically for him. The date was June 30, 1973, and Jones was three years out of high school. The headlines were all about the Watergate hearings, which had begun the month before, and pet rocks were the craze of the day, but another sort of mania had a grip on Judy Jones. "I was caught up in the whole Secretariat phenomenon," she said. "I'll never forget watching the Belmont Stakes race at home with my mom and both of us goin' nuts as he came down that stretch. My friends were all horse crazies, too, so, of course, when we found out he was going to be at Arlington, that's what we lived for."

Jones remembered how crowded Arlington was—"packed to the gills." She and her friends were familiar with the backside, having been there on many occasions for other things, and they actually got to talk to Eddie Sweat that day. One of Jones's friends was handy with a camera, but her film did not advance for some reason and all her precious shots of Secretariat came to naught. Jones revealed the latter detail with anguish, still acute more than thirty years after the fact. She made a face and groaned as she spoke of the lost film.

"What did Eddie say?" I asked her.

"He just talked about the horse and we asked him some questions."

"Like what?"

"Oh, it was so long ago. . . . Oh, I remember one. We asked if Secretariat had a special diet, and Eddie told us the horse drank Hinckley & Schmitt bottled water and they brought it with them."

The Arlington visit barely whetted the appetites of Jones and four other horse-mad young women for the horse called Secretariat. Jones made many trips to Lexington while still living in Chicago in the 1970s and 1980s—a round-trip of almost eight hundred miles—always to see Secretariat. She became a regular at Claiborne, saw Buckpasser and Hoist the Flag, Tom Rolfe and Nijinsky II—all horses now buried at Claiborne—and got to know one of the grooms who handled Secretariat in those days.

"We used to feed Secretariat peppermints," Jones said. "He loved peppermints. We had made an appointment at Claiborne—myself, Diane Viert, and Helen Hayse, we all went out there." The groom showing Secretariat asked Judy if she would take a picture of him with his charge. The horse, meanwhile, had spotted the peppermints in Diane's hand. "The groom was standing close to the horse," explained Jones, "and as Diane showed the peppermint, Secretariat went like this with his head"—and here Judy Jones made a sudden lifting motion with her own head, though her motion surely had nothing on his.

"He was asking for the peppermint," she said, "and he hit the groom right in the nose and knocked him out. He fell down, broke his nose. It wasn't any meanness. Secretariat was just asking for the peppermint and the groom was in the way. Oh my God . . ." No Joe Louis uppercut ever had that kind of power, but the groom looked like he had gone ten rounds with the champ. He was down for the count and then some, and farm staff had to carry the bloodied man away on a stretcher.

Jones, her friends, the horse—all were in shock. Jones grabbed the lead shank and held Secretariat while trying to stifle her own mortification, but Claiborne staff were gracious. "Accidents happen," they told her, and all was forgiven. As for the groom, he later had to have surgery when his nasal passages failed to perform in the usual way. Moral of story: Do not stand between a great horse and his peppermints.

"I was in awe," said Jones, "that they let us get that close to the horse. I even have photos of one of my friends brushing him." Here Jones put a hand to her mouth and looked dubiously at the tape recorder. She expressed the worry that the groom, now deceased, had surely overstepped the bounds in allowing such contact and that naming him might sully his reputation. Let the groom, then, go unnamed.

But Jones will always be grateful to that groom for letting her touch a magnificent horse. "I especially remember," she said, "how beautiful his head and eye and neck were. He had that 'look of eagles,' we call it. But the thing about him was he was a very kind horse. I'm sure he could have his moments, like any stallion, but he was a really sweet horse. He let us touch him and never ever laid an ear back or lifted a foot or anything."

The only thing that bothered Jones about these visits was the burgeoning weight of the horse as the years passed. "He had that big, cresty neck and they let him get too heavy. At the end, he looked almost quarter-horsey in a way. He was just chunky."

Jones and her husband—formerly a track photographer for the Ontario Jockey Club—moved down to Kentucky in 1989. John Jones had photographed Secretariat's last race at Woodbine, but he never got to see the horse in the flesh in Kentucky. And when the horse died that fall, Judy Jones sent flowers to be laid at his grave. She got back, in return, a handwritten note from Seth Hancock, Claiborne's owner.

For Jones the artist, Secretariat was an inspiration. She spoke with awe and affection of his lovely face, his little ears, his chestnut color and those distinctive white markings—horse-show people call it "chrome," Jones said, "and Secretariat had a lot of chrome."

To draw Secretariat, she would have had to measure him, and she had those details, too, tucked away in her brain. "Horses, ideally," she explained to me, "if you were to measure from the withers to the ground, and then from the point of the shoulder all the way back to the end of their body—a perfect horse would be in an exact square. Secretariat measured a little bit taller than he was long. That's because his legs were a little bit longer and he was short-bodied, very compact."

Jones spoke in a kind of rapture about his musculature, his desire, his heart and biomechanics. "He was just gifted from God," she said, "as all great athletes are."

⁓

I am in the spacious trailer workshop of a saddler, watching him methodically take my saddle apart while a propane heater utters what sounds like applause in the background. The saddle elf has picked a cold day to make his rounds and come to my stable in southeastern

Ontario. He wears a black toque with NEWMARKET in bold red at his forehead as he works. The hat was acquired on a trip to the English horse mecca.

An English saddle should fit a horse like a leather glove fits a hand. But the insulating material inside the leather of a glove can shift and flatten; a saddle's padding can do likewise. My saddle is in need of what the saddler calls "a fine-tuning."

After he has added stuffing where he thinks it warranted—imagine cotton candy being poked into a saddle's recesses with a long shoehorn—he pauses to admire and feel the result. He smiles, admittedly amused by his own smugness. He tells me his wife teases him when he complains of the little aches and pains his profession makes him prey to, saying he likely hurt himself patting his own back.

I give him a line uttered by an erstwhile colleague at the daily newspaper in Nelson, British Columbia. I must have liked something I had written and said so in the newsroom. My fellow reporter offered a mocking, stop-the-press headline: REPORTER BREAKS ARM PATTING SELF ON BACK. Christian Lowe, my saddler, laughs robustly. We have been talking as he works about this thing that occurs between horses and humans. I tell him how torn I am—how one day I am convinced there can be a profound connection between some humans and some horses, and the next day a like connection smacks of something else.

Under the latter category, I tell Lowe—a quiet, competent professional who is so genuinely nice and enthusiastic, you want to pass his business card around at parties—about a horse handler I met at Kentucky Horse Park, Tammy Siters. Her charge, and he had been so for years, was the aforementioned John Henry. (Kirsten Johnson, a horsewoman I'll come to shortly, once saw John Henry being walked to his paddock in the company of several people. She was describing how some horses exude dignity and bearing. "John Henry would walk twenty feet," she said, "then stop, and all the people would stop—until *he* wanted to go.")

Siters claimed that old John is conversational, that he understands much of what she tells him. And one day, just outside John Henry's stall, she described to me a kind of negotiation she once had with the horse over the administration of a nasal vaccine. A park employee there to do the job was terrified of going into John Henry's stall, and Siters had the following chat with the horse.

"What's it going to take?" she began. "A peppermint?" The horse shook his head.

"Two peppermints?" Another shake of the head.

"Three peppermints and a carrot?" The horse nodded. Tammy Siters assured the technician that a deal had now been struck, and the vaccine was administered without incident.

I tell Chris that if the relationship between Secretariat and Eddie Sweat is one shining example of the depth of understanding between a horse and a human, surely this other example between John Henry and his handler illustrates just how naïve some horse-centric people can seem. And I want to know which camp he belongs to—the mystical bunch or the more clear-eyed.

To my surprise, Chris chooses the former. He still works as he talks, his right pinkie encased in protective black leather while he drives a curved needle in and out of the saddle's bottom and pulls the heavy black thread taut. He tells the story of a Thoroughbred stallion he once gentled when the horse was four. Chris had done some ground work with the horse, a black, almost sixteen-hand Thoroughbred called Sailor, and had been astonished at how easily it had all gone.

"My experience with stallions at that point," Chris tells me, "was nil, but I don't think he was aware he was one, so no special precaution was needed when working around him. He was the type that never had to be shown anything twice and he seemed to be doglike in his need or want to please. If he had one habit, it was sucking on my boot whenever we stopped on loose rein. I don't know what the horsemanship guys would say about it, but I lapped it up as a sign of affection."

And then one day, after just two weeks of working with him on the ground and when no one was at the stable, Chris got on Sailor. It was the first time *anyone* had backed this horse. Not a wise move, Chris now admits—best to have an observer there in case of injury— but this was a measure of his confidence in the horse. There was an indescribable connection between them, and nothing the horse would not do for him, and they soon began training for eventing. Chris did not own the horse, but he rode him with the owner's permission and blessing. Kinship, it seemed, had nothing to do with ownership.

But one day, six or seven months into the project, when Chris was away from the stable on a trip, the owners of the horse sold the stallion—"sold him out from under me," is how he put it ten years after the fact. And, while the saddle business puts him on the road almost constantly, making the notion of getting another horse impossible, Chris has concluded that, in any case, there would be no point. He is sure he will never see that stallion's like again, that no horse could possibly measure up to Sailor.

There can be a bond between horse and human, I take him to say, and sometimes it soars. The connection—that is the word Chris uses— is unfathomable and, once felt, unforgettable. Eddie Sweat likely took that truth to his grave.

Ten years after losing him, in his own private way Christian Lowe still mourns Sailor.

I am sitting in the library at Kentucky Horse Park, which doubles as office space for the museum's staff. Someone has dropped a piece of birthday cake and a cup of tea in front of me and is telling me about a certain volunteer—one of many working on preparations for the bronze-unveiling event slated for the weekend. The volunteer's name is Vicki Blood and she is, says the librarian, an acknowledged Secretariat nut. Said nut happens to be in an office close by, and the librarian fetches her.

Vicki Blood plops down beside me at a round table, where I have spread out my clippings on Secretariat. A lively, upbeat woman and a longtime volunteer at Kentucky Horse Park, she settles in like an old friend, for any friend of Secretariat's is a friend of Vicki Blood's.

We eat cake and talk Secretariat. I want to know why she still cherishes the memory of that horse so long after he ran. "It's something that stays in your heart, that doesn't want to leave," she says. "And it goes way beyond horsey people. Just say the name Secretariat. People stop and turn."

She was once describing to a friend in a gift shop an article in *The Blood-Horse* magazine on the details of Secretariat's funeral—how Claiborne staff had fashioned the oak casket, then covered the horse in Claiborne's yellow racing silks. And Vicki Blood became aware that all business in the shop had ceased and a small circle had formed around her as she talked.

"He's in my heart; he's always going to be in my heart until I die. And if I should die," she says, as if death for a horse lover were only a possibility, "I'd like to get permission from Claiborne Farm and have my ashes sprinkled over his grave." But she laughs long and loud after saying this, so I cannot be sure if she means it or is just mocking her own besottedness.

⌒

You can't have just one nut, right? The phone rings in my room at the Springs Inn in Lexington. A woman named Janie Hinson has heard I am looking to interview ardent fans of Secretariat, and she is sure that describes herself.

We talk, and later we run across each other at the bronze unveiling. She has Vicki's horse-centric good cheer, almost a giddiness, the kind of zeal an evangelist loves to see from the pulpit. All the tents hawking Secretariat stuff, the clubbiness of it all, the shared sensibility: A Secretariat party is Janie Hinson's kind of party.

She was twenty-five when Secretariat was making his run at the Triple Crown. Hinson was living in Virginia at the time, and, because Secretariat was born in that state, some state pride kicked in. Kentucky always got the glory when the Derby came around; now it was Virginia's time to shine. After Big Red won the Derby, then the Preakness, Hinson and her fiancé made arrangements to watch the Belmont at her folks' house. "The TV went on the fritz," she recalls. "I was beside myself. My mother got on the phone, ordered a TV, and it came just before the race. I remember Secretariat pulling away down the stretch and me screaming, 'Run! Run!'"

His pride, his beauty, his energy—all drew her to the horse. She began collecting Secretariat prints, and the album is now jammed— four inches thick. There are, she tells me, pictures of him on her walls, along with a plate signed by Ron Turcotte. Hinson has the magazines, of course, *Newsweek, Sports Illustrated,* and *Time,* with himself on the covers. She has bought photos of him on eBay. She bought the Secretariat chocolate bars and countless T-shirts, though she drew the line at the two-pound bobble-head doll—"too cartoonish," she says.

Hinson is thrilled with the Bogucki sculpture, and gets emotional just talking about it on the telephone with me. She remembers going to Kentucky Horse Park in 1997 and seeing the statue of Secretariat at the entrance. "Man o'War," she says, "was looking so majestic down the lane. Then I saw the statue of Secretariat. I have never been so disappointed. It had no movement or spirit." The new bronze, says Hinson, beaming, "does him justice."

～

One of the videos I saw at Kentucky Horse Park showed Secretariat getting a bath. Afterward, the handler at Claiborne circles the horse, and what is strikingly apparent is not just the horse's power and beauty but his intelligence. The camera pans in close on his head, and the eyes radiate charisma and focus. He looks bright and curious and keenly interested in what's going on around him.

Heywood Hale Broun—the author, actor, sportswriter, and broadcaster, who died in 2001 at the age of eighty-three—once talked of the way Secretariat carried himself: like a champion who knows he is a champion. Broun said that horses in a race will often drift to the outside from sheer fatigue. "Secretariat," he said, "is the only horse I ever saw who went wide out of centrifugal force, rather like those characters in cartoons. He's going wide because he can't hold himself in." Broun apparently carried in his wallet only two photographs: one of his family, one of Secretariat.

～

Bill Cooke is director of the International Museum of the Horse at Kentucky Horse Park, and when he sits at his desk, he can look across his ample office to the opposite wall and see a triptych of framed color photographs.

The one on the far left shows a young chestnut rolling in his paddock, all four feet in the air. Happy, happy horse. The middle shot has him just starting to rise, his back legs beneath him, his front legs about to lever his impressive body up into the air. It is an image of power. Finally, the third shot: He is shaking his whole body and the dust is coming off his left side in a little storm. This is a gleeful, contented horse.

It is, of course, Secretariat, at Claiborne. The photographs were taken by a doctor in Saratoga Springs, L. J. Hoge, who had become infatuated with the horse after watching him run in the Hopeful Stakes at Saratoga in August of 1972. There is, it seems, an innocence about the images. The horse is not posing; he is not about to work or to finish working. He is a relaxed horse, a horse at play—rolling in the dirt to satisfy an itch, to keep off the bugs, or just because it feels good.

A horse will shake after a roll in the dirt and, by some biomechanics known only to four-legged animals, will employ just about every muscle in his body. A horse's shudder is not like that of a dog, who will do something similar upon leaving the water. A dog's shake starts at the head and works its way to the tail, the water being shed as the energy moves along his torso, as if the almost violent back-and-forth shaking of the head has sent ripples down the body.

A horse's shake does not start at the head. A horse's shake is a whole-body shake, a shudder shake, as if every muscle in the horse's body were doing the rumba. Imagine sitting on a washing machine during the helter-skelter spin cycle with the load unbalanced. A horse will shake after a roll in dirt and, sometimes, after a long hack (a trail ride). I feel good, I take the horse to say, and I'm glad to be home. The first time my horse shook with me in the saddle, his head down low like Secretariat's, I thought I would pitch off. I cannot imagine the power of a Secretariat shake.

Bill Cooke has witnessed that shake dozens of times. "I must have been out at Claiborne twenty or thirty times while Secretariat was there," he tells me. "It was one of my favorite trips." Sometimes Cooke went alone, sometimes with potential donors to the museum. "Never in all the times that I was out there did Secretariat fail to put on this wonderful show. You'd come up to his paddock and he'd see the cameras and the people and his ears would perk up. He knew he was the star and he'd do his victory lap around the paddock, come charging up to the fence right toward the people and kinda slide to a stop and then look noble for a minute. And always, after that, he'd go out to the center of the paddock and find him a nice dusty or muddy spot— depending on the day—and do the biggest roll you could possibly ever do if you were a horse."

"Like that," I say, pointing at the triptych.

"Like that," Bill Cooke replies.

Snow, too, delighted Secretariat. Those who were at Claiborne when snow fell reported that he would prance in it, roll over on his back, and kick at the flakes as they fell.

Cooke has seen many great horses in his twenty-seven years at Kentucky Horse Park, but he has never seen a horse with as much personality as Secretariat. Forego, John Henry, and Cigar all had it, but with Secretariat, said Cooke, *it* was amplified tenfold, for the horse knew he was special. "They are," Cooke says, "these blessed beings that can do things their counterparts can't even contemplate."

Cooke speaks in a deep baritone, a voice many broadcasters would love to have. It lends authority. He takes me into the museum's basement, a wonderfully cluttered place full of saddles and sculptures and art—all pieces donated to the museum and either formerly on display or awaiting their turn. Housing dozens of paintings is a tall metal closet affair, with each piece of art in its own framed bracket so the art can be wheeled out and examined, then returned, like a book to its shelf. Cooke wants to show me the half a dozen or so Secretariat prints and photographs and paintings. Even here, in the museum's basement, the horse continues to have a meaningful presence.

Cooke makes the point that, if anything, Secretariat has only grown in stature over time. He was the first Triple Crown winner in twenty-five years, and when that feat was followed in quick succession (though less dramatically, by Affirmed and Seattle Slew), those who follow horse racing began to minimize the achievement of winning those three spring races. What happened, says Cooke, is that three great horses came along in the same decade. The fallow years since have driven home the point that great horses are rare, and the Triple Crown is hard-won.

⌒

The smell of a horse up close is always sweet. Where my dog, bless her, cheerfully breathes into my face her own vapors of old tuna and sour socks, my horse smells of green grass and red apples. (How *I* smell to my horse is another matter.) The only thing that smells better than a horse's muzzle is a baby's head.

So I envy in a way those whose contact with Secretariat is not through videos or photos, paintings and magazine covers, but through his blood. They ride or own his offspring.

In 1997, a plumber named Nick Corini purchased a small ranch near Hollister, California, and acted on a long-held dream—to breed a champion horse. In 2000, he bred one of his mares to Academy Award, a son of Secretariat, and got a chestnut colt. In 2003, he bred all four of his mares to Tinner's Way, a son from Secretariat's last crop (born just months after his death) and winner of $1.8 million on the track.

"Why did I breed everything to a son of the champion," he wrote me, "knowing that every expert states that His sons are below standard as breeders? Because I want to be a part of this great horse."

As he wrote, Corini said he could see on his office wall nothing but Secretariat: individual framed photographs, framed programs from each Triple Crown race, eight framed magazines with the red horse on the cover, the horse's postage stamp, his commemoratives, news of his victories as a two-year-old—all in frames and under glass.

Nick Corini is sixty years old now, and has ten grandchildren. And although he never saw Secretariat in the flesh, he and his three young sons watched and cheered as he won the Belmont Stakes. Now Corini is what he calls "a small breeder," one with a dream. At the time he wrote me, three of his four mares were in foal.

"I cannot contain my enthusiasm," he wrote, "when I see these mares daily. Three grandchildren of SECRETARIAT"—whenever Corini wrote the name, it was all caps—"will be on the ranch this year. I am still part of the greatest horse that ever lived. . . ."

⌒

Tobi Taylor was a horse-mad eight-year-old girl in 1973, and the one horse she loved most was Secretariat. She had posters of him in her room; she spent her allowance money on magazines featuring him on the cover; she even wrote a letter to the folks at Breyer, imploring them to mold a model in his image. (And maybe young Tobi planted a seed, for eventually Breyer did just that. Breyer manufactures six-inch-high plastic horses, models of particular champions and breeds, for kids and collectors.) By 1997, Tobi Taylor had owned several horses and was working for a dressage rider and trainer in Scottsdale, Arizona, who asked her one day to ride a chestnut called Twinkie.

The chestnut, it transpires, was a son of Secretariat—out of one of the three test mares, this one a draft mare, bred in 1974. Twinkie (his registered name is the much more noble Statesman) was twenty-five when Taylor described all this in the March 2000 issue of *Dressage Today*. Statesman had been a stud, a jumper, a polo pony, and was then a kind of "steady Eddie" on the trail—a calming influence on other, younger horses. Children would stop the riders to admire "the pretty red pony," the one, wrote Taylor, who had surely inherited his father's enormous heart.

⌒

Angela Crandall rides My Lucky Gem, a granddaughter of Secretariat's. She was looking for a younger horse to take her on long hacks into the redwood mountains of Humboldt County, California, where she lives. Her first horse—bought when she left home and even before she had purchased a car—can no longer manage such treks. On the notice board at a local stable she spotted her dream horse: a tall, muscular dark bay "with a kind eye." Only when she spoke to the owner did Crandall learn of the horse's pedigree.

She calls the mare "Lucky," and cannot ride her without thinking back to the old man. "I feel," she wrote me, "the importance of what Secretariat was to many whenever I saddle up to go on a ride, or whenever I just go outside our kitchen door to lay my head on Lucky's silky shoulder."

Like Nick Corini, Angela Crandall hopes one day to breed My Lucky Gem, to keep alive "the famous blood."

⌒

Renee Attili says she will always remember where she was and what she was doing when she heard the news of Secretariat's death in 1989. She had been planning a visit to Claiborne when the news came.

"Secretariat," she wrote me, "was the horse that made horses truly come alive to me when I was a young girl. Until Him"—yes, she capitalized the word—"my experience with horses had been limited to shaggy, sad (but still beautiful to my little-girl eyes) ponies at the local fair and petting zoo, photos and Breyer Horse models. He was the most majestic, noble, powerful horse that I had ever seen."

Attili went on to become an exercise rider, working with green Thoroughbreds at Buckland Farm in Virginia. She once rode a filly by Secretariat called Secretary's Story: "I felt like I was riding royalty. Riding her was truly an honor. She had a similar beauty and air about her. She actually had been born missing an eye, but, like her sire, she ran because she loved it. She went on to do pretty well from what I heard. Even though she was of His blood, as were many others, none has compared to Him. He was simply His own horse."

Though Renee Attili never saw Secretariat in the flesh, she has seen the video of one of his morning workouts. As an exercise rider, she has a certain eye, and what she saw was "truly something not of this world. The way he worked with such power and at the same time easy, was simply awe-inspiring."

"That is why I cried at the news of His death," Attili wrote, "why I still get the chills thinking of that early morning workout, hearing that BRRAAPP BRRAAPP BRRAAPP sound, and why after more than thirty years he still moves my spirit."

⌒

I cannot get John Henry out of my head. If Secretariat was the all-American hero, John Henry is the bandit with his face on WANTED: DEAD OR ALIVE posters all over the West. Even in old age (a remarkable thirty-one years old as I write this), he remains a dangerous horse, and yet the record shows that if you could get him on your side by dint of charm or courage, or both, then John signed on the dotted line and was sweet on you for life.

At Kentucky Horse Park, I kept going back to the Hall of Champions just to peer into his dark stall. A sturdy ornamental grate—like the screening that separates priest and confessor in the darkness of a confessional—covered the inside of his stall door, ruling out any possibility of a child, say, putting her fingers between the bars and losing said fingers to the horse inside. A sign by John Henry's door further warned visitors that horses may bite (all the stalls had such a sign), though they might have added, "This one more than most." Age has not dulled the old sourpuss. Tammy Siters, his longtime groom at the park, told me he still gets frisky in cold weather.

His race record is stunning. Between 1977 and 1984, he had a jaw-dropping eighty-three starts. John won thirty-nine of his races; he placed fifteen times and showed eight times. He was in the money 75 percent of the time over an unearthly span of eight years. All this from a gelding who once sold for eleven hundred dollars.

John Henry was twice named Horse of the Year, the second time when he was a stately nine years old. No horse had ever done that, and up until he did, no horse had ever won $6.6 million. Small, at 15.2 hands, and decidedly plain, he had a particular way of going. George Pratt, the professor of electrical engineering and computer science at Massachusetts Institute of Technology, once examined John Henry's stride, as he had done Secretariat's. Pratt called John Henry's stride "a thing of ice-cold efficiency . . . the changes of lead are wonderfully smooth—a Ferrari going through the gears." And it was a massive stride, too: Red pole markers at Kentucky Horse Park put his stride (25.5 feet) right up there with the big boys—Man o'War (28 feet) and Secretariat (24 feet).

Pratt's comments were contained in an article in *Equus* magazine in 1985: A panel of experts—veterinarians, scientists, even a psychic—was assembled to fathom this notorious horse. An ultrasound imager determined that he had a huge heart—up to 25 percent larger than average. Linda Tellington-Jones, who has made touching a horse into both a science and an art, remarked on his sense of superiority and determination to lead. Veterinary surgeon Dr. Matthew Mackay-Smith, summing up the panel's findings, called John Henry "self-confident, aloof, alert, studious, wise, and, it must be said, more than a bit theatrical."

But here's the thing. In the book *John Henry,* by Steve Haskin, is an award-winning photograph of the horse with his racing groom, Jose Mercado. Taken when the horse was in his prime, the photo shows a burly groom in a checked short-sleeved shirt, a carrot in his right hand and John Henry—the very devil himself—leaning into the man's chest, the horse's visible left eye half-closed and dreamy, as if Mercado were a cherished uncle telling him his favorite bedtime story. The photo is very like others I have seen that capture the horse–groom bond: Eddie Sweat and Secretariat, Tom Wade and Seattle Slew, Sandi Patterson and Big Ben, Will Harbut and Man o'War.

Mercado had passed the horse's test: One of John Henry's favorite tricks was to inch toward the stall wall during grooming, until he had the groom pinned. The horse was mean, said Mercado, "and I had to be a little rough with him at times," but once he had the horse's respect, he never lost it.

Tammy Siters told me that John Henry has broken her nose with a cow kick, and once reared up on her and charged her. At the last second, she took the lead shank and smacked him over the shoulder, thus stopping the charge and perhaps saving her own life. Then it was John Henry's turn to be petrified, and he shook in the corner of his stall until Siters made peace with some mints. He broke the toe of another handler by stepping on her foot, and, on another occasion, bit the same handler on the thumb, drawing blood. "It's like he has a split personality," Siters told Haskin. "He wants to be good and there is a real good side to him, but sometimes that evil John just has to come out." (When I last spoke to Siters, just days before Christmas of 2005, she reported that John Henry was in fine form: He had bitten three park employees—though not Siters—in the previous ten days.)

On the other hand, John Henry abides birds in his stall, and he got along very well with one trainer's Labrador retriever, named Opie, who used to sleep close by the horse in the stall. They would nibble at each other and play. But when a goat, Ba Ba Louie, was offered as a paddock pal on John Henry's arrival at Kentucky Horse Park in 1985, the horse almost killed the hapless creature. The park had to pay several hundred dollars in vet bills to stitch him up.

And yet John Henry has embraced certain people in his life, and he has *consistently* been loyal to them. Between 1990 and 1997, Rosemary Honerkamp was the stud groom at Kentucky Horse Park. "Their relationship," Siters told Haskin, "was something right out of *Black Beauty*. John truly loved Rosemary and never once even looked cross-eyed at her." (Siters later modified that story, telling me that John Henry did stomp on Rosemary's feet a few times, but was otherwise a prince in her presence.)

John Henry did not like the handler assigned to take him out to his paddock one day, and he let her know it by blocking the entrance to his stall with his own prostrate body. Honerkamp came along, said, "John, get up," which he promptly did, and she led him peaceably outside.

And I am left wondering, What does Rosemary Honerkamp possess that has enabled her to penetrate the horse's aloofness? Is it pure confidence, or confidence disguised as kindness? What qualities does she share with Eddie Sweat, Will Harbut, Tom Wade, Sandi Patterson, and Jose Mercado that made Secretariat, Man o'War, Seattle Slew, Big Ben, and John Henry not just warm to them but enter into a pact that these horses would always honor, sometimes until they were put in the ground? Tammy Siters had called it "something right out of *Black Beauty*." But what? Horses know, but we may never know.

⌒

"Taxi for Scanlan!" the bartender shouts.

I am watching—what else?—horse racing on the big screen of the bar at the Springs Inn, and sipping a Killian's Irish Red, a beer with a horse's head on the bottle.

A gaggle of six Irishmen and one Irishwoman is in the bar, and they look comfortable, as if settling in at their local for evening pints of Guinness. I recognize the liquor blush, the brogue, the sharp tongues—they remind me of the Irish priests who taught me in high school. The Holy Ghost fathers specialized in clever sarcasm and cheerful mockery.

Among the seven Irish are several Scanlon brothers (the spelling becomes clear when I chat them up). One Scanlon has called for the cab, and it's now out front, but they seem in no hurry. I show one brother, the eldest, my driver's license, thinking that a Scanlon from Ireland might be amused to meet a Scanlan from Canada. He is not. I suppose he thinks I'm tugging feebly at some distant Irish roots, and he has no time for Danny Boy nostalgia. He humors me, for a bit.

"Are you here to buy horses?" I ask him.

"Mebbe," he replies coyly. "And why are you here?"

"To write a book," I say.

"Ah, that'd be easier," he replies. I take him to mean that they have come to Lexington to pan for gold, to find the next Secretariat, but gold and fool's gold look much alike. The Irishman had it right: Anyone can write a book, anyone can memorize Thoroughbred bloodlines, and on auction day all the horses look gorgeous. One in a million has the right stuff.

The next day, Tuesday, July 20, 2004, is the second day of the Kentucky Summer Yearlings sale at Fasig-Tipton on the Newtown Pike, just north of Lexington. Some five hundred Thoroughbred horses are up for sale. Seattle Slew was sold on these grounds. So was Unbridled. Every now and again, lightning strikes.

Sales catalog (or "hip book") in hand, I wander the vast grounds and, within minutes, spot the Scanlon brothers. The loud palaver from the bar is gone now. It's solemn business buying horses. I have found the Irishmen by chance: I saw a horse listed in the catalog (a "hip number"—literally a black number on a white oval affixed to the horse's hip—is often the only identifier) and went to see him back at one of the barns. The money this horse's sire and dam had earned impressed me, as it did the Irishmen. One Scanlon, looking Joycean with his glasses perched on his nose, gazes intently at the young horse being circled in front of him.

Does the man from County Meath like the movement, more graceful than that of any model on a runway? Does he like the horse's princely bearing? The roundness at the rump, the way his shoulder comes off the body, the straightness of the legs? Or is he seeing a flaw in the horse's assembly—at the knee, the hip, the neck? Is the shoulder too straight, the back too long or too short? I leave him to his pondering.

Amy Gill, the equine nutritionist, has agreed to meet me here and help me understand the sale process. I gather that coming to the sale is common sport in Lexington—99 percent of the onlookers have come not to buy but to watch others buy.

Amy points out the former governor of Kentucky, in a cowboy hat and holding court in the indoor walking ring. Outside, in the middle of the outdoor walking pavilion, is the trainer extraordinaire Bob Baffert, in his trademark sunglasses (he is allergic to hay and horses, and the glasses mask his chronically red eyes). Leaning on the rail close by is John Veitch, trainer of Alydar. There are men in cowboy boots, Japanese men in suits, Arabs in headdresses—and everyone is on a cell phone.

These buyers, Amy informs me, have been going around to Kentucky horse farms, looking at prospects, for weeks. They have examined X rays and vets' reports; they have pored over bloodlines and considered the recommendations of their own trainers and agents. They know exactly which horses they want. Or do they?

The parade of horses unfolds in chronological order according to hip number. Each yearling is walked several times over the rubberized brick pathway on the outdoor ring while a hundred or so onlookers lean on the rail and eye the passing horse. Then the horse is led into the indoor ring, where the filly or colt is again circled in each of the four corners, with more gawking and note taking. Finally, the yearling is led through the doors and onto the sales pavilion's stage—an enclosed theater where an auctioneer in a high, polished pulpit takes bids as the horse is circled over pine shavings and finally sold, or not. All day long, the auctioneer's voice is the music in the air and the dance is the dance of horses circling, always circling.

The auctioneers' "What am I bid?" prattle must be exhausting, for they relieve one another constantly, like tag-team wrestlers. Men in black suits roam up and down the aisles, catching bids. I cannot tell *who* is bidding, let alone by what means. I know only that I would love to take a young horse home, to be a player in this grand old game.

The horses being sold are seventeen and eighteen months old. They have been preened and clipped, buffed and polished, like sports cars in a showroom. Some firms hire "preppers"—professional horse beauticians who paint the hooves, lay on the ShowSheen, and make the client gleam. I watch one groom as he gingerly, delicately, slowly plucks a bit of hay, as if it were nitroglycerin, from a young colt's tail as he passes. Pity the poor grooms.

These wide-eyed horses are truly babies, and should be forgiven their spookiness, but any outburst—any dancing, any swinging of the rear end, and, heaven forbid, any rearing—would offer prospective buyers one more reason not to buy that horse or to bid less. The blare of the auctioneer's microphone, all these strangers and strange surroundings—a young horse would have cause.

One dark bay filly by Fusaichi Pegasus, with dollops of blood from Northern Dancer, Riva Ridge, Mr. Prospector, and Nijinsky II, goes this day for a cool $450,000. But sometimes a horse fails to garner even the rock-bottom price—maybe seven to ten thousand dollars—set by the seller. "Sold to Woody," one auctioneer will proclaim, his own euphemism for "back to the seller."

A jet black horse whom Amy Gill and I both admired—for his look, his bearing—appears to suffer that fate. Hip number 126, one of the few horses at auction with a name (Available Light), is a bay colt with a link to Secretariat: The colt's sire's second dam (grandmother, in human terms) was Terlingua. We dash around the corner and into the sales pavilion to see how he fares. But the lordly young horse fails to impress much and sells for a mere thirty thousand dollars.

I try to imagine what it's like to come here as a buyer empowered to bid up to, say, $500,000 on a horse. To be a player. Maybe you like the dam In Excelsis Deo (you are an old Catholic). Or Seattle Belle because you are a Slew guy. Or My Irish, because your name is Scanlan, or Scanlon. Or, on a hunch, you take a horse by Songandaprayer. (The records will later show that agent Robert N. Scanlon bought Hip number 6, a black colt by Songandaprayer out of Peppy Lapeau, for $200,000.)

Or you decide to hold off. You have read that Seattle Slew covered a mare, May Day Ninety, before he died in 2002, and that the dark bay filly is coming up for sale at Saratoga Springs in August. That hip book, too, is free for the taking here, like some freshly baited hook.

(And that hook continues to catch fish. A fourteen-day auction at

Keeneland in September of 2005 took in close to $400 *million,* a record, with 40 of the 3,545 horses sold fetching $1 million or more.)

I go back to the bar at the Springs Inn, but there is no sign of the Irishmen. I watch more TVG—simulcasts of horse racing all over North America. A young horse almost flips over in the starting gate; long shots come through and favorites hang on; jockeys flail their mounts down the stretch.

In the morning, I see the smallest of the Irish bunch—I take him to be the jockey among them—outside the inn's little breakfast nook.

"Did you buy any horses yesterday?" I ask him.

"Mebbe," he replies.

⌒

For Amy Gill, being at the sale is a chance to meet friends and network. Every five minutes, it seems, she encounters a client or an acquaintance. One such is Kirsten Johnson, and within minutes of meeting me, she is extending an invitation to her clinic, just outside Lexington. Called the Kentucky Equine Sports Medicine and Rehabilitation Center, or KESMARC, it offers help for the hurting horse.

Amy, Kirsten, a scribe from Canada: We lean on the rail, watch all the pretty horses, and our talk turns to Secretariat. The Belmont, of course. "I can *still* see it," Kirsten says. "It's timeless. It is absolutely timeless." The Derby. "The most amazing thing about Secretariat, though," says Amy, "honestly, this is the greatest thing: that he ran each quarter of that Derby faster. No horse has ever done that."

And the two women talk about the Smarty Jones stab at the Triple Crown, and how that horse (whose pedigree traced back to Secretariat) tugged at them. "It's the feeling," says Kirsten. She is a strawberry blonde with a natural passion for the world of the horse. "We all want the same feeling we got when Secretariat ran," she says.

"There isn't anybody in the business who isn't searching for that horse. It's a kind of greatness that leaves the equine realm." Like a couple finishing each other's sentences, Amy and Kirsten together tell the story of Jack Nicklaus on his knees in his den, weeping as Secretariat played Pegasus in the Belmont.

Both women express the wish that the contemporary science of computerized photography existed in Secretariat's day, so that his biomechanics, stride, and motion could all have been analyzed and, better, cataloged for posterity. It seems that Amy Gill and Kirsten Johnson want to see Secretariat run again, but in slow motion, up close, so his legs fill the wide and split screen, fold and touch, fold and touch, over and over again.

⌒

Out on Shannon Run Road, a chestnut filly is going for a swim at KESMARC, aided by two men with fifteen-foot blue lead ropes clipped to either side of her halter. As the horse churns the water and makes counterclockwise circles of the pool, each man must stay just ahead of her. This is tricky business, for the men must watch both the horse and what lies ahead—such as the little raised bridge to the pod that lets one man stand and turn in the middle of the pool and that enables this whole procedure. The handlers, especially the one making those wide outside turns, are getting almost as much exercise as the horse.

Kirsten Johnson is giving me, as promised, the grand tour. Her clinic offers sports medicine for high-end equine athletes—mostly Thoroughbreds, but horses from all breeds and all disciplines are treated here. The center features a fourteen-foot-deep pool, a submerged hydraulic treadmill, a mechanized horse-walking machine, a miniature track, and fifty-six stalls.

"We deal with everything here," says Johnson, "from minor arthroscopic surgery and horses that just need a freshen-up to what could be catastrophic life-threatening and career-ending injuries—and everything in between." A horse might, by degrees, go from treadmill to pool to light workouts on the track—with its soft footing of crushed polymer. A rider is up as we cross the track, and I feel like a pedestrian on a crosswalk, looking both ways. There is a busyness to the clinic, with horses just arriving, or getting a bath, some going to their treatments or being turned out. About a thousand horses come to the center every year.

A horse, says Johnson, will *tell* you what is wrong. Even a back problem can be diagnosed simply by applying touch to the horse's pressure points. A flinch, a hard turn of the head, pinned ears—all might be tantamount to "Ouch!" Enter the chiropractor, the acupuncturist, the therapist with massage machines.

There is also a hyperbaric oxygen chamber, whose healing powers Johnson calls "profound." A decompression chamber like the ones used to treat divers with the bends, this one is barrel-shaped and large enough to accommodate the tallest horse. The gleaming white chamber looks like a space capsule and strikes me as claustrophobic, but for a horse it is no more menacing than entering a trailer. The idea is to have the horse breathe pure oxygen and thereby to get more oxygen into the bloodstream, which induces a cascade of effects: Any inflammation decreases, and a good thing, too, since swelling may impede the antibiotics meant to kill an infection. Both blood and medicine reach the problem area.

As we walk the grounds and peer into stalls, I am reminded—for all their rugged size and power—just how delicate and fragile the horse is, especially the sport horse. A Thoroughbred takes a mere six strides from the starting gate to hit forty miles an hour and start taking in five gallons of air a second. The force of all that weight and speed exerts an impact on the horse's cannon bone of ten thousand to twelve thousand pounds. I know this courtesy of a display at the National Museum of Racing and Hall of Fame in Saratoga Springs. The so-called red line in racing is dangerously close: At eighteen thousand pounds, the stress on the cannon bone is too much to bear. A moment of imbalance, a push from another horse, lousy luck, and the bone may snap like a branch.

Some horses at KESMARC have taken "a bad step." But toss in parasites, bacterial infections, respiratory ailments, torn ligaments and tendons, and nature and man have many ways to fell a horse.

When I ask Johnson about the state of the Thoroughbred breed, she says she worries about the lack of diversity in breeding, wonders about the soil in pasturelands not possessing the nutrients it once did, wonders if some of these immensely valuable horses are babied, kept indoors when maybe a day in the rain is not a bad thing, may even be a good thing.

I expect Kirsten Johnson to say she loves her work, and she does not disappoint. "I grew up a hopeless romantic with horses as a child," she tells me, "and I must say I don't feel any different about them today than I did then." Only one thing has changed, she says. "I have better taste. I have the knowledge to enjoy a great one."

But if the track is a world of light and dark, Kirsten Johnson is by no means spared the latter. "I see the best," she said, "and I see the worst. Don't ever think that I don't have horses that come in here where I don't want to shoot whoever did it to 'em. It doesn't make me feel any less for the horse. I refuse to become skeptical. I refuse to stop trying to educate, because a lot of it comes from ignorance. Trust me. I live both sides. There are farms here I won't work for. There are trainers I won't take horses for."

Kirsten's tour of the center began in her office, where both she and the office secretary have photographs of Secretariat on the wall by their desks. Kirsten's, taken in 1988, shows her nose-to-nose with Secretariat, the horse in his paddock and Kirsten on the other side of the fence. And it is there in the office, as she tucks into her sandwich at lunch, that I put the question: "Why, with all the improvements in equine nutrition, breeding expertise, track conditions, has no horse challenged the chestnut's Triple Crown times? While human runners set new records every year, why are equine athletes unable to best times set in 1973?"

"He was just that good," Kirsten says. And for whatever reason, she adds, the training of racehorses has not changed in all that time. But Kirsten then tosses the question over to KESMARC's bookkeeper, Terry Trossen, who is a horseman from a family with deep roots in the horse-racing industry. He thinks training *has* changed since Secretariat's time.

"Horses today," he says, "are bred and built for speed. Some of those records you're talking about are for longer distances, endurance. Horses are just not trained that way anymore. Trainers get them as two-year-olds and they're trying to break twenty seconds for two furlongs. That's what they're selling. They're selling speed. They want 'em to win early because they have to recoup their investments."

Times for six- and seven-furlong races and the mile: Those are all tumbling, says Trossen, as owners and trainers take the money and run. But the Triple Crown tests speed *and* endurance. The Derby is a mile and a quarter; the Preakness a mile and three-sixteenths; the Belmont a grueling mile and a half. If horses could talk, Funny Cide and Smarty Jones would surely say how hard it is to be both a sprinter and a stayer.

Secretariat was not supposed to be both. He was a son of Bold Ruler, and those genetics were supposed to gift the colt with dash that would peter out over the longer distances, races that track people call "routes." Maybe the Princequillo blood on his dam's side kicked in—Princequillo get "can run all day." We can only guess. Secretariat was a freak of nature and he remains, says Johnson, his own point of reference. No true horseman, she says, casually compares a contemporary horse to Secretariat. "The comparison to Secretariat," she says, "is saved and very rarely used. And when it is used, it's used in a very careful way."

~ ADULATION ~

I'm in a diner in Ocala, Florida, with Charlie Davis, Secretariat's old exercise rider. Before we leave our corner spot by the window, I show him a photograph taken at Saratoga Springs—most likely in August of 1973 (the time of the loss to Onion). Charlie had never seen the image, even though he is in the photo, wearing the Meadow's blue and white, and he is up on Secretariat.

They are on the track, the tote board behind them. There is white lather at Secretariat's loins and chest and his mouth is nicely foamed, so they have clearly just finished a gallop and are walking back to the barn. The summer wind has tossed up the horse's mane, and his coat shines as if someone had taken steel wool to a penny. Charlie looks pleased, his hands low on the horse's neck, his stick lined up with the angle of his lower leg. The horse was two, Charlie thirty-two.

I had casually mentioned to Sonny Sadinsky, a friend of mine in Kingston, Ontario, that I was working on a book about Secretariat and his groom. And Sonny said, "You should see this photo I have." The image, on heavy stock, was small poster size—fourteen inches wide by eleven inches high—photographer unknown.

I brought with me on my trip three color photocopies of that image, two to be signed for friends back home, one for Charlie. His eyes brightened when he saw it; then he kissed the photo and said he was going to frame it. "Ohhhhh," he kept saying, as if someone had given him a birthday present months after the date.

As we leave the restaurant, Charlie proudly shows the photo to three waitresses huddled at the cash register. Charlie, it seems, is a regular.

"It's him!" one waitress shouts.

"Yes," I say, "and the horse he's on is Secretariat!" Instant bedlam. The waitresses fall over themselves in a rush to hug Charlie, who doesn't mind a bit. And in that moment, I get a sense of what it must have been like for Eddie, to be that close to all those hosannas, to feel the adulation.

~ 7 ~

The Ghost of Eddie Sweat

"We live on hope," Joe Riggs, Jr., said that July day in 2004 at his farm in Kentucky. He was walking me to my car, and I took a last, lingering look at the broodmares and foals in his sloping fields and that gutted shell he hopes one day to call home. ("Hope springs eternal in the human breast," wrote Alexander Pope. "For fools rush in where angels fear to tread" was also his turn of phrase.)

Where there is hope, maybe faith is close by, but what about charity? One of the abiding myths of the racetrack is that the track "looks after its own." In my travels for this book, I heard of several trainers helping grooms weather storms in their lives. The aid offered was discreet, and when I asked one trainer if he had ever helped out one of his grooms, he denied it—though his old partner had earlier assured me he had. Why would a trainer hide his own generosity? Because if you help one groom, they'll all want it? By what name do we call such kindness? Is it philanthropy? Or paternalism (its poor cousin)? And however defined, was it denied "the groom of grooms"?

I am still searching for the words to describe how I feel about Eddie Sweat lying there in his pauper's grave. Mystified, appalled, angry: All variously apply. But what I feel most strongly is an overwhelming sadness. Eddie had played a critical and acknowledged role in the success of perhaps the greatest racehorse who ever lived. ("Smart, informative, a groom's groom," Bill Nack called Eddie Sweat. "The one person the colt visibly responded to, the one he recognized and waited for.") But like gold miners who must empty their shoes and pockets of gold dust at the end of every shift, Eddie Sweat worked with gold but took home almost none of it.

Did Eddie bring on his own poverty by trying to support his offspring, his many siblings and their families? Did Lucien Laurin, whom Eddie looked upon almost as a father, ever shortchange him? To what extent did Eddie—by his drinking in the later years, by giving away money to every outstretched hand on shed row—invite his own Dickensian end? What role, if any, did Eddie's color play? Why is Tom Wade, Seattle Slew's groom, sitting pretty, while Eddie's sole legacy to his children was a tiny plot of land? Were Eddie's savings poorly or badly managed? Should any of the owners and trainers Eddie Sweat worked for in his lifetime on the track have dug into their own pockets to ease his plight, or were any of them even aware of how badly off he was in his final days?

Everyone I talked to had a different explanation for Eddie's frightfully impecunious end. The various parties, some of them, clung to self-serving notions. No one had a clear or untainted grasp of the truth. And even were he alive, Eddie, I'll wager, would not point fingers. He would shield and protect reputations. Privacy, a jockey once told me, is much honored at the racetrack, and Eddie would have felt bound by its rules and governances. And so, at a point late in my quest, I stopped trying to fathom Eddie's cruel deathbed finances, stopped weighing the stories and sifting through them, stopped seeking some final truth. I would let the stories run, let them jostle and butt against one another—like bumper cars at a small country fair.

It seemed to me that the only easily comprehensible and undeniable aspects of Eddie's life were two elements: the man's essential kindness and his gift with the horse.

When Eddie Sweat died in 1998, Penny Chenery told *The Blood-Horse,* "Eddie was very important to Secretariat, and to me. . . . He respected the horse, but he was never afraid of him. I used to say that he was an important part of the team, but he really was the team."

On other occasions, Chenery dubbed Eddie "one of the finest men around a horse I ever saw" and a steadying presence for Secretariat when fans, reporters, and photographers besieged the horse. She called Eddie "Secretariat's stability."

Eighty-three and still rebounding from a severe heart attack the previous fall, Chenery talked to me in the spring of 2005 about what set Eddie Sweat apart as a groom. "It was his devotion to his horses," she said on the telephone from her home in Lexington (she has since moved to Denver). "He was a very *professional* groom. He knew exactly what his job was. He was never late, and he *loved* his horses. Secretariat was feisty, and a less skilled and intuitive horseman might have tried to fight with Secretariat. Eddie would say, 'Now c'mon, Big Red.' He would kid and jolly him and dodge him if he kicked out. The only negative thing," she added, "was that we forgot to give Eddie advice on attire." Eddie's dandyism, those plaid pants on

Derby day, did not go down well in the Chenery camp. It wasn't that she disapproved of those loud clothes, but she did think they were "unprofessional."

Penny Chenery and Eddie Sweat did not have actual conversations. Most grooms and owners don't. "Eddie was class-conscious," Chenery said. "He was a 'Yes ma'am' and 'No ma'am' kind of man with me."

She well recalls the friendship between Eddie and Charlie Davis. She told me, "Charlie was the clown; Eddie was the professional. I remember after Secretariat won the Derby, someone sent a case of champagne to the barn at Churchill Downs. We"—she was with Lucien Laurin and Ron Turcotte—"were stuck with the press for an hour. We get back to the barn and here's Charlie, three sheets to the wind. The horses were walking Charlie. He's singing, 'How sweet it is to be loved by you . . .'"

Eddie had gone along, and he posed with a glass of champagne for a picture with Secretariat. But he took only a sip and tossed the rest. There was work to do.

Often called "the first lady of racing," Penny Chenery has for decades promoted the sport, its charities and worthy foundations (including the Grayson–Jockey Club Research Foundation, which funds equine research—about $800,000 annually—from a $20 million nest egg). We have the Ed Bogucki sculpture of Secretariat because Penny Chenery auctioned off most of her Secretariat memorabilia in 1999. Sold were, among other things, a Secretariat horseshoe with dirt still caked in it, a feed bag from the Meadow, a bridle worn by Secretariat, the blanket awarded after the Belmont victory, dresses the owner wore to his races, seat tickets, dried carnations. The Belmont Stakes blanket fetched $43,000, the Bogucki maquette brought in more than $44,000, Secretariat's tack box went for $13,000, and the Triple Crown bridle and bit fetched $28,000. In total, $336,675 was raised.

When Chenery was trying to save the family farm back in 1973, with estate taxes looming after the death of her father, she formed a syndicate. Thirty-two shares, worth $190,000 each, entitled the holder to breeding rights to her superhorse. The Chenery family retained four shares, and the six million dollars raised did indeed save the farm. Grooms almost never partake in this division of spoils. But Eddie Sweat, at least late in his life, apparently did not accept his fate or take it as a given. He was, some insist, resentful (though others close to him vehemently deny this).

I think of another man, a black man, from Secretariat's early days. Howard Gregory, seventy-eight years old, worked at the Meadow for thirty-one years and was around the young colt from the day he was born. *The Blood-Horse* tracked him down in 2002 and got him to reminisce. He remembered, for example, burying Somethingroyal, Secretariat's dam, when she died at thirty-one—an advanced age for a Thoroughbred.

Howard Gregory loved his work, and he thought there were no nicer bosses in the world than Christopher Chenery and, later, his daughter, Penny. Money, Gregory said, was never a problem then, and they all got bonuses and shares in winnings. When Gregory wanted to build his own house, Christopher Chenery helped him out. "I live in a six-room house on five acres, and it's all mine," he said, still thankful to the man he calls "Mr. Chenery." Growing up, Howard Gregory would have heard himself referred to as "Negro," "colored," "black," "African-American," each age with its own nomenclature for the pigmentation of a person's skin. But a black person of his era—Eddie Sweat's time—would have always referred to his white employer as "Mr."

Gregory busies himself these days with little landscaping jobs and fixing engines. He lives on Riva Ridge Road, part of a settlement known as Duval Town, built after emancipation to house freed slaves. In the early 1970s, when Secretariat was growing up, grooms at the Meadow were black and most lived at Duval Town. A farm truck would pick them up in the morning and take them to the Meadow. Sadie Lane, in Duval Town, is named after "Aunt Sadie," who cooked for Penny Chenery's mother in the 1940s.

Raymond Woolfe told me that "Mr. Chenery was a class act all the way. All his instincts were in the right place." I wonder where his spirit of kindness went to and why the racetrack seems to follow his example more by exception than as a rule. Was his generosity like some rare orchid that thrived on the Meadow's Virginia soil and only under his tending, defying any attempt at transplanting? Did it, like the fraternity of black grooms, simply fade away?

Penny Chenery, as the owner of Secretariat, would have paid Lucien Laurin 10 percent of purses won. She managed the Meadow Stable; she saw the checks going out. The groom was supposed to get 1 percent of that take, and Chenery finds it hard to believe that Lucien Laurin would have pocketed any money meant for Eddie. As for the groom's unseemly circumstances at the end of his life, she learned of it only after the fact. Eddie had faded from view. It was why, Penny Chenery said, neither Eddie's family nor Charlie Davis were invited to the Secretariat unveiling in Lexington. No one in her circle, she said, could find them.

Even Ron Turcotte, with all his contacts and despite issuing many feelers, could not track down Charlie Davis. "I would have paid his way," Turcotte told me. "I wanted him to be there for the unveiling." As for finding Eddie Sweat's relations, there are so many Sweats around Vance, South Carolina, it could easily be called Sweatville. Eddie's son and siblings would have attended the unveiling had they been invited, and they were not happy, at all, about the oversight.

When I asked Penny Chenery how we might improve the lot of grooms, she had no easy answer. "Give them better horses," she said, joking just a little. The better the horse, of course, the greater the chance of victory and of a groom sharing in the spoils. "Grooms," she conceded, "are an exploitable pool of labor, and many trainers do shortchange them. They *should* be adequately paid. I would hate to advocate unions. Maybe if tracks insisted on standards of accommodation, maybe if there were more inspections. And fewer gyp trainers."

I was struck repeatedly as I did my research by how valuable grooms are and yet how invisible they are. Everyone at the track has a hand out, hoping for a bonus or a share, and virtually the last hand is the groom's. Only the hot walker stands more removed from whatever largesse track society is willing to bestow.

I remember wading through files at the Keeneland Library and finding an article on Secretariat in the December 1997 issue of *Western Horseman* magazine, and being struck by the caption beneath one of the accompanying photographs. The photo showed Secretariat in the winner's circle after the Derby, and the jockey, trainer, owner, even the owner's sister, were all named. The black man holding the horse was tagged an "unidentified handler." The author or editor of the piece had not bothered to look up his name. Eddie was dying when that piece was published—he was buried the following April—and I trust he never saw the insult.

This book was written in praise of Secretariat and other great horses and their grooms, but if the fabled horse was the book's inspiration, Edward "Shorty" Sweat became its enduring ghost.

⌒

At nine o'clock on the morning Eddie died, his firstborn son, Marvin, got a cold chill, and he knew in that instant his father was gone. Marvin was in Miami and set to board a flight to New York later that day. The two men had talked on the phone the night before.

"My father," said Marvin Moorer, "was a strong, strong man. He went to work every day of his life, whether he was sick or not. I never heard him say he was tired. But that night, he said, 'Son, I'm so tired.' 'Hold on,' I told him. 'We're coming up tomorrow on a plane.' 'I'll try,' said Eddie. 'But I'm so tired. . . .' "

The next day, Marvin saw his cousin Vincent Walker come around a corner with tears in his eyes and he knew without being told. "I could always call him and I felt better after," Marvin said. "And sometimes he gave me tough advice. He might say, 'You got yourself into this mess; now you get yourself out.' Now I couldn't call him anymore."

I have seen photographs of Marvin, and he is the spitting image of his father, just a half foot taller. Like many of the Sweats, Marvin was athletic in his youth—he played point guard one year for a semipro basketball team based in Chicago. His cousins played college baseball or football and one tried out for the Miami Dolphins.

Eddie Sweat, said his son, was nineteen years old in 1958, when he met a local girl, Laverne Moorer, then seventeen. She bore his child, Marvin, but her father blocked Eddie's proposal of marriage, insisting his daughter was too young. Later, it was Laverne who wanted marriage and Eddie who declined. They would have a love-hate relationship for the rest of their days.

"I saw the look in my mother's eye the day of the funeral," said Marvin. "I heard her say to the casket, 'I always loved you and now you're gone.' That touched my heart, but there were days, I know, when she wanted to throttle him."

The church was filled to capacity on the day they buried Shorty Sweat, and there were some white people in attendance—exercise riders, mainly, and staff at Holly Hill Training Center, who had come to pay their respects. And while the jockey, in his wheelchair back in New Brunswick, was excused, the family did wonder why no owners or trainers were there.

"Had Lucien ever shortchanged Eddie?" I asked Marvin, for I had heard that charge often.

"There was a bit of that," he replied. On the other hand, Lucien, said Marvin, had offered Eddie a nice home in South Carolina, and an opportunity to run Holly Hill Training Center. But Eddie refused to leave New York. Eddie was also offered training partnerships, and more lucrative offers with other trainers. But he would not leave Lucien. "He was loyal to Lucien," said Marvin, "and he didn't want the responsibility of being a trainer."

As for Eddie's awful finances, Marvin offered a simple observation. He remembered Linda Sweat taking him shopping when he was fourteen. Marvin was living with his mother in New York, and seeing Eddie and Linda on weekends. "She was more of a spender," said Marvin of his stepmother, who taught preschool children. " 'If you like it, get it' was her advice. I had always been taught to conserve. I used to do my father's banking. I'd deposit his checks, and he had quite a bit of change. This was in 1994 and 1995." What role, if any, Linda Sweat played in Eddie's descent into poverty and where the money went, no one really knows with certainty. (Linda Sweat and her two daughters declined my request for an interview, as did Marvin's mother, Laverne Moorer, who was in poor health and recovering from brain surgery.)

The home in New York was lost in a dispute over back taxes, and whatever nest egg Eddie had amassed, including land and investments, not to mention all the silver plates and trophies, the detail of the Bogucki bronze, and other Secretariat memorabilia, disappeared down some deep dark hole.

"It was so bad," said Marvin, "that I had to put in fifteen hundred dollars to help pay for the funeral. The Jockey Club paid for part of the casket. All my father had to leave his kids was two acres of land, and I just gave my share to my sisters."

Eddie's youngest sister, Geraldine Holman, had to pay funeral home charges in both New York and South Carolina, along with the cost of transporting Eddie's body, and she even bought the blue suit he was buried in. "I went broke paying for all that," she told me, "but I know he's in a better place, looking down on all of us with a big smile on his face."

For all his money woes at the end, Eddie, his son said, had no regrets. "Until Secretariat," Marvin told me, "my father was day-by-day, happy-go-lucky. Secretariat got him recognized. That was a great moment in his life. I have never seen him so happy. He had a nice house, a real nice house. One time we were in Saratoga, and we couldn't walk anywhere without being stopped for autographs. He was on the cover of *Ebony* magazine and *Jet* magazine in 1973. But he hadn't forgotten his friends and relations back in South Carolina. He got his nephews jobs on the track, with much more money than they were getting in South Carolina."

"Did your father," I asked, "try to help too *many* people back in South Carolina?" This was another accusation circulating on the Eddie Sweat grapevine.

"He would say he didn't help enough," Marvin replied without hesitation. And I thought, Marvin, you are your father's son.

Marvin wishes he had known about the unveiling of the bronze in Lexington. "All Penny Chenery had to do," he said, "was contact Holly Hill Training Center. I'm really not happy, but there's nothing I can do about it now."

There's a kindly swagger about Marvin Moorer. ("I *think* like a seven-footer," he told me, laughing as he recalled his basketball days. He fondly remembered playing one-on-one with the prominent trainer Nick Zito, who, he said, "*loves* punishment.") Marvin will admit that the father-son relationship wasn't always the best, especially during his teenage years, when he was doing badly in school and loudly resenting his father's absence. They had confrontations, long periods apart. But in 1983, when Marvin was twenty-four and just out of the military, he started working with Eddie at Belmont, an arrangement that continued until 1987. For the first time, father and son "talked as men."

Marvin fondly remembers a man who loved baseball and rhythm and blues (Tyrone Davis and Johnnie Taylor especially), who loved to cook and dearly loved a joke. Eddie laughed easily and often, and he did not lack for confidence. He died convinced that he could have saved Secretariat from laminitis, could have protected him from the disease and, failing that, could have treated it. Sweat's genius with horses and his racetrack fame, though, were always tempered by something else.

He was a black man from the Old South. "My father," said Marvin, "had a tendency to look down on the ground, with his hands in his back pocket, especially when he was talking to Roger or Lucien Laurin. I was raised in New York and I was taught to look a person in the eye when you're talking. I didn't grow up with the race thing."

One day not long before our interview, Marvin Moorer was driving through Lexington and he stopped for a meal at a restaurant. The chef must have spotted him and came out from the kitchen to tell him that he looked very much like a man he knew and admired, one Edward "Shorty" Sweat. There was a painting on the restaurant wall, which the chef proceeded to show Marvin: It was the Richard Stone Reeves painting, of Eddie holding Secretariat, with the blanket on the ground between them.

"That's my father," said Marvin, who pulled out from his wallet his father's obituary in the *New York Times*. There followed a great commotion, with the chef taking Marvin around and introducing him to patrons, who now sought Marvin's autograph. "My father was a special man," his son told me. "I miss him a lot. He was not a religious man, but he had God in his heart."

~

David Walker, son of Birtha Lee Walker, Eddie's eldest sister, adored his uncle. "He was bigger than life," said this former groom, who had worked for more than a decade at Belmont. "When he walked into a room, the whole room would light up. He had an air about him." I wondered if it was a princely air, and thought of Ted McClain's first words to me about Shorty Sweat: "Eddie was a prince."

Walker talked to his uncle in the last days of his life, and he does not believe that Eddie ever regretted his time on the backstretch. "Eddie was supposed to get one percent of race winnings," said Walker, "and he didn't always get what he was promised." But bitter? No. "Other trainers desperately wanted Eddie to work for them. They knew that any horse with quality, in Eddie's hands, would be better. Many trainers tried to seduce Eddie with offers of more money. He refused. He was loyal to Lucien Laurin."

In 1973, when Eddie delivered Secretariat into the hands of the grooms at Claiborne Farm, Seth Hancock—then and still the farm's owner—offered Eddie a job at the farm. Taking it would have meant steady hours, a solid wage (and not one that rose and fell with racetrack luck), relief from all the travel, and even the company of the horse he loved. But Eddie turned Hancock down. I have to think that he later regretted not taking that offer, but the thought of uprooting his family must have seemed too much at the time. And the backstretch still tugged at him.

This, too, is speculation, but perhaps Eddie—out of kindness and consideration—spared his blood relations any hint of his own rancor as he lay dying. His siblings adored him, and they might have found it unbearable to know that both cancer *and* regret were gnawing at him during his final days in that hospital bed in New York City.

His sister Mary Lee Council, the eighth of the nine Sweat children, told me that she and Eddie as very young children used to sleep in the same bed. Eddie called her "Duke" (she can't remember why) and she raised one of Eddie's sons, Eric. "He was real friendly and nice," Mary Lee said of Eddie. "Always had a smile. I loved him and I miss him. He was a happy man." And the family was close, she said. "The Sweats, we all stick together."

In the days and weeks before finally succumbing to the Job's list of ailments that assailed him, Eddie admitted to his nephew that he hadn't taken care of himself, hadn't always gone to the doctor when perhaps he should have. Eddie also admitted to David Walker that Secretariat's death nine years beforehand had taken a lot out of him. Drinking did not dull the pain and may have compromised his health even further.

"What should my take be on your uncle?" I asked his nephew. "Was he a lucky man who had doubts at the end, or was he content with his life?"

"Your take," advised Walker, "should be that he was a great man with a lot of great horses. He never complained. It's a happy story. He had a joy ride. The only sad part is that Eddie Sweat wanted to be the first groom to enter racing's Hall of Fame." What does it say about the sport of kings—whose history in America goes back several hundred years—that its hall of heroes recognizes only horses, trainers, and jockeys? There is no category for owners, which is understandable, but none for grooms, either, which is not. They should bend those rules at Saratoga Springs, make an exception, so Edward "Shorty" Sweat can get his dying wish.

⌒

I asked Ron Turcotte why he had given a thousand dollars in cash to both Charlie Davis and Eddie Sweat in the wake of the Triple Crown victories. "They were doing most of the work," he said, as if his gesture were self-evident. "I always took care of the boys in the barn. Those guys were sleeping on cots in front of Secretariat's stall!" Racetrackers call it "staking"—an owner, trainer, or jockey shares the wealth with the bottom rung when a horse posts a win. Ron Turcotte remembers an owner at Woodbine walking down the shed row and handing out fifty-dollar bills.

There is charity on the backstretch, but it's hit-and-miss, and backsiders never know when they'll need some or where it will come from. In 1972, set to ride Riva Ridge to victory in the Kentucky Derby, Turcotte flew to Louisville assuming that either the owner or trainer had booked a hotel room for him. They had not, and, at the eleventh hour, there was no hotel room for a hundred miles. On the street, Turcotte crossed paths with a trainer and a racing secretary he knew and they let him bunk in their hotel room. The night before the Derby, and the winning jockey was sharing a bed. Next year, with Secretariat, it happened again. Turcotte once more had to lean on the kindness of friends.

This is how it is on the track. There is benevolence in track society, and there is its opposite, and those on shed row cannot know which will come their way. The image of an owner handing out fifty-dollar bills—or a jockey a thousand dollars in cash twice over—is an arresting one, but it points ultimately to the variable and patronizing nature of the rewards system on the backstretch. There are always shouts of glee when loaves of bread are cast to the poor or candies are tossed at children, but the scramble that results is often rough-and-tumble. And always, it lacks dignity.

⌒

Bill Nack finds it hard to believe that Eddie Sweat died a sour man. Nack finds the assessment too blunt, too simplistic. He is a fine writer, one with a sense of life's complexity, and he would argue that opposing truths can coexist: that a man can feel hard done by and privileged on the same day, even in the same breath.

"I knew Eddie thirty years," Nack told me from his home in Washington, D.C. "I'm sure there were moments in his life when he looked back and wondered. Lucien Laurin was like a father to him. He loved Lucien. So Eddie must have been conflicted at times, because the father didn't look after him." Nack said he had heard both Eddie Sweat and Charlie Davis say that they never got out of the Secretariat experience what they deserved. But neither man wanted to see that complaint in print.

Bill Nack reported in an updated version of his biography on Secretariat (published in 2002) that Eddie Sweat died "virtually penniless." The Jockey Club Foundation, which administers a fund to help track hands down on their luck, helped pay for Sweat's funeral. Roger Laurin paid the airfare so that Eddie's widow and children in New York could attend. "The man," wrote Nack, "had spent, given away or lost what money he had saved from his heyday as a groom."

"The fate of Eddie Sweat," Bill Nack told me, "is one of the great shames of the track. When I wrote my piece in *Sports Illustrated* on grooms ["Nobody Knows Their Names"], that was my statement. And I was really criticized by the racing establishment for that story. When grooms started to organize back in the 1960s, you'd think it was Lenin out there organizing workers. The reaction by rich owners was that severe. The haves don't want to share anything. Why didn't someone set up a trust fund for Eddie? One cover by Secretariat would have done it."

Nack has devoted his life to writing about the track, and if the racetrack's romance pulls him in, its cruelties wound him. "Are you a little conflicted about the track?" I asked him, "or a lot conflicted?"

"The latter," he replied.

"When Ruffian broke down on the track in 1975, that was a seminal experience for me. It was disillusioning. I'm not saying that Ruffian got cortisone, but it was around that time that trainers started using cortisone on horses. And the cortisone set up breakdowns because it dulled the pain. Go For Wand broke down. Prairie Bayou. Horses were dropping all over the place, and it took the romance out of it for me."

Nack understands why writers are drawn to the track, where the affluent stand shoulder-to-shoulder with the downtrodden. "That color, those kinds of contrasts, made the track so attractive to Damon Runyon," he said. "Hemingway loved the track, and Red Smith said he loved the track because it was so full of stories about poor people. And poor people are more colorful: They wear their hearts on their sleeves."

Nack does not remember Eddie drinking in all the time he knew him. What Nack remembers of his friend is his feeling for horses: "He was a horse whisperer before that term was even invented." Nack remembers how clean Eddie was, always, and what a snappy dresser he was on race day. Nack has a memory of Eddie dancing in a disco at Saratoga Springs one time. The great groom, it seems, was also a great dancer.

～

Eddie Sweat was what a friend of mine calls "a forelock tugger"—someone convinced of his own peasant stock and just about everyone else's blue bloodlines (especially if they were white folks).

Shirley Bogucki, the wife of the sculptor Ed Bogucki, picked Eddie up at the airport in Milwaukee once early in 1991. "He seemed," she told me, "like a really nice person. Well dressed in a suit and tie, very polite, and *really* into horses. We are all very horse-oriented in our house and we could talk to him forever about horses, especially about Secretariat. He was so pleased to be talking about Secretariat."

But despite Ed Bogucki's best efforts to dissuade him, the groom kept saying to him, "Yes, boss. Yes, boss." "I find it heart-wrenching," Shirley said, "to think of what he had to do to ensure he was 'keeping his place,' so to speak. He was astonished to see himself in that statue. He never imagined he'd have that recognition. And I know he got a lot of satisfaction at being close to Secretariat."

Eddie Sweat gave an interview to *Canadian Horse* magazine when he was in Toronto in 1973, and the magazine subsequently ran both its writer's questions and his answers. Readers of that piece got a real sense of the man's voice, his dignity, his professionalism and generosity. Eddie was asked, for example, about how he handled all the fans and reporters coming around, first to Riva Ridge's stall and then to Secretariat's. "It's something I've got to put up with," he said, "because they both are champions. But I helped them to be famous, and they helped me be famous. You have to put up with the people asking you all kinds of questions. You don't want to get snotty with people 'cause people are people, and I love people."

The reporter had earlier noticed Eddie giving a woman a few strands of Secretariat's mane hair. "Actually, I shouldn't do that," Eddie said, "but she asked me so kindly. . . ." Another woman asked for Secretariat's droppings, said she was going to enclose the precious stuff in glass, and, of course, Eddie obliged when the horse did.

The magazine asked Eddie about his finances and whether he was better off having won—with Riva Ridge and Secretariat—five of the six Triple Crown races in 1972 and 1973. Eddie sidestepped the question and alluded only to getting a higher salary than usual, but he seemed not too concerned then about wages. "Aside from money," he said, "I've met more people and people respect me more now than when I was rubbing the other horses. . . . Wherever I go, there's always someone who knows me or read about me and all that has made me feel very proud of myself, to know that there are people all over the world saying nice things about me. It's really something to have somebody come up to me and say, 'Are you Ed Sweat?' "

Heady stuff for a boy who grew up picking cotton and tobacco in backcountry South Carolina. He was a posthole digger and a construction worker. Then he got close to the greatest racehorse of our time, maybe of all time, and many looking on envied him. His loyalty to his horses was deeply felt and unassailable: During a wildcat strike by backstretch workers in 1960 at Aqueduct and Belmont (bricks were tossed and one man was killed), Eddie refused to join in and looked after seventeen horses by himself. He explained then that he didn't attend union meetings for one reason: no time. Eddie put the horses' welfare before his own and that of his fellow workers—which is either admirable or deplorable, depending on your point of view. Undeniable is that for several years he was a celebrity groom.

"Did it compensate?" is my question. I hope that proximity to equine greatness did compensate in some way, but I wonder if that always sustained him near the end. Eddie Sweat was working for Roger Laurin and sounding tired when he talked to the *Daily Racing Form* late in 1992. He had five and a half years left to live, but he was already struggling in every way.

"Right now," he said, "I'm just hangin' in there; I got no choice. I'm fifty-four years old . . . gettin' old, gettin' old. I'll take a horse over to the paddock and I'll be out of breath half way there. But who knows? Maybe one day I'll get lucky and come up with another big horse."

Ever the horseman, Eddie was hoping that luck—or a great horse—would rescue him. But if Secretariat and his long legacy could not do the job, no horse could. Eddie told a Louisville newspaper, the *Courier-Journal,* in 1993—just before the running of the 119th Kentucky Derby—that he had earned a 1 percent take of Secretariat's $1.3

million in track earnings. (Eddie's friends—Jimmy Gaffney, Charlie Davis, and Gus Gray—all scoffed at this when I put it to them.) If so, that still only comes to thirteen thousand dollars. But Eddie groomed, remember, *many* winners over his almost forty years on the racetrack. Whatever he took home, it was enough, Eddie said then, to help him buy a house between the Aqueduct and Belmont racetracks, in Queens, New York.

One room in that house, he said, had been set aside as a shrine to Secretariat, with memorabilia, photographs, trophies, plaques, and newspaper clippings. A china cabinet, his sister Geraldine remembers, was chock-full of silver plates, medallions, and four or five models of Secretariat. And for safekeeping, he had folded into a trunk the duds he had worn to the Derby in 1973: the plaid pants (the vivid white-black-and-red pattern that had raised the eyebrow of Penny Chenery), the white jacket with the blue shoulder patches, and the sporty white hat. Eddie loved his lids: tweed caps, porkpie hats, floppy hats, fisherman-style hats. For twenty years, he had kept pinned inside his tack box—the one that followed him as he roamed from track to track until the life ebbed out of him—a color photograph. It was dog-eared and fading, but he must have been proud of it, for he showed it to the Louisville reporter that day in 1993. The photo showed a proud groom leading the winning horse from the track on Derby day.

"Only way that horses will win," Eddie Sweat once told Bill Nack, "is to sit there and spend time with 'em. Show 'em that you're tryin' to help 'em. Love 'em. Talk to 'em. Get to know 'em. Now, that's what you gotta do. You love 'em and they'll love you, too. People might call me crazy, but that's the way it is."

This was, as far as I could determine, the man's essential philosophy on horsemanship. Eddie had also predicted to Nack, "They'll take me to my grave with a pitchfork in my hand and a rub rag in my back pocket." And he was not far wrong about that.

"My wife and I," Eddie said in Toronto in 1973, "have a very good understanding." He talked about how proud she was of him, how she would take the silver plates home and put them on the mantel. But think about it: Her husband enjoyed fame but not fame's wages. If Linda Sweat, or his children—Marvin, Michelle, Tiffany, Eric—wanted to see him, often their best bet was to turn on the TV or read a magazine.

A line leaps out from that interview in Toronto: "She's taken it pretty well." *It* sounds like some unfortunate circumstance, a death in the family, some malady requiring fortitude. Was Eddie talking about his fame? Or about his absence from hearth and home?

His family insists that his absence was *not* an issue. "He was always gone," his sister Geraldine told me, "but even his kids didn't object. He kept in touch; he sent money home. They loved him." When his stepdaughter, Michelle, had a baby, she named him Edward.

Shorty Sweat had worked almost every day of his life, even into his last year, when several illnesses were consuming him. When he died at North Shore University Hospital in Manhasset, New York, on April 18, 1998, he was fifty-eight years old. There would have been, in any case, little by way of pension or benefits to look forward to in his old age; certainly no golden handshake.

"What hurt us," Geraldine Holman told me, "was that we was looking for someone from the track to say something at his funeral. Nobody showed up. They sent flowers, which was nice. But he had devoted his life to the track, and we expected something back." Maybe, had a formal invitation been extended to certain owners, trainers, and jockeys, emissaries would have come. It would have meant the world to the family to have Eddie's worth recognized, to see some respect paid, but the emissaries did not come. Rock Hill Church's pastor gave the eulogy at Eddie's funeral.

Eddie's death, said his sister, "took a toll on me. He was everything to be proud of. My brother was a kind man. He'd give you the shirt off his back. We would watch the races and we would see him. We were thrilled. We couldn't believe that our brother was on TV!"

The Secretariat Center—a twenty-two-acre farm for retired racehorses—opened in 2004 at Kentucky Horse Park in Keeneland. In a perfect world, there would also be Eddie Sweat Place, a retirement home for distinguished grooms who have given their lives to horses. The two places would be close by each other, the retirement home high on a hill so old grooms could watch the foals gambol in the fields of bluegrass and clover down below.

⌒

I think of something that Ted McClain, the former trainer, told me, about how practically living with a special horse—as Eddie did with Secretariat—would force a reaction. "You'd either hate each other or love each other, one of the two," McClain said. "You'd be so damn glad to see him go, or it would kill you."

When Eddie Sweat and Charlie Davis, Secretariat and Billy Silver flew to Louisville in late April of 1973 before the Kentucky Derby, Eddie was well aware that he was taking on a huge task. On the road to the Triple Crown, Eddie worked virtually round the clock— groom by day, watchman by night. He would rouse himself every half hour. "Down here," he said at the time, "I want the job done right, so I'd just as soon do it myself. Not that I don't trust 'em" [hired security] but it's my horses, and if anything went wrong, it'd be my responsibility." *My horses,* and, in a way, they *were* his horses.

Eddie Sweat once talked about the pressure, the lack of sleep, and the worry that were part and parcel of grooming a six-million-dollar horse. "At Louisville and Baltimore," he said, "I was never more than twenty yards away from him. The only time I would leave him alone was when we came back here for the Belmont. Even then I'd get up at all times of the night, hoping daylight could come so I could go to work."

He told the *Daily Racing Form* in the fall of 1996, not long before he died, "I guess you could say I was his main man." Eddie's fondest memory of Secretariat was the last time he saw him, about 1983. Eddie told a reporter with the *Lexington Herald-Leader* that he had gone to Claiborne to say hello and he remembers being at the paddock fence and making the duck sound that was always part of the chatter between them. Secretariat trotted over to him and listened as Eddie spoke softly to him.

"Do you remember when you won the Belmont by thirty-one lengths?" the groom asked his old charge. Secretariat's response was to continue biting his wooden fencing. Eddie smiled as he told this story. He remembered aloud how, on Derby day, he had trouble getting Secretariat over to the paddock to tack him up because all the horse wanted to do was stand and pose for pictures. Eddie told the reporter that Secretariat was "an old, big ham" and "a rascal."

I have the sense that Shorty Sweat got a taste of something extraordinary when he was grooming Secretariat, a kind of exultation in his bones. The source was that magnificent chestnut horse and the heat and light he seemed to cast on everyone, but especially on those who got close to him. No one got closer than Eddie in 1972 and 1973. During the twenty-five years that followed, until they laid him in his grave at Vance, South Carolina, Eddie yearned to feel once more that special warmth on his face, but he never did. Some might say that a great horse is a curse, for a groom can spend the rest of his life trying to recapture the experience.

I put to Gus Gray one night in a restaurant in Ocala, Florida, much the same question I had put to David Walker, Eddie's nephew. Is the Eddie Sweat story a sad story or a feel-good story? "It's both," said Gus. Charlie Davis piped in with this thought: Long after Eddie had given up Secretariat, the groom would be nodding off to sleep at night and the face he saw in the dark was Secretariat's. Big Red was in Eddie's head and there was no letting go.

There is an old saying around the racetrack: It is not what the people do to the horses that is interesting; it's what the horses do to the people. As Gus Gray so eloquently put it, a great horse had passed through Eddie Sweat.

A stallion is not like other horses you can turn out with the herd so he can form his own allegiances and find his place in the hierarchy. A stallion turned out with another stallion would fight to the death. The only contact a stallion ever gets with another horse is when he brushes the competition in a race, enjoys the company of a track pony before and after the race, or when he covers a mare at the stud farm.

The Thoroughbred stallion, especially, is simply too valuable to risk being put out in a paddock—even with an aged gelding or two. He will never stand, as horse pals do, head-to-tail with another of his species so they can swish each other's flies. He will never enjoy mutual grooming, each horse working the other's body with bared and careful teeth.

The stallion, then, is ever alone, with fences and stall boards between him and his horse brethren. He can see, smell, and hear them, but six-foot-wide pathways typically separate a stallion paddock from other paddocks, so touch is a fleeting pleasure. The stallion is a herd animal deprived of the herd.

The Thoroughbred stallion, then, whether still active in racing or retired to stud, must find friendship, if he can, with his groom.

~ 8 ~

PILGRIMAGE

FEBRUARY 19, 2005. At noon, I cross the border between the United States and Canada at Niagara Falls and start heading east, following the green highlighter line I have drawn on my map of New York State. Another odyssey has begun; the course is set—east, then south, to the sacred places in the lives of Secretariat and Edward "Shorty" Sweat. Every map of every other state along the way—Pennsylvania, Virginia, North Carolina, South Carolina, Florida—has been assigned its own lime green line for me to follow.

One minute into the United States, the driver/navigator makes his first error. He misreads a highway sign (takes 190, not I-90). The one goes north, the other east. Imagine his surprise, only twenty minutes into his odyssey, as he joins the line of cars to cross the Canadian border at Niagara Falls. But he is most grateful for a small mercy—a last-chance duck-out lane on the left that spares him an embarrassing explanation at both customs checkpoints and sets him back on his wayward way.

An inauspicious start, and it gets worse before it gets better. I wake up in a Ramada Inn at Clarks Summit, Pennsylvania, cast the curtains wide, and see almost a foot of snow on the ground and on my car—actually, my father's car, which I have borrowed for the trip. I call his big Buick "Snowbird 1" and use that designation every time I call home to report on my progress, or lack of it. I am not used to Pop's power windows and locks, and I inadvertently touch a button as I step outside at Clarks Summit to brush off one last bit of snow from the driver's side window. When I go to reenter the car, I find every door locked. Snowbird 1 is idling, the heater blasting, the keys inside, and I am shouting a bad word in the hotel parking lot.

Dusk is close when I get to the Meadow, the farm near Doswell, Virginia, where Secretariat was born. I can hear what sounds like a distant waterfall and the insistent honk of geese overhead, heading back north (without the aid of either maps or lime green lines). Otherwise, it's dead quiet here, which seems appropriate, because this is for me, and many others, hallowed ground.

I have, of course, read and reread Raymond Woolfe's book on Secretariat and pored over the countless photographs he took of the Meadow and its most famous leggy foal. I know the horse farm's story—how Christopher Chenery bought back the old family inheritance, filled the pastures with classy broodmares and foals, made it all grand. Woolfe's photos paint a bucolic picture.

But my first hint that the Meadow is grand no more comes when I get close to the white posts and long lines of horse fencing: The paint is peeling, and some boards are broken and rotting. I know that Penny Chenery has sold the farm, that it has passed through several hands and suffered its share of bad luck, but I have also read in Woolfe's book that someone has bought the Meadow, intent on restoring it. Yet there is no sign of life in the place—no cars parked, no staff milling about, not one horse in the pastures.

A flashy green pickup truck with horse art airbrushed everywhere emerges from the training barn, and I stop the driver, hoping to learn something of the Meadow's current circumstances. Sandra Jones and her teenage daughter Whitney have Morgan horses at home, on nearby Peaceful Lane. The two women had kept foals at the Meadow in recent years.

The state of Virginia, they tell me, has bought the property for use as the future site of the state fair, but in the meantime the buildings are being dismantled. Scavengers, with the state's blessing, have been ripping up useful lumber and poles from the track. Mother and daughter are on just such a mission: Meadow track poles lie in their truck bed.

"It's a sad time here," says Sandra Jones. She is the spitting image of a woman who works in my home stable: upbeat, apple-cheeked, horsey to the core. "When Secretariat was winning all those races, it made everybody happy here. This is an awesome place. If I had enough money, I'd buy this place in a heartbeat." She would need, in a heartbeat, millions of dollars to outbid the state of Virginia. For all its decay, this farm is still the birthplace of Secretariat, and that fact has surely driven up the price. For years, I have read about plans to create a Secretariat museum on these grounds. I asked about the project in a state of Virginia welcome center the day before.

"They're still talking about it," the greeter replied, sounding a tad world-weary.

Sandra Jones remembers the Meadow in its glory, how the young Secretariat in his paddock would rush to the fences to greet any visitor. And for years, Whitney Jones says, pilgrims would come to the track and scoop up dirt in a bottle to take away as a souvenir.

Whitney—who was born in 1989, the year Secretariat died—knows the horse only in a secondhand way, through books and videos and the memories of her father, who saw him run. But you cannot live so close to the Meadow and not love its greatest foal. Whitney tells me that if you come to the Meadow track in the middle of the night, you can sometimes hear the sound of a horse galloping. She and her mother have heard it, and so have friends. Several years ago, the friends had a foal rejected by the mare, so they stayed at the Meadow training barn every night for months hand-feeding that baby. They heard the strange galloping many times, though there was clearly no horse out on the track. The sound of a lone horse breezing was always heard at the same time: three o'clock in the morning.

"Does that story frighten you or comfort you?" I ask the two women.

"Well . . . it's kinda weird," says Whitney, sounding a little worried, and then both women erupt into nervous laughter.

"It's the spirit of Secretariat," Whitney says with a teenager's certainty. She is wearing heavy beige coveralls and looks the part of the tomboy farm girl. My bet is that she is unafraid of work or getting her hands dirty. "One morning," she says as I listen at her rolled-down passenger-side window, "we came out and opened up the gate and you could feel something strong run through you, but we didn't know what it was."

Both women are curious to know why a Canadian writer has come all this way and what interest Secretariat holds for him. And I tell them about Eddie Sweat and his extraordinary bond with the horse, and I describe the photo Ray Woolfe took on the plane to Claiborne—Secretariat and Eddie nose-to-nose, the horse gripping his groom's jacket with his teeth. And both women, in unison, offer that sound people make to convey how touched they are: "Awww . . ."

After the two women leave, I walk down to the training barn inside the oval track, or what remains of it. The stalls, including the one that was once home to the foal named Secretariat, are still intact. But any signs over doors, certainly any with THE MEADOW or SECRETARIAT printed on them, have been lifted. Some outbuildings' roofs have caved in, the screening in doors is torn, and everywhere is evidence that rust and mold and neglect have been winning the battle. Bring on the bull-dozers.

I leave at dark, but not before scooping up a Styrofoam cup of light sandy red soil from the track. I know, because Sandra Jones has told me, that the track was resurfaced in recent years, so Secretariat never actually ran on this particular dirt. But I take my scoop anyway. It is what pilgrims do.

That night, it pours rain in Virginia, and the pelting keeps me awake. I have a notion of driving to the Meadow track to see if I can hear the sound of one horse galloping. But the notion fades—unlike the muffled roar from Interstate 95. There is no sound of a "distant waterfall" at Secretariat's birthplace, just the dull and constant whine of passing engines—that other horsepower.

⌒

Next morning, I am back at the Meadow, intent on seeing the foaling shed where Somethingroyal gave birth to a Bold Ruler foal named Secretariat almost precisely thirty-five years ago.

The white shed, with its two twenty-foot-square stalls, lies across a busy road from the track and training barn. The previous night, the road was quiet, but by day it comes alive. Highway 30 east cuts the Meadow in two. The foaling shed is set off from any other barns and outbuildings, and a long fenced alleyway leading up to it lends a little grandeur. But the 17A sign over the side door, which I noticed in Ray Woolfe's book, is gone.

And while the roof is intact and the framing still solid, the blue paint—blue and white were Meadow Stable's colors—is chipping off the Dutch door. Inside, I see where the gophers have been making their passageways, the hornets their nests, the spiders their webs. The previous day's visit should have prepared me, but despite the warm and welcome Virginia sun, I still feel an emptiness as I stand in front of the foaling shed. Even in present circumstances, I expected a little honor to the old boy's memory.

Up past the sprawling Georgian house, built by someone in the post-Chenery period, are parked several heavy trucks with STATE FAIR—VIRGINIA painted on the side doors. Some wag has put on one truck's roof the kind of small plastic markers that funeral home staff place on the hood of your car as you join the procession to the cemetery. This may be a workman's prank, and nothing to do with the Meadow, but it seems to fit the mood of this once-splendid property falling into ruin.

I stop at the All-American Travel Plaza, a sprawling truck stop, to seek out Charlie Ross, one of Secretariat's first grooms. These days, he cleans shower stalls, not horse stalls. But he seems harried, unsure of when he might get off later in the day, and not terribly keen on talking about the horse in any case. "Secretariat," he tells me, "that was a long time ago." I am disappointed, but I try to see things from his vantage point. I did notice, in Ray Woolfe's book, pictures of Charlie Ross—a white rub rag dangling from his back pocket, grooming a young horse after a gallop, giving a rider a leg up. Thirty-three years younger, he was part of something then; he was a black man grooming good horses. Charlie Ross must have valued his work, must have been valued.

He would have watched over the years as the fortunes of the Meadow, his old workplace—not five minutes down the road from the truck stop—rose and fell, rose and fell in the Chenery wake. Now someone stands before him, a man in a white Secretariat ball cap looking eager and hopeful, tape recorder in hand. What does Charlie Ross see but a bone picker. Small wonder he would rather take a pass.

I get back on I-95 and drive south along the long green line. Next stop is Holly Hill, South Carolina, where Eddie Sweat was born and laid to rest.

⁓

The interstate's temptations—"the world's smallest church," the Ava Gardner Museum, Pedro's theme park (and the hundred or so billboards that herald it)—hold no sway with me. The cold meat and bagels, the apples and bananas, the mixed nuts and jujubes, the hefty juice and water bottles I had packed before crossing the border reduce my dependence on interstate food fare, and a good thing, too.

Every time I gas up the silver-gray Buick, the air feels warmer. The colors are changing. I left the snow back in Pennsylvania. Virginia was gray and brown. North Carolina offered the bloodred of the redbud tree and the lime green of new shoots and tender grass. A winter-addled Canuck is pleased to feel the sun on his face.

The shadows are long when I get to Holly Hill, South Carolina. The white librarian in town is helpful but does not know where Rock Hill Church is; a black patron does and gives me directions to the cemetery where Eddie Sweat is buried. The graveyard is north of Holly Hill, not far from Vance. And if you look in the telephone book for the Vance and Holly Hill area, you will find thirty-four Sweats listed.

I see, among others, Adolph and Lucile Sweat, Banetta Sweat and Blease Sweat, Lurene Sweat and Marquett Sweat, Marvin Sweat, Nettie Lou Sweat, Rajohn Sweat (there are two Rajohns, both on Hill Street, a few houses apart); there are Rhodell Sweat (Eddie's sister-in-law) and Rufus Sweat, Tahesia Sweat, Tahersia Sweat and Tenika Sweat, Vanessa Sweat and Willie L. Sweat.

Rhodell Sweat told me on the phone that Eddie was "a nice guy, real nice guy. He was very helpful with my kids at Christmastime, stuff like that. Always trying to help. And he loved his horses."

There is even, I will learn during my time around Holly Hill, a Sweat Street. A Mr. T. Sweat lives on Sweat Street, and I wonder if he moved there for a lark. I also wonder if an ancestor of Eddie's did something noble, but the naming of the street—the local librarian will later inform me—has more mundane origins. When the 911 service was recently introduced, many streets, heretofore called by highway numbers, were given names. And since Mr. T. Sweat (no relation of Eddie's) had lived on the street longest, county officials named it after him.

The Rock Hill Church cemetery, not ten minutes from Holly Hill, lies at the confluence of three dirt roads: Rock Hill Road, Chateau Lane, and Po Chance Drive. There is no sign to identify the cemetery, no wrought-iron gate or fencing, nor is there here the grim geometry of the dead that I am used to: neat rows of gray stone markers, the heads of the dead all perfectly aligned, lest anyone get a head start on heaven, or any other destination. In the graveyards I know, the dead are tightly spaced, elbow-to-elbow, everything rectangular or square.

The dead of Rock Hill Church seem more randomly situated, next to bushes or trees, the graves often festooned with wildly colorful arrangements of plastic flowers. These are not small, discreet bouquets at the base of granite markers, but bold and flashy circles and crosses, often tall and wide, and they are everywhere. It is my first, and strongest, impression: that wash of color, every color under the sun, color to nudge the dead. In this cemetery, shaped like a ragged triangle, some heart-shaped wreaths and bouquets have been dispensed with, tossed into the woods that flank one whole side. It's as if

the flowers were real, had lost their bloom, and had been left to com-
post on the forest floor.

Some graves lie close together, but there are many airy spaces, too,
an invitation to the living, perhaps, to walk here. The longer I stay,
the more I like this back-road cemetery, its quiet verve, the white-pine
forest that surrounds it, the big old trees in the middle with their
hanging moss, the dry crackle of curled oak leaves underfoot.

The light is fading as I make my rounds, head down, looking from
grave to grave. Some, I see, have coins on them, a little pocket money
for the afterlife. A full moon has already risen and baying hounds are
calling to it, as are the frogs in the lowland meadows. There is a pleasant smell in the air, maybe from the white pine—"hard pine," they
call it here. Or maybe it is the sweet smell of spring.

When I do find what I am looking for, a grave right on the edge,
just kissing the forest, I am surprised by the little jolt of emotion that
courses through me. I did not know the man, never met him, never
saw him or heard him speak. But I am moved to see the ground-level
concrete bunker that houses his remains, the plain alloy and glass
marker that names him—plain, as Secretariat's stone was plain. Just
name and dates: Edward Sweat, 1939–1998.

At the head of the grave, someone has placed three plastic Breyer
horses, none more than six inches long. A black horse, a bay, and, no
mistake, Secretariat. (Only later, when I got back home and more
closely examined my photographs, did I realize that I *was* mistaken.
The horse was only a rough facsimile of Secretariat: The chestnut
color was right, but this horse had four white feet, not three, a blaze,
not a stripe, on his head. What is unmistakable was the gesture. I
would wonder for months who had put those horses at Eddie's grave,
and Geraldine Holman, Eddie's sister, finally solved the mystery for
me. She and Linda Sweat had been to the grave just days before I arrived. Geraldine had provided the black horse; Linda had set down

the dark bay, the chestnut Secretariat look-alike, and the blue and white plastic flowers.)

This I have not planned, but I go to the car, get the white Styrofoam cup with the sandy soil from the track at the Meadow, sprinkle it at the plastic horse's feet, as if the chestnut would like the smell of home and the feel of familiar turf, as if his old groom would appreciate the token in all its sentimentality.

⌒

"Oh Lord, there was so many people. The church was packed when my uncle died," says Willie Perry. "And that's a *big* church." It is indeed a big church, Rock Hill Church, redbrick, with a white steeple and a white cross on top. The church is not far down the road from the cemetery; hymns sung in the church carry that distance. Down the other road that flanks the cemetery is Holly Hill Training Center, where Eddie learned his craft. Were it possible for a dead man to hear hymns or a horse's hoofbeat, he is close enough.

Eddie was born nearby on August 30, 1939. Home was a fifteen-acre farm where David and Mary Sweat raised nine children, Eddie the sixth among them. The bus he took to school as a boy went right past Holly Hill Farm. He would work after school on nearby farms, picking cotton, corn, soybeans, watermelon, potatoes. The wage was twenty-five cents a day. But he was also interested in horses and got a job working for Lucien Laurin at his training center, digging holes and building fences. By the age of seventeen, he was hot-walking and grooming, and he would walk the two and a half miles between home and work.

This was Eddie's world: Lake Marion to the north, Lake Moultrie to the east, the nearby towns of Vance, Eutawville, Wells, Sand Ridge, Four Holes, Holly Hill. Eddie would become a racetrack gypsy, driving

Lucien Laurin's red van, but when it came time to put Eddie in the ground after he died in a New York City hospital, there was no question of where. They brought him home to South Carolina.

His sisters Birtha Lee Walker and Mary Lee Council told me that Eddie loved "country food," and when he came home for visits, this is what he ate: corn bread and beans, collard greens, fried chicken, rutabagas, and sweet potato pie.

"The kids [his nephews and nieces] loved him to death," said his oldest sister Birtha Lee, whom Eddie called "Sis." "He used to tease them. He'd grab the food right off their plates with his hands, then hide it and claim to find it by accident. He was their favorite uncle. It was happy days when he came around." Eddie would amuse the children with magic tricks, with quarters that appeared and disappeared in his hands and behind his ears. Some of the adults around Vance called Eddie "Big Bubba" (*bubba* is a word in the Geechee dialect that means "brother"), but the children found that a mouthful, so they called Eddie instead "Uncle Big Bull"—and that nickname stuck. The uncles, meanwhile, also loved to see Shorty coming, for he would have a little bottle of whiskey for each of them.

Willie Perry is sitting on his porch on Camphorwood Road, a dirt road a stone's throw from the Holly Hill track. We sit on rough wooden furniture in front of his not-so-mobile home with its tin roof, and I riffle the pages of Raymond Woolfe's book, hoping they will stir this man's memories.

Willie Perry remembers, and he smiles a lot as he does. "He was a good man, I tell you what. Every time you see him, he laughin.' When he come down here, he loves everybody. He just was a good person, real good. He loved his work, definitely, and it was shockin' to everybody when he died. I ain't never seen him mad. No suh. Never. He talked about Secretariat all the time, all the time. That was his big horse. He said it was *his* horse; he loved that horse. That was all he could talk about when he come down here, was Secretariat and Riva Ridge. My uncle thought he was a lucky man, and he never complained. Never."

Willie Perry, a shy, short man in his fifties, looks on as I continue flipping the pages of a book he has never seen. He is a mechanic at the garage in Vance, and he has taken the morning off to accommodate me and my project. (Charlie Davis, Secretariat's old exercise rider and one of Eddie's best friends, had previously given me his daughter's telephone number in Vance, and she, in turn, gave me a number for Willie Perry and told him I would call. "The Holly Hill gang," as Ted McClain put it, had kicked into gear.)

"What goes around comes around" is a tired expression, but one that conveys a time-honored truth nonetheless. It occurs to me that all the people I talk to on my journey are not just being kind, though they are that, too. They know I am going to write about Eddie, so a kindness to me is a kindness to him. My hunch is that he earned in his lifetime among friends and relations a great stack of IOUs, and that seven years after dying, he is still calling them in.

Willie Perry—destined to die of a heart attack in August 2006—this day wears blue jeans and a purple sweatshirt and smokes cigarettes on his porch. He is a man of few words, but he speaks with great affection about his maternal uncle. The man on the porch always thought his uncle had money, and if he dressed with flare, it was "for the horses." If Shorty had a genius with horses, "he learned if off his own." Eddie taught Willie some of what he knew, as well as Willie's brother, Johnny, now a foreman at Belmont. "Shorty was the best, man," says Willie Perry. "The best."

⁓

Holly Hill Training Center is as neat and polished as some trailer homes on these back roads are swaybacked and crestfallen. Home to almost one hundred horses, the farm's several outbuildings and barns feel unified by their Lincoln green–colored steel roofs and the black horse weather vanes on top. The track and starting gate across the road are classy; the farm's iron gate opens and closes to those with security passes; even the chain on the horse gate, I notice, has recently been oiled.

This is where Eddie worked, when Lucien Laurin ran the show. Willie Perry worked here for a year and gave me some names of men who had worked with Eddie. More members of the Holly Hill gang.

Pedro Olin is one, and I happen to meet him by the farm gate. He cannot chat long, for work on the farm tractor beckons, but he does tell me that "Eddie really loved his job and his horses. He was happy in his work." But the man I want to talk to, Olin tells me, is Randy Jenkins, and he points out his whereabouts.

In the ample tack room, amid the saddles and bridles, I find Jenkins, a distant cousin of Eddie's, who worked with him before and after Secretariat. "He taught me a lot," says Jenkins, who puts down his sandwich. "He was one of the best. A good man, a good, kindhearted man. Laughin' all the time, never sick."

Randy Jenkins is a quiet man in his mid-fifties. He used to ride with Eddie in that red van and he remembers softball games and barbecues with Charlie Davis and other men from around Holly Hill. "The homeboys," as Jenkins puts it.

He says that Eddie had a scar on his shoulder where a horse called Bold Marker bit him: "He was a tough, rough horse. Used to tear Eddie's clothes off all the time. That horse had bad legs, but Shorty worked on him . . . good leg man." Randy keeps returning to that compliment, as if it were the nicest thing that one groom could say of another. Eddie did not repay Bold Marker's violence with his own; he rubbed the horse's legs and gave him back his speed.

Randy Jenkins had heard that Eddie suffered a severe beating at the racetrack, and Eddie's nephew David Walker later confirmed the story. It was early in Eddie's career; he and some other backsiders were leaving the track in New Orleans to celebrate a win, when they were set upon by a group of men, robbed, and savaged. One minute, Eddie was elated by victory and had some cash in his pocket; the next, the pocket was empty and he was licking his wounds.

I think of something Raymond Woolfe once told me, about his book on Secretariat. "The general public wants a fairy tale," he said, "and I gave 'em one. If I had put in all the crap I knew . . . I rode steeplechasers for fourteen years and I had my heart broken so many times. Horses dying, getting killed needlessly. The racetrack is an incredible theater of life. It's a hypnotic place to many people. It's hypnotic to me, for God's sake. I'll always feel like the track is home."

But there is a dark side to the track, said Woolfe. I had many conversations with him on the phone, and I would think he was just about to sign off, and then he would set some new course, but always come back to Secretariat, Eddie, the track, the backstretch. Thoroughbred racing both repulses and attracts, and I sensed in Ray Woolfe a genuine sadness and anger about the fate of Eddie Sweat, as if the track itself had swallowed a happy man—"always laughin'"—and spit him out.

But I cannot be sure. I am gathering a kaleidoscopic picture of a dead man, relying on the testimony of friends and relations who loved him. Not many of us speak ill of the dead, in any case. And if Ray Woolfe peddled a fairy tale, what mythology am I pursuing about a chestnut horse and his black groom?

Jimmy Gaffney rode Secretariat during those dawn workouts throughout 1972 and into the summer of 1973. But during the Triple Crown run, Lucien Laurin and Gaffney had a falling-out. The rider thought the trainer was stinting in his bonus money; the trainer accused the rider of grandstanding on Secretariat. So Laurin turned to his most trusted exercise rider, the one who had ridden Riva Ridge— George (Charlie) Davis.

I knew that Charlie Davis was a Holly Hill alumnus, that he had been as close to Eddie as anyone, but for a long time I had trouble tracking him down. My queries to the Jockey Club and like agencies led nowhere. Then the same luck that produced Ted McClain turned up Charlie Davis early in 2005.

A friend of mine, a trick-horse trainer in Ocala, Florida, named Carole Fletcher (we had worked together on her memoir, *Healed by Horses*), said she would put out the word. And word came back almost immediately. Her friend and fellow trainer Danny Jenkins is a starter who also certifies horses for the starting gate. Jenkins, it transpires, is pals with a horseman in Ocala named Gus Gray, who is fast friends with Charlie Davis, who also works in Ocala. Ocala, then, will be the last, and, in some ways, the pivotal stop on my journey.

⌒

I link up with Gus Gray at a gas station in Ocala, but I am late for our meeting—I got lost, of course. A big, round-shouldered bear of a man with a beaming smile, Gus Gray is the yearling manager at Double Diamond Farm in Ocala. He is devoting his lunch hour to hooking me up with Charlie Davis, and I follow Gus's red LeBaron convertible to Charlie's house (no one home) and then to the Ocala Training Center, where Charlie works and where we finally find him. As we arrive, he is supervising a small crew using a forklift to relocate a round feeder. "The number-two boss man," as he calls himself, Charlie Davis also oversees foaling at the center.

He is sixty-five, a grandfather to twenty-eight grandchildren and a great-grandfather to three others, yet he seems as loose and nimble now as when he rode Secretariat. I watch his face and sometimes see a toll there from a hard life; other times it strikes me that a small electrical current runs through him, as it did when he was a boy. He weighs 122 pounds, just three more than his riding weight from 1973, and his hands are big, all knuckles. Lucien Laurin, a former jockey, thought the world of him as an exercise rider and would tell all who would listen, "Watch his hands; watch his hands." In his youth, he galloped all of Laurin's good horses—Riva Ridge, Upper Case, Spanish Riddle, and, of course, Secretariat.

Davis is dressed youthfully—white ball cap, a red-checked shirt over a blue-checked shirt over a white T-shirt, with charcoal pants and new white running shoes. He has high cheekbones, a wide black mustache, shining coal black eyes: an eager, open face. And he can talk all day about Secretariat, the tales all told in his rich South Carolina dialect. Charlie will arch his upper body back and squint his eyes to make a point; he will fall into pantomimes to create pictures, make sounds to add audio to the video.

Charlie leans against a tree near the stables at the Ocala Training Center and tells story after story. "And so, and so . . ." he says, linking the stories. He has two listeners, and it is hard to tell who is enjoying this more—the animated narrator or the rapt audience. I begin to worry about Gus getting back to his job, for his lunch hour is surely past.

"Am I keeping you?" I ask Gus, who is from Alabama.

"Oh, thas okay," he says, delivering his one-hundred-watt smile. "I just love to hear Shorty talk." Charlie's nickname is one he shares with Eddie, and eventually I get my Shortys (Charlie is five four; Eddie was five five) all straightened out. Later, I will hear Charlie referred to as "Choo-Choo Charlie." The track, it seems, has no time for real names.

Charlie vividly remembers his first moments on Secretariat, and his impression—as he walked the horse onto the track—was of a colt who was either slothful or lame, or both. "I hear trainers sayin', 'That horse is sore.' I thought he was sore. He was lazy, laid-back. When he first came from the farm—the Meadow—he was muscular, big. At Hialeah, we wanted him to see the flamingos in the fields." Many horses spooked at the sight of these strange luminous sticks exploding by the hundreds into pink flight, swirling and turning like a fan. The idea is to expose a young horse to all sorts of unnerving distractions.

"Secretariat," said Charlie, "went out there like he been there ten years. I take my stick, he swish his tail. He in no hurry for nuthin. Other two-year-olds, they all down the track. I say to myself, 'What Lucien Laurin doin' bringin' this big, fat, lazy son of a bitch down here for?' Second day, same thing"—and here Charlie does a mime of a man with his eyes half-closed, as if just roused from sleep. "Only time he move when you put his feed in the tub." Charlie makes a drumming sound with his mouth to imitate Secretariat frantically rooting around in a plastic feed pail.

Secretariat, Charlie says, was a very smart horse. Still a baby, he nonetheless knew that a morning workout was just that—a workout, not a race. The horse was saying, as Charlie puts it, I can't make no money in the mornin.'

Secretariat would gently drop his head if he wanted Charlie to loosen up on the reins. Other young horses would have shaken their heads, pulled and protested more loudly. Secretariat, in a quiet, assured way, was telling his rider to *relax,* to take it easy, and reminding him who was in charge. Charlie will tell me over and over again—and we will get together four times when I am in Ocala—how much he wished that Secretariat could have talked. Charlie is sure the horse would have told him, I am the pilot. You is de copilot.

Riding Secretariat, says his old exercise rider, was like riding a plane. "But not a DC-ten," Charlie insists, "not even a seven forty-seven. He was the Concorde. When he drop that head, he comin.'"

Charlie remembers sitting on the back of Billy Silver, Secretariat's track pony, when Secretariat made his late charge in the Kentucky Derby. Charlie was standing in his stirrups, hand-galloping, scrubbing away, and the Appaloosa gelding did not flinch. He knew his rider was elsewhere, that his body was not to be taken seriously. Charlie also makes the point that—contrary to what has been written—Secretariat did not shun Billy Silver's affection. They were good friends and would often graze together on the grass behind the track at Belmont.

Charlie Davis remembers, too, walking Secretariat before the Belmont Stakes and hearing someone nearby rattle a pail. The horse rose up on his hind legs, pawed the air, then landed before circling majestically, kicking dirt and stones against the nearby sheds. A little show of power, like a wizard setting off fireworks by winking.

Later, at Carole Fletcher's house, I sit beside Charlie as we feast on barbecue pork and watch his old Secretariat videos. We are sitting together on a little bench, Charlie's left leg touching my right leg, and his limb is hammering like a piston. On the screen, Secretariat is starting one of his patented charges, and Charlie makes that *eeeeoooooooooowwwww* sound—the sound of a Spitfire, say, as the fighter plane banks and plummets to the attack. Some nights, he tells me, he will go home and pop those videos in his machine. He never tires of seeing that horse run, of reliving that extraordinary time in his life. That night at Carole's, he arrived with his videos and Ray Woolfe's book in its special cardboard sleeve, both items tucked under his arm as a preacher would tote his Bible.

"Do you have every race in your head?" I ask him.

"Yessss," he replies.

"Every race?" I say, pressing him.

"Oh-ho-ho-ho-ho-ho," he says, as if daring me to test him. The race at Garden State, November 18, 1972, for example, showed Charlie Davis what a great horse Secretariat already was and gave him an inkling of what was to come. The record showed Secretariat last of six horses at the quarter turn, fourth at the halfway point, and third three-quarters through the mile-and-a-sixteenth race. The *Daily Racing Form* said he "rallied boldly around horses on the final turn." Charlie Davis has his own language to describe the move: "Excuse me, ladies and gentlemen, Secretariat is gettin' in gear!"

"I thank the good Lord," Charlie tells me, "that I got on the greatest. He be my boss man! He was the horse of the century!"

Despite their apparently modest places in the world, people like Charlie Davis and Gus Gray do not lack for confidence. They walk with a big stride and fool you with their hat-in-hand manners. Charlie says, without boasting, that he was "one of the best" exercise riders of his day. Maybe not *the* best, but among them. Gus boasts that he is the only black groom ever to have a race named in his honor—the Gus Gray Handicap was run, only once, at Gulfstream several years ago. Gus has written a book about his life as a groom for the legendary trainer Fred Hooper, who died in 2000 at the age of 102. (Self-published, *They Call Me Gus,* authored by Gray and a ghostwriter, sold some five thousand copies.)

A self-made, self-taught man, Fred Hooper had made a fortune in the construction business and had won his first Kentucky Derby in 1945 with the first Thoroughbred he had ever owned, one called Hoop Jr. His horses would win one hundred stakes races and $55 million at the track.

Gus left us to go back to work, but not before telling me that

I should write a book about grooms—not grooms and horses, just grooms. Charlie and I went off to a modest little restaurant, where he tucked into one of his favorite meals—liver and onions—and we talked about Eddie Sweat.

"We been through somethin,'" Charlie said. "We were like brothers." Charlie grew up at Eutawville, a few miles northeast of Holly Hill, where his father broke horses and grew potatoes, corn, and cotton. Charlie's friendship with Eddie dated back to 1957, when both were teenagers and working for Lucien Laurin at Holly Hill. Later, at Belmont and on the road at tracks all over North America, they would eat together, bunk together in rooms the size of a horse stall, go to the races together in the afternoons.

"We always keep a hot plate," Charlie said. He was the designated chef (and still fancies himself a good man in the kitchen). "And when we were short of money, we'd buy a can of beans, three or four hamburgers, a bag of rice and cook up a big pot." He looked back fondly on the memory. "That was the good old days."

Both Gus and Charlie remember a time in the fifties, sixties, and early seventies when the backstretch was the domain of black people from the American South. Some trainers, perhaps superstitiously, hired only men from a certain state. Fred Hooper hired blacks from Alabama; Lucien Laurin was partial to blacks from South Carolina, and especially his old haunt of Vance. Gus and Charlie saw the backstretch as a family then, and you could leave your room unlocked and everything would be there on your return. Now there are double padlocks on the doors, and the black men are mostly gone, replaced by white women and Hispanic men.

But if the backstretch was ever a family, it was a dysfunctional one. Both men remember beatings. Gus was fifteen and working at Aqueduct when an older man held a butcher knife to his neck after Gus had refused to give him "a loan" of ten dollars. "You gonna need a friend," the knife-wielding man said, and the scene sounded like something out of a prison movie, where the tough old con offers the younger con "protection"—for a price. Only the intervention of another racetracker saved Gus's life.

Fair to say that on the backstretch, you *do* need a friend. Charlie Davis and Eddie Sweat, two home boys from Holly Hill, were like two peas in a pod. Charlie could remember only one time when he and Eddie got angry with each other. They went to the races and did not talk for a whole day. That night, Eddie acted like nothing had ever happened. The reason for the stony silence has long since slipped Charlie's mind.

What he will not soon forget is Eddie's dutiful grooming. "To Eddie, the horse was his child," Charlie explained. "Before he go home, make sure the hay last all night. Another flake, clean water. He wash all the feed buckets like he washes dishes." Above all, said Charlie, he set an example for the others, Charlie included, to follow. "He made me think," said Charlie, pointing to his head. He is full of admiration and affection for his lost mate.

"How important was Eddie to Secretariat?" I asked.

"Eddie was his father," said Charlie. "Any time Eddie walked that shed row and Secretariat or Riva Ridge heard his voice, the heads would come up. Both heads would come through the door." There was magic in Eddie's hands, and the horses knew it. Charlie made a curling, lifting motion with his right shoulder to show how Secretariat would lean into Eddie's massage. It was "like you rubbin' your cat at home," Charlie said. The magic came through his fingers and that sponge."

Several times during the lunch, Charlie got what he termed "full"—the tears would gather in his eyes, and he would cover them and apologize. At one point, he was talking about Eddie's proficiency at bandaging a horse, and Charlie echoed Randy Jenkins's phrase—that

Eddie was a "great leg man"—and then added, "He was the master." That word *master* seemed to buckle Charlie, and he had to pause and gather himself.

Charlie talked about Eddie's vigilance as a groom. Eddie would watch Riva Ridge and Secretariat eat, take note of how fast, or slow, they ate. He would constantly check their teeth, take their temperatures. Shorty Sweat was like a nurse in an intensive care unit.

Later, we talked about money. Charlie seemed immensely proud of the fact that he had put away enough money to buy five acres of land near the track at Holly Hill, along with two mobile homes, all paid for. He doubted that Eddie had managed anything similar. Charlie completely agreed with Ted McClain's assessment of Eddie— "a prince," someone who would do anything for anybody. But Charlie also implied that Eddie drank more than was good for him, at least in the later days, and that he gave away to siblings and friends more money than he should have. "Put it this way," said Charlie. "I wished he'd left more for the wife and kids. His heart was huge. . . . "Something always happen to the good, not to the bad," he said through tears. "I wish today that Eddie was here and tell you the same thing I'm telling you. When you think you got a friend, you ain't got no friend." I took Charlie to mean that backstretch "buddies" saw Shorty Sweat as a soft touch and drew from that well of generosity until the well ran dry.

⌒

I had promised Gus and Charlie I would buy them a supper for all their trouble, but I got a little anxious about my beleaguered pocketbook after everyone piled into Snowbird 1 and Gus directed me toward the fancy steak houses of downtown Ocala. I need not have worried. We pulled into the Golden Corral, where, for ten dollars, you could belly up to the buffet—whose range and size were mesmerizing—all evening long.

Over their plates, Gus Gray and Charlie Davis told stories of back-stretch society, its attractions, its hazards.

Gus, who had been a groom for a long time, knew the territory. A groom looking for work, he said, should be able to say, "I rubbed so and so." If you can't name a big horse, they don't want you. Imagine what kind of passport Eddie Sweat carried around until the day he died. "I rubbed Secretariat."

"Sometimes," said Gus, "a great horse passes through you, and that's what makes a groom. You get a good horse and the light hits you. . . ."

I was thinking he was waxing poetic, Alabama-style. But I asked all the same. "What light?"

"TV lights," said Gus, but all that attention can fold in a hurry. He used to rub a good horse called Tri Jet, and when that horse was winning, some people called Gus Gray the horseman of the decade. "Now they say," observed Gus, "you used to be a dang good groom."

"It's cruel, isn't it?" I said.

"Yeah," replied Gus.

"Just like losing in front of your kid," Charlie added. He said he had had precisely that feeling on the day that Secretariat left his home barn at Belmont to stand stud at Claiborne. "I went into my room and cried. I didn't put the TV on; I just sat on the corner of the bed. I remember peeking through the blinds and watching Ronnie Turcotte kiss Secretariat." (Ray Woolfe captured the moment in his book.) "On that day, it seemed to me that was one of my kids leavin.' My firstborn."

The Muzak played in the Golden Corral, patrons filled and re-filled their plates and bellies, and two men who had spent all their lives on the track tried to help me understand what can transpire between a racehorse and a groom. Gus said that when a groom talks of a previous race, he will say, "I was running against . . ."—as if the groom himself had been competing in the race. It is a measure of how much a groom begins to see life through a horse's eyes.

"You with those horses more than you with any member of your family," said Gus.

"There we go," agreed Charlie, like a one-man chorus in a Baptist church.

"You take those horses going to the Kentucky Derby," said Gus, pronouncing it *Ken*-tucky. "That's the groom's life, okay? And one groom gonna come out smellin' like a rose in May." He described the campaigning for the Derby in May, how it starts in March of the previous year. Trips to Florida, California, Arkansas. That horse's groom, explained Gus, "feels his pain, everything. All o' that go with you. When he hurt, you hurt. When he smiles, you smile. 'Cause that the only thing that you got. That's all the family you got."

But surely, I countered, the groom has an actual family, too. Maybe a wife and kids. Where do they fit in all of this?

"But here," said Gus, "something that took over now. This is something big. That horse, he your son, your daughter, and everything." Gus said he had seen grooms become so obsessed with a particular horse, so unwilling to leave the barn, that the owner was forced to separate man and horse. A groom's life can take a strange twist.

"That's why," said Charlie, leaping in, "Eddie start to drink so much. Because Secretariat was like one of his kids, and one of his kids just died."

Think of it. A groom never rides the racehorse, never hits him with a stick or makes him work. The groom only comforts him, feeds him, bathes and massages him, tucks him into bed. The nature of their contract is skewed. A grandfather or grandmother doting on a grandchild might not be a bad comparison.

Gus talked about the day he went to the funeral of the farm manager, Fred Hooper's son. The hearse passed the barn, and Gus took a moment to look in on Tri Jet, something he did twice a day. He described finding the twenty-nine-year-old horse dead in his paddock. Gus had to deal with his own awful grief, but he could not pass on to his employer the terrible news. Everyone feared that losing Tri Jet and his own son on the same day would kill the old man.

Then Gus, now dewy-eyed, asked the question: "You got to ask yourself, say, do a grown man supposed to cry about a animal?"

"Yes, they do," Charlie piped up.

"If you part of the animal," said Gus, "you got to cry. That's when the sad moment comes." And he described that day in the paddock, how the tears ran down his face as he mourned Tri Jet. There is a painting in his house of the black horse, which he had earlier shown me, and the man proudly holding the horse in the painting is, of course, Gus Gray.

The investment—emotional, physical, financial—that some grooms make in a horse is wholehearted and unstinting. It is beyond measuring. Or is it? If the horse feels safe, confident, and loved, if he does not ache despite his workload, if his moods are respected and that special spot behind his ears is scratched daily—all because an attentive groom knows about it and has seen to it—surely the horse feels better, runs faster, gives more, offers that noble effort at the finish line. Maybe it is the difference between first and second, between a Triple Crown and something close to it. The bond between horse and groom, I would argue, can pay dividends.

An owner or trainer can exploit that groom's commitment, take advantage of it, use it, make money off it. And yet the groom who attends the horse, the exercise rider who tunes him up, the hot walker who prevents him from tying up, they share only a little in the glory and hardly at all in the windfall. Is that fair? I asked my dinner mates.

"No, it's not fair," said Gus, still smiling. "I'm glad you said that. Now you gettin' to be a writer."

Only occasionally, said Gus, will an owner look out for a groom. He cited the case of a horse called Kauai King, who won the Kentucky Derby in 1966. That horse's groom, known widely as "Popeye," got a five-thousand-dollar bonus. (A horse called Amberoid, trained by Lucien Laurin and groomed by Eddie Sweat, would beat Kauai King in the Belmont that same year.)

Charlie Davis said that his entire bonus for riding Secretariat at the time of those Triple Crown victories and afterward was one thousand dollars, and it had not come from the trainer or the owner. Jockey Ron Turcotte approached him one day after those races with a wad of cash. "Merry Christmas," he told Charlie, presenting him, and later Eddie Sweat, with a bundle of bills.

⌒

The next evening, Carole and Gary Fletcher put on a splendid barbecue at their small farm outside Ocala and included Charlie Davis and Gus Gray on the guest list. An equine artist came, as did an exercise rider bearing fresh scars on his face from a horse's hoof. Gus, meanwhile, hobbled about the place with a cane. That afternoon, he had been walking a yearling onto a trailer, when the horse nailed him— hoof on knee. Gus was clearly in distress, but the pain made no dent in either his appetite or his broad smile.

Also on the guest list was Danny Jenkins. The word *colorful* does not begin to describe him. He is a lean six-two, a Vietnam vet, winner of the Bronze Star (with a *V* for valor), a recovered alcoholic, and a confident horseman, whose fragrance is often a blend of cologne, cigarettes, and coffee. In Vietnam, he was the point man, the one who called in air strikes and was most vulnerable to enemy fire. Danny has a glint in his eye and does not lack for courage.

~

The next day, I meet Danny Jenkins at the starting gate at Ocala Breeders' Sales-Company, with its full-size track and green metal starting gate. Here, several mornings a week, he certifies horses. Once certified, a horse is eligible to run at any track in North America.

I have come to watch Danny and his colleague, Dave Jacobs, go through their paces. It's a sunny, windswept Saturday, and the horses are slow to arrive, so there is time to muse on the state of racing and the art of the starter.

Danny lays out on the white plastic rail beside the starting gate what he calls "the tools of the trade": buggy whip, chain and shank, standing shank, lead-up, good leather gloves, and a flipping rig (like a slimmer version of a horse collar, and used with horses intent on flipping backward in the starting gate).

The so-called problem horse, Danny says, is often just plain sore and therefore rank. Maybe, I suggest, we should listen when the horse says he is sore.

"Yes," he says, "but there's a lot of greed in this game. And people run 'em, run 'em, run 'em, run 'em, run 'em, run 'em. And never hardly give 'em a break." Danny, who has worked on the backside for thirty-seven years, laments the lack of expertise in today's trainers, some of whom operate without even basic knowledge of horsemanship. In the old days, a trainer had to pass both a written test and a barn test administered by track stewards to ensure that he or she could at least correctly apply bandages and saddle and bridle a horse. Today, anyone can buy a trainer's license.

Horsemanship, says Jenkins, takes time, and no one seems to have time anymore. Danny says horses are often run before they mature, and buyers who spend millions on a young colt or filly put enormous pressure on themselves, and on the horse, to recoup the investment. Danny argues that a "mature" horse is a three-year-old; some experts claim the age is more like four or five years old. But whatever the cause of horses breaking down on the track (hard surfaces, young horses, overwork), this veteran starter is seeing more horses going down.

Still, Danny Jenkins loves the adrenaline of the track and he counts himself blessed to have learned from some gifted old-timers, to have worked the Breeders' Cup and the Kentucky Derby. He loves the crowd and the rush. But he is sometimes appalled by what he sees. "A lot of people wouldn't come to the track if they knew what happens on the backside," he says.

"Like what?" I ask.

He eyes my tape recorder as if it were a venomous snake and makes a show of walking away. He is only half-joking.

He tells me that in the old days of Thoroughbred racing, there was no starting gate, just men on steps holding out long buggy whips in front of a line of horses. When a bell was rung and the whips were dropped, the race began. A kinder starting method than the starting gate, he says, would be something similar to what Standardbred racers do: A truck trailing a wide metal frame slowly drives away and gradually accelerates, then peels off to the side as the metal frame folds like a butterfly's wings. Thoroughbred racing's metal starting gate—fixed in place, its doors all opening simultaneously—offers an explosive and dramatic start to a race all right, but it's hard on horses' bones. Too bad, I guess, about horses' bones.

"I can't change things," says Danny. And he utters that old prayer: "God grant me the strength to accept the things I cannot change, the courage to change the things I can." What he *can* do is teach horses about courtesy and confidence at the starting gate.

This morning at the gate, I look on and I see little victories. Take this one, for example. A female exercise rider approaches the gate on an obviously nervous filly, so nervous that she is literally quaking, her legs shaking as if she has been out all night in an ice storm. I learn the horse's story: Her owner, also a rider, had taken her through the gate weeks before, but the young filly panicked and badly cut herself with her own hoof. Blood sprayed as if from a garden hose. Danny had been direct with the owner: You're out of your league and you're "hindering" the horse. Get a good exercise rider for the next time.

Now the filly is back, and clearly terrified at the prospect. The new rider, Terri M. Bailey, is stroking the horse's neck, smiling and talking to her, giving the gorgeous wide-eyed filly all the reassurance in the world, while Danny, from the ground, likewise pats her belly. "Hold on, sissy," Danny tells her, then calmly leads her through the gate and just lets her stand there and breathe a little. Then he instructs the rider to ease her out and gallop her down the track a ways. The lesson for the filly is that the starting gate might not be a horse-eating monster after all, and they will build on that prospect.

"That's enough for today," Danny yells out to the rider. (Later, as I exit the grounds and pass the stables, I spot Bailey. She is *still* smiling, still praising the young filly, still stroking her as she dismounts.)

Danny Jenkins has a party piece. He takes out his bottom plate of teeth, then the top plate, to show what is left after horses' hooves have had a go at a man's smile. The gums are all pink and bare, like a newborn baby's. Later, Danny sits in his truck to do some paperwork and to seek shelter from the wind.

"What's your horse's name?" he asks me.

"Dali."

Danny fills out a little white card, writes in the date (2/26/05) and the place (O.B.S.), and signs it before handing it to me. Saroma Dark Fox Dali, my stout Canadian horse, is now good to go (blinkers "on") at any racetrack in North America.

Before I leave, and just as Danny Jenkins and Dave Jacobs are about to call it a day, two horses and two riders arrive close to 11:00 A.M. The horses seem calm and the two men usher them into place and close the gates, giving me the task of pressing the starter button—a red button at the end of a long black rubber tube.

I think of another button, a yellow one. Some years ago, I was in Ottawa, boarding the train to Kingston, and met a friend in the station. He was that train's engineer and he wondered if I'd care to ride with him up front all the way home. Every time we hit a railway crossing, I hit that yellow button and held it. Two longs, one short, one long, like shouts of joy. I was ten years old all over again.

Ocala, Florida, and I'm that boy again. From his place on the starting-gate pedestal, Danny sends me a look that says all at once, This is a lark all right, but it is also serious business. He is not smiling. He is Danny Jenkins, starter.

"On three, Larry. . . . One . . . two . . . three."

When I press the button (holding it longer than is necessary), the loud school bell sounds as the gates clang open, and the two horses charge down the track. There is no race, no crowd, nothing but two jockeys chirping loudly and spraying up clods of earth as they playfully sprint their horses down the backstretch. So why is my heart beating? Why do I follow them with my eyes to see which horse pulls ahead? Why can I not stop smiling?

Geraldine Holman, Eddie Sweat's sister and the youngest of the family of nine children, vividly remembers going up on the train from South Carolina to New York one time with two of her sisters to see Eddie, and being joined by Linda, Eddie's wife.

"It was hot," Geraldine told me, "so hot, I passed out at the train station. Eddie thought I was sick, and he was very worried, but it was just the heat. And when he was sure I was fine, he started telling me about Secretariat and how we all had to get to the track right away. He was so excited. 'I gotta go get my baby.' 'Let's go, let's go.' He kept saying before the race, 'Watch how my baby gonna run.' And I said to him, 'Edward, you love that horse more than you love your wife!' Linda was right there. She heard it, and she accepted that. She knew that horse was his life."

During the race, Eddie was almost beside himself. Geraldine could hear him screaming, "Come on, baby! Come on, baby! That's my baby! That's my baby!"

After the race, which Secretariat won with ease, Geraldine watched as her brother hugged Secretariat, kissed him, and posed for the photographers, then told his sisters and wife that he had to go off and attend to the horse. "I gotta rub my baby now," he said before addressing the horse in the same way. "You're my baby," he kept saying into the chestnut's ear as he led him away. "You're my baby."

⌐ 9 ⌐

EULOGY FOR A HORSE

"EVER OWN A GREAT HORSE?"

The man asking the question was Preston Madden, the owner of Hamburg Place farm in Lexington, Kentucky. His question came as a response—impatient, clipped, bordering on testy—to a question of my own, one I thought I knew the answer to but had asked anyway.

"Why," I had asked Madden, "do we bury some horses?" Implicit, I think, in the response of this elder horseman was his certainty that I had never owned a great horse myself, for if I had, I would have known and understood the need to honor that horse. For Madden, my question was a foolish one, impolite at best. But I was curious about the horse cemetery marked on my map of Fayette County and environs, and my hope was that Preston Madden would know something about it. I had picked up the map in the state tourist office on a hot, steamy day in July 2004.

It was a day of stark and swirling opposites, of slicing rain beyond the sweep of my car's frantic wipers, and, coincidentally, sun so bright that I had donned sunglasses. When had I ever worn shades in the rain? The water lay gleaming on the highway, bright as liquid silver, and the suffused light in the sky seemed divinely inspired, as if heralding some important tidings from above. I remember remarking, as I crossed into Kentucky from West Virginia, on the boldness of the Bluegrass State—where sun and rain, fire and water, seem to coexist happily. I remember a slight giddiness at arriving in the state that claims to offer horse heaven, or, at least, heaven for horse lovers. As I drove west on Interstate 64, past limestone cliffs of layered rock—gray over white, black under beige—and got closer to Lexington, I saw what I expected to see: Greek Revival mansions with tall white pillars straight out of *Gone With the Wind,* rolling fields boxed and divided by plank horse fences, elegant horse barns topped by horsey weather vanes, bronzed horse heads on proud stone gates. But no horses. And the thought came, maybe horses here are too expensive to be left out in the rain.

I had already circled on the map of Lexington the places I wanted to visit—the Keeneland Race Course for its track and magnificent library; Kentucky Horse Park, where Man o'War is buried; the Fasig-Tipton sales facilities, where the yearlings would be showcased a few days on; Claiborne Farm in Bourbon County, where Secretariat stood at stud and is buried.

Horse farms were marked on the map of Lexington as red horseshoes, open end up, as always, lest the luck run out. My map was well stamped with red horseshoes, close to a hundred of them, some of the farms' names legendary in the world of Thoroughbred horse racing—like Three Chimneys, where the great Seattle Slew was king of the stud, and Hill 'n' Dale Farm, where he is buried. There, on Versailles Road (Ver-*sails,* as I would hear locals pronounce it) was the storied and oft-troubled Calumet Farm with its elaborate fire engine red iron gates. Claiborne Farm lay to the northeast, just by Paris, Kentucky.

I made one more circle on the map. Just south of Winchester Road, and just east of the New Circle Road, was marked in red the words *Horse Cemetery.* And, over the next several days, I tried hard to find it amid the car washes and strip malls and new houses on Liberty Road in the ever-burgeoning city of Lexington. No one I asked knew of the horse cemetery's existence and they seemed surprised to see it listed on my map.

I put my pursuit aside. Only later, back at home, did it occur to me that perhaps someone at Hamburg Place farm, just south of the cemetery, could tell me something. I called them and got through to Preston Madden.

He let it be known that he was busy and had little time for questions. He told me to be quick. I offered to call back later, when he had more time. Now or maybe never, I took him to mean. Later, I wondered if Madden was not so much lacking in southern hospitality as trying to protect himself. Perhaps he simply had no stomach for discussing on the phone with a stranger the details of presiding over the burial of beloved horses.

It turned out, and this Preston Madden did allow, that the horse cemetery was his and had been part of the family farm for a hundred years. He described it as an acre and a half in size, well concealed, and now closed to the public. The nearby highway was being widened, and one thousand acres of Hamburg Place farm were gradually going the way of many horse farms in Kentucky. Some horse fences, some neatly carved paddocks, some graceful arcing meadows would give way to bulldozers, surveyors' red stakes, new houses with double-car garages. (Another one thousand acres, though, would remain a horse farm.)

"The point is," Madden told me, "some horses *deserve* a burial."

Among the fourteen horses buried in the cemetery are several illustrious runners from the Standardbred and Thoroughbred ranks. I now know this, and in precise detail, in part because Dr. Deirdre Durkis, an anesthesiologist and, in 1998, an archives volunteer at the Kentucky Derby Museum in Louisville, has painstakingly recorded all the horse cemeteries in the area and privately produced a book on the subject. *Where They Sleep: Burial Sites of Thoroughbreds in the Bluegrass Country of Kentucky* describes the cemetery near Hamburg Place farm as "an oasis of tranquility" amid the traffic sounds of Lexington.

I was sorry I had missed it. I thought of Père Lachaise cemetery in that other Paris. The vast and ornate graveyard is, I am guessing, the quietest spot in the city, and apartments overlooking the stone bunkers of the dead have what most Parisians lack—a place to hear themselves think. Buried there, among other artists, are the writers Apollinaire, Balzac, Proust, Molière, and Wilde, the actor Sarah Bernhardt and the singer Edith Piaf, the composer Chopin, the painters David and Ingres, Delacroix, and Géricault.

The one site that gathers more crowds than any other is that of rock star Jim Morrison, late of the Doors. His tomb became so defaced by fans leaving worshipful messages that the tomb is now guarded round the clock, and the stone-slab top has been replaced by a kind of sandbox. On the day I was there several years ago, the sand was home to candles, Métro tickets, single cigarettes, handwritten messages, flowers, cards, a scarf, and a jar of homemade jelly with a green gingham frill on top.

Horse graves, I would learn, draw their own red-eyed pilgrims bearing flowers and gifts for cherished runners. But before there can be a monument, some horse owner must choose a spot, dig the grave, bury the body, compose wording for the marker—the horse's years, sire and dam, championships won, something about the horse's character and place in the human heart.

The cemetery by Hamburg Place farm, according to *Where They Sleep,* contains the remains of some fourteen horses in the Madden family who were buried between 1906 and 1995. Here lies, among others, Bel Sheba, a daughter of War Admiral and dam of Alysheba, the latter the Kentucky Derby and Preakness winner in 1987. Also here are Lady Sterling and Star Shoot, dam and sire, respectively, of Sir Barton, the Canadian-owned, Kentucky-bred Triple Crown winner in 1919 who raced against, and lost (like every other horse but one, named Upset) to, the great Man o'War. Star Shoot, ranked among the greatest sires of the early 1900s, had been blind for several years when he died of pneumonia. T. V. Lark, champion grass winner of 1961, died of a massive hemorrhage after an allergic reaction, possibly to an insect bite.

The listings seem cool and detached, and they only hint at the emotion and grief that must have darkened these burial ceremonies. One marker, for example, remembers Springtime, a Madden family member's "gallant polo pony who died during a match."

I took note of the *who* in that phrase, not the more usual *that.* I have written or coauthored eight books about horses, riders, and trainers, and invariably this question arises during editing: Is it "the horse *who*" or "the horse *that*"? Is a horse a *he/she* or an *it?* I have always been on the *who* and *he/she* side of this debate.

Reading Durkis's book (one of two, by the way, on horse cemeteries in Kentucky; the other is *Etched in Stone: Thoroughbred Memorials,* by Louisville's Lucy Zeh), I was also struck by *how* some of these horses died, details that must have underscored the sense of loss at the time of the horse's death. Sir Martin (1906–1930) was leading and about to win the English Derby "when he fell." The horse, though, must have recovered, for he died "as a pensioner, provided for in John Madden's will." Bel Sheba, meanwhile, was "buried in a small, private ceremony at the Hamburg Place Cemetery, presided over by Mr. Preston Madden."

I tried to imagine that scene in 1995. Did a mournful rain fall? Did Preston Madden weep? Were words spoken? Were certain mementos or favorite foods tossed into the grave before the ground was covered over? Maybe silence is the right thing when a great horse is laid to rest.

Had I been better versed in Thoroughbred racing history, I would have known the name Madden. Only later would I learn that John Madden, Preston's grandfather, rose from modest beginnings to become the top Thoroughbred trainer in the United States for eleven consecutive years in the early part of the twentieth century. To breed a stakes winner is one way of measuring a horseman's success: John Madden bred 182 of them. His first champion was a horse called Hamburg—bought for $1,200 and sold for $40,001 (thus enabling Madden to make the claim that he got "more than $40,000"). At one time, Hamburg Place farm encompassed two thousand acres, all just a gallop away from downtown Lexington. *Six* Kentucky Derby winners were foaled at this farm: Old Rosebud, 1914 winner; Sir Barton, 1919 winner; Paul Jones, 1920 winner; Zev, 1923 winner; Flying Ebony, 1925 winner; Alysheba, 1987 winner.

An article on John Madden in a 1929 edition of the *Thoroughbred Record* described "a real vein of sentiment beneath his burly exterior." The article pointed to "his kindness to employees and attachés, his devotion to the fame and memory of many a great horse or horseman." His celebrated equine graveyard at Hamburg Place was said to contain the graves of "horses he kept enshrined in his 'heart of hearts' forever, it being unendurable to him that they should pass into oblivion when their race was run."

It seems a fair bet that John Madden was unusual in his desire to honor the equine dead (and maybe his grandson shares his grandfather's sentiment). This much is true: The cemetery at Hamburg Place farm is the oldest recognized horse burial ground in the Lexington area, and maybe the prettiest. One photograph I have seen of it shows a serene-looking field behind a low limestone wall and a tall line of trees. The centerpiece grave, behind a wrought-iron fence, is that of the Standardbred mare Nancy Hanks, with a horseshoe-shaped series of stone markers all around it, as if the horses buried below are all paying homage to a great mare. (The cemetery at Hamburg Place farm has since been relocated to a new spot on the farm. Preston Madden calls the cemetery "a sacred trust" and he says he intends to replicate the original quite precisely.)

Lucy Zeh's book describes grave markers for close to five hundred horses in the bluegrass region of central Kentucky. The monuments range from simple headstones to the massive bronze statue of Man o'War, which stands almost 25 percent larger than did the actual horse. In their varying sizes and shapes—from flat stone markers set into the ground to towering obelisks, from modern granite memorials with bas-relief images carved on the granite's face to the older, simpler style with gently arcing tops—the stones mimic what you would find in human cemeteries.

The odd marker makes it abundantly clear that a horse, not a human, lies below. The eccentric champion Nashua (1952–1982) was a son of Nasrullah (Secretariat's grandsire), and was once described as "a playboy who found distraction in everything." He would rear in the walking ring and toss his handler about like a tail on the end of a kite; he would eye fans in the stands, shy from cameras, was "fractious at the post." Still, he was Horse of the Year in 1955 and the first horse to fetch a selling price of more than a million dollars. Nashua's memorial is a bronze statue showing the horse being led by his groom of twenty-five years, a black man named Clem Brooks. Much in the manner of Will Harbut with Man o'War, Brooks would entertain visitors to Spendthrift Farm with stories about the proud and cantankerous Nashua.

Sometimes an owner has had etched into the stone marker a phrase or sentence to capture that horse's spirit. The grave of Forego (1970–1997) features a flat stone marker that simply lists his name and dates and this accolade: "A towering champion, he had the speed to win at seven furlongs, the staying power to win at two miles, the strength to carry greater weight than all rivals and triumph with brilliance." The gravestone of Count Fleet (1940–1973) is even wordier, but one phrase leaps out: "Never out of the money."

The names of some runners in these graves would be familiar even to the casual racing fan. To the ardent follower, the names have the ring of psalm: Alydar, Bold Ruler, Citation, Hail to Reason, Hoist the Flag, Mr. Prospector, Nasrullah, Nijinsky II, Raise a Native, War Admiral, and, of course, Secretariat.

Since 1973, when Secretariat made his spectacular runs, some one million Thoroughbreds alone have entered the stud books. That represents just one breed, and only its registered horses at that. The American Horse Council puts the number of horses in the United States at just under seven million. Since Secretariat, millions of horses in North America have come and gone, and they did not all die in the loving embrace of their handlers. A small scandal erupted a few years ago when it was learned that Ferdinand—the 1986 Kentucky Derby winner and Horse of the Year in 1987—almost certainly ended his days in a Japanese abattoir. He had been a disappointment at stud and passed from one owner to another until that last ignominious day. Many were aghast to read that story, but they should not have been.

Remember the advice that Black Beauty's mother gave him when he was a colt? "I hope you will fall into good hands," the mare tells him; "but a horse never knows who may buy him, or who may drive him; it is all a chance . . ." Anna Sewell wrote these words in 1877.

⁓

The young girls who flock to some summer equestrian camps might wonder why the horses change from year to year. The answer is plain: It is simpler, and cheaper, to load the ponies and horses onto slaughterhouse trucks at summer's end than to keep them in hay and lodging all winter long. Next spring, the camp will buy a new bunch, who will go the way of the old bunch. Not every camp does this, but some do. Grim economies often govern the births, and deaths, of horses.

I once asked a man who runs a small riding academy near my home in southeastern Ontario about the fates of aging horses who have been used to give lessons at the academy. He is a kind man, an astute horseman, but he is horse-poor and cannot afford sentimentality—or vets to euthanize horses. The special horses, he told me, the ones who have rendered noble service to the farm, are shot in the head. Death is quick and painless and the horse is spared the ignominy and hardship of an awful trip on the dreaded truck. I have always admired this man for his good cheer and I thought more, not less of him, when he told me that he undertakes this terrible duty himself.

⁓

Recently, I spoke at length with a friend whose horse had just died. I knew the horse; he and my horse were stablemates and paddock mates for years, so I keenly felt her loss. There I was, transfixed by my friend's grief as she poured out the details of her horse's tragic death—caused by a hunter's stray bullet and an ensuing infection in the bone. I was, I hope, sympathetic and attentive, and I commiserated with her. I gave her my best advice: write a eulogy for your horse (which she did). The writing, I told her, will do you good and will keep alive his memory, his kindness, his quirks, and his glee.

But another part of me, the writer part, recognized the value of the moment, its essential truth and power. And even as I listened on the phone to my friend's grief, I was thinking how her testimony might warrant a place in these pages and shed light on the connection between Eddie Sweat and Secretariat.

You see, there occurred this ceremony, if we can call it that, in the barn before my friend's horse boarded the van that would take him to the equine hospital in Guelph, Ontario. A certain mare in the barn, who any other time would have nipped this timid old gelding, this time greeted the gray warmly. She bussed him on the cheek, took in the smell of him, got as close to a hug as a horse can get. One pony licked the gray as he passed. Another horse grabbed hold of his halter and would not let go. And though all the horses in the barn had been fed and had no cause to nicker, they were *all* nickering. My friend said she had never heard the barn so loud, and to her it was clear: The horses were all saying good-bye. They knew the big gray was not coming back.

Is this horse-centred mysticism? Horse owners do and say wacky things, and I am an old reporter hard-wired against such silliness. At the same time, I wonder, Is there a whole world of animal-to-animal communication we know nothing about? Do some of us wish we were Dr. Doolittle, that fabled man who could talk to the animals? This I do know: A study done several years ago at the University of Pennsylvania found that 98 percent of pet owners talk to their animals, as if to a sympathetic friend. But I wonder how many *listen* to their animals, in the way, say, that Eddie Sweat listened to Secretariat—listened with his ears, his heart, listened in his bones.

⌒

I have often pondered what will become of my own horse should I outlive him. (He is a vigorous twelve, and I am a healthy fifty-seven as I write this, so maybe we will both peter out at about the same time.) I could not bear to see him loaded on a meat truck, and I am not the rifle sort. In answer to Preston Madden, I would say that I *have* owned a great horse. My horse deserves, and will get, an honorable and painless farewell.

I cannot imagine the scene, but I suppose I must. The strange thing is that I have already thought through the burial of my dog—the ash box I will bury her in, even the spot where I will bury her—by the cabin, in the high grass in which she loves to roll on her back. It is partly the size of horses that confounds our plans for burial, because the logistics of burying a horse go far beyond a weeping human with a shovel in hand. A horse's grave requires a backhoe to make the hole, a winch to place the horse in his grave, or a meat truck to haul the carcass away if the soil is too thin. You see why I draw the curtain on such images.

Perhaps I will, should I outlive him, bury Saroma Dark Fox Dali in a small private ceremony, maybe in the north field under the white pines I planted myself ten years ago. As I age, as my time with my first and only horse enters its eighth year, as I look back on all that we have been through and all that I have read and written about horses, what grows ever more real to me are the powerful feelings that can arise between human and horse.

⌒

Only a few days into my stay in Lexington, I was having supper in a Ruby Tuesday, across the road from the accommodation I had settled into. The Springs Inn is a sprawling place that also features a quiet and separate back section well away from the road. Not the quiet of Père Lachaise cemetery, but close enough.

I had in front of me at the restaurant a great sheaf of articles photocopied in the library of the Keeneland Race Course. I was wading through the pile, pen in hand, sifting for gold nuggets. My waitress, meanwhile, had spotted the name Secretariat on one of the headlines and said she happened to have served a couple the day before who had driven all the way from Texas just to see Secretariat's grave at Claiborne.

"They had always been fans," my wide-eyed server told me, certain I would want to know. My waitress was six years old when Secretariat ran, but she knew the name nonetheless; just about everyone in Lexington does. The Texans had apparently spent a lot of money on a limited-edition print of Secretariat crossing the finish line. I know the one: All four feet are off the ground and the horse looks to be flying. The couple's pure delight in their purchase, a delight they had cheerily shared with their waitress, had remained with the young woman, and she was passing it on to me.

A few days later, I was myself at Secretariat's grave site. Claiborne Farm is technically closed to the public, but if you call ahead and arrange a time, one of the stud-farm managers will show you the horse's old stall (with his name in brass alongside those of Easy Goer, Unbridled, and Bold Ruler), the ample paddock he used to gambol in, and the spot where he is buried.

Some who bury their horses obey a time-honored ritual that sees head, heart, and hooves (and, in the case of mares, the ovaries) placed in the grave. On learning this, I chose not to dwell on the mechanics of how these body parts are separated from the whole (the awful business, someone later told me, is accomplished through instructions passed on to the slaughterhouse). In any case, what remains of the horse's body is typically sent off to the rendering plant. Even in death, horses serve.

⌒

On the morning Secretariat died at Claiborne Farm, groom Bobby Anderson clipped a shank on him and led him into a two-ton van. "Big Red," Anderson whispered to him in the van, trying to soothe him. "Big Red." The horse was then given a lethal injection of barbiturate. Anderson called it the saddest day of his life.

It was thought that Secretariat would continue to cover mares well into the 1990s, but laminitis hastened his death at 11:45 A.M. on October 4, 1989. Laminitis is a horseman's nightmare. Still something of a mystery but often blamed on excess grain or lush grass in the horse's diet, obesity, hormonal imbalance, or toxemia, it comes on like a wasting disease. The hoof can literally disintegrate in a matter of days, the pain is agonizing, and the horse can no longer bear his own weight.

Laminitis is not always a death sentence for a horse. But Secretariat had the disease in all four feet, and it must have been heartwrenching to watch his precipitous decline. He was nineteen years old. Many remember the day Secretariat died, how flags in Lexington flew at half-mast, and the genuine grief in Kentucky and around the world that marked his passing.

⌒

Peel back any story, and you find layers. Some stories peel like an onion, and you almost wish you had not gone that extra layer.

I asked Penny Chenery if she was there when they buried Secretariat at Claiborne, and she told this story: "When Secretariat died, I was living in New York. I was unprepared. Seth Hancock had called me on Monday afternoon to say that Secretariat was in bad shape. On Tuesday morning, a reporter called me to ask how I felt about Secretariat's death. I said, 'It can't be. Seth would have called.' But poor Seth, he was overwhelmed. What a blow to Claiborne. Later, I heard how they had made Secretariat walk into the van where they euthanized him. He was in so much pain."

"What should they have done?" I asked Chenery. "What would have been better?"

"They should have put him down at his stall," she replied, "then used a winch to haul the carcass into the van."

Gus Koch, Claiborne farm manager, was shocked that Penny Chenery had such an image in her head all these years. "I was there," he told me. "Secretariat's hooves were not 'practically falling off,' as some stories suggest. It did not cause Secretariat discomfort to walk into the van, which we brought right to his stall. He'd suffered a relapse and we did the right thing by the horse. It was the most dignified thing to do. He was always handled with the utmost respect."

If Secretariat's last day at Claiborne bothered Penny Chenery, so did his first day there in 1973. "Their means," she said, "of keeping a horse off the track from being too active in his paddock is to pare his feet to where it hurts to walk. Someone took a picture of me that day at Claiborne when we gave him over. I'm walking up a hill; my back is to the camera. I couldn't bear to watch him being led to his paddock. They could have tranquilized the horse, introduced him slowly to the paddock."

Gus Koch, though, says Secretariat simply had his shoes removed, and his hooves were rounded up with a rasp. To a horse who had worn shoes all his life, he says, it would have been a new sensation—like walking barefoot.

Penny Chenery had asked Eddie Sweat if he would accompany

Secretariat on the plane that day. She was in the hold of the plane; she watched as Ray Woolfe took that unforgettable black-and-white photograph of Eddie and Big Red nose-to-nose.

"Eddie," she said, "had a temperature. He was sick with a cold. He made the trip because I asked him to. It was a great gift." Both Riva Ridge and Secretariat were nervous on that flight, and Eddie never once left them, moving from one to the other to comfort them.

Later, when Ray Woolfe's book was published, someone saw that other photograph—the one of Eddie shot from behind, weeping—and sent Chenery a poem called "Alone on the Wall." Penny Chenery had told me about the poem and offered to send me a copy when I expressed interest in seeing it. A search through her papers proved fruitless at first. Moving from Kentucky to Colorado, she wrote in a note, "messed up my poor filing system." But eventually, the poem did turn up.

The thirty-two lines of rhyming couplets, by Joyce Embrey Patci, pay homage to Eddie Sweat, his artistry as a groom, and his grief that day. Woolfe's photo speaks of a love story between a man and a horse, and Patci had clearly been moved by the image. Moved enough to compose the poem and send it to Penny Chenery in 2002. That poem, Ed Bogucki's bronze, this book: All owe something to that photograph.

Secretariat was like no other horse and he was accorded a rare honor: He was buried entire in a six-foot-by-seven-foot oak casket three feet high and his body was wrapped in a bolt of felt—the color of Claiborne's yellow racing silks. The burial was a private ceremony, with about twenty people present—farm president Seth Hancock, his sister, and certain farm employees. One who was there likened it to "a death in the family."

Gus Koch was then the stud manager at the farm, and he stayed that night until eight o'clock, handling calls from radio stations all over the United States, Canada, and Europe. "By nightfall," he said, "the whole area around the grave, inside the hedge, was covered in flowers. It was an amazing sight." I could imagine the scene, an area maybe fifty feet by fifty feet thick with funereal flowers. When Secretariat was alive, some ten thousand visitors a year went to see him in his paddock. A steady stream continues today to visit his grave site. The flowers, likewise, have not stopped coming, but the bouquets are especially frequent on anniversary days: the day he was born, the days of each Triple Crown race, and the day he died.

Eddie Sweat, meanwhile, was shattered by the death of Secretariat. "He was so out of it," his sister Geraldine Holman remembers. "He said it was like he had lost his best friend. 'I can't believe my baby's gone,' he told me."

She once reproached her brother for the way he treated Secretariat. "Eddie, he's not human," Geraldine told him. "Yes he is!" Eddie insisted. Eddie was convinced that the horse knew what his groom was telling him, and Eddie always spoke to the horse as if he did fully understand.

When Secretariat died, Eddie cried a long time. He wouldn't eat and went into an extended period of mourning. "He loved that horse so much," Geraldine told me. "Secretariat was his heart. I never saw a grown person cry over an animal like that."

~

Only on autopsy was an astonishing fact revealed: Secretariat's "great heart" was not just a turn of phrase to explain his many dramatic come-from-behind wins on the racetrack, but an anatomical fact. The horse's heart was twice the normal size and a third larger than any horse's heart the veterinary surgeon had ever seen.

Dr. Tom Swerczek, research and diagnostic pathologist at the Gluck Equine Research Center at the University of Kentucky in Lexington, did the autopsy on Secretariat. "The heart was perfect," he said at the time; "there were no defects. It was simply the largest heart I've ever seen. We didn't weigh it but we visually estimated it at between twenty-one and twenty-two pounds."

In 1993, Dr. Swerczek did an autopsy on Secretariat's old rival Sham from the 1973 Triple Crown races. Sham had died on April 23 of that year in his stall, the victim of an apparent heart attack. This time, Dr. Swerczek did weigh the heart. At eighteen pounds, it was the second-largest equine heart he had ever seen. Said the pathologist, "I thought it was ironic that Sham was still finishing second to Secretariat." Poor Sham was second to Secretariat in the Derby, second to Secretariat in the Preakness, and second to Secretariat in one pathologist's heart-size stakes.

When Secretariat died, the *New York Times* ran his obituary, with cameo photo, on the front page. The writer observed that the horse had become "a symbol of brilliance and beauty beyond his breed." But if the newspaper of record noted his passing, so, too, did the popular press. In its obituary, *People* magazine answered the complaint that Secretariat's offspring were merely good, not great. Such critics, the magazine declared, "asked the impossible, for that was a task for the gods."

After Secretariat's death, Penny Chenery was inundated with letters expressing condolence. "There were people who wrote to me," she later said, "as if I had lost a son. True bereavement letters, from close friends as well as from people I'd never met. I think people understood how important this horse was to me." When she visited the grave site not long after Secretariat was buried, there were a dozen visitors there. "It was as if they were viewing a body lying in state. Nobody caught my eye, or poked each other and said, 'There's the owner.' It was as if they were on a pilgrimage."

Secretariat's marker is a plain stone slab, the gray fading to white under the hot Kentucky sun, with the name Secretariat in bold type above and his years below: 1970–1989. The ground has settled a little around his grave, as if he were down there playfully pulling the earth toward him. On the day I was there, a small bouquet of white and blue silk flowers lay just to the right of the stone.

"Did someone at the farm put those flowers there?" I asked Joe Peel, the Claiborne employee who had been the guide on my personal tour.

"No," he replied. "A couple were here just the other day. It was an extraordinary thing. They had come a long way and the woman just broke down at the grave. She lay over that stone and wept, just shaking and trembling. You would think her own son was buried in the ground below." Claiborne staff are used to such outpouring of emotion, and everyone who has ever worked at this sprawling farm, with its ponds and white swans, its century oaks and gracious stone entryway, has stories to tell of men and women unraveling at Secretariat's grave site. But this episode had clearly left its mark on my guide.

"Was the couple from Texas?" I asked him.

"Yes," he replied. "I believe they were."

⌒

Big Red, they called Secretariat, but he was not the first big chestnut to bear that appellation. Another horse had come many decades before him, and some still call him the greatest racehorse who ever lived, greater even than Secretariat. Horse-racing sages endlessly debate the point, in the way that boxing aficionados joust over who was the greatest boxer of all time—Muhammad Ali of the modern era, or his counterpart from the 1930s and 1940s, Joe Louis.

Those on the Man o'War side argue that the horse wore heavy iron shoes (lighter aluminum shoes came later), was handicapped by excessive weights, and ran on slower tracks. The Secretariat camp insist that their horse faced much tougher competition, recorded better times, and left a bolder legacy.

Though the horses differed in temperament (Man o'War was tempestuous before races, while Secretariat was agreeable), there do exist some striking similarities between them. Both bore the nickname Big Red, both were tall and massive chestnuts with similar markings, a huge stride, and a voracious appetite, both were claimed to be the Horse of the Century, both had won races by staggering margins (Man o'War by one hundred lengths, Secretariat by thirty-one), both had a deep and abiding affection for their black grooms, both ended their careers by running their twenty-first, and last, races in Canada, both would ham it up and pose for photographers, and both horses were adored and accorded heroic status. It has been variously estimated that one to one and a half million people went to visit Man o'War during the twenty-seven years he lived at Faraway Farm outside Lexington. Fifty thousand people a year went to see him and to be entertained by the horse's groom, Will Harbut, who became a celebrity, as would—albeit in a quieter way—Eddie Sweat.

Though his bones were later disinterred and reburied under a massive statue at Kentucky Horse Park, Man o'War was first laid to rest at Faraway Farm, in what was surely the most remarkable funeral ever accorded a horse.

A crowd (one estimate put it at two thousand people) gathered at the farm on that cold gray day of November 4, 1947. The great horse had lain in state for several days in a six-foot-by-ten-foot oak casket lined with the farm's black-and-yellow racing colors. Man o'War died with an enormous erection, and the cloth discreetly covered that fact. The big stallion was thirty years old when he died. A picture of him taken that year ran with one of the obituaries, and what struck me was how fit he looked. Man o'War was frolicking in his paddock like a colt, and his coat had a fine sheen.

Because the horse had to lie in state inside the farm's stallion barn for several days, preservation became necessary, so farm staff did what few people have ever done: They embalmed the horse. The norm for humans is two pints of embalming fluid; Man o'War required twenty-three.

Past Man o'War's open coffin, hundreds of people slowly filed. One newspaper report noted that "some reached down quietly to touch him; others leaned far down to pat his neck or stroke his flank. Others just looked, or hoisted children high in the air to see the magnificent Thoroughbred in repose."

The death of Man o'War was front-page news around the world. In Kentucky, merchants wreathed their storefronts in black and teachers had their students memorize the tribute to war horses in the Book of Job: "the glory of his nostrils is terror. He breaketh up the earth with his hoof, he pranceth boldly . . .")

The funeral was broadcast live on radio nationwide, with the prominent Kentucky horseman Ira Drymon serving as master of ceremonies for the thirty-minute service. "Truly," he told his rapt and silent listeners, "Man o'War was a memorable horse. Almost from the beginning he touched the imagination of men and, though they saw different things in him, one thing they will all remember is that he brought an exaltation into their hearts."

Man o'War had done for Americans of the 1920s, who were desperate for a hero after World War I, what Secretariat later did for Americans in the 1970s, when they needed respite from Watergate,

Nixon, and Vietnam. Two generations fifty years apart pined for something to believe in. And those in both eras had chosen to believe in a brilliant copper horse called Big Red.

Cameron Lawrence, writing a few years ago in *The Backstretch* magazine, had a nice line to describe Man o'War: "the colt the color of sunlit rum." Joe Palmer, a great turf writer of the day, said of Man o'War that "he was near to a living flame as horses ever get and horses get closer to this than anything else." The starter of the Travers Stakes called the horse "so beautiful it almost made you cry, and so full of fire that you thanked your God you could come close to him."

When Man o'War was retired to stud in 1920, the Lexington Chamber of Commerce announced a plan for local schoolchildren to strew flowers in his path from the railway siding through town and along the route to the farm. Man o'War's owner, Samuel D. Riddle, nixed the plan with a terse telegram: "He's only a horse."

The horse, who retired as a three-year-old after setting five world records, would know only one groom, Will Harbut, for the last fifteen years of his life. Theirs was an extraordinary relationship. Man o'War died just a month after Harbut died, and many at the time believed that grief had hastened the old horse's death. Harbut, almost surely, would have seen it as a blessing not to have witnessed the passing of his great friend. Harbut's obituary in *The Blood-Horse* magazine listed among his survivors a wife, six sons, three daughters—and Man o'War.

Those who met Will Harbut remarked on his smile, his rich baritone voice, his rumpled felt hat. In his character, in his joy, in his feeling for his charge, Will Harbut sounded for all the world like Edward "Shorty" Sweat. Will's son Tom, who still lives in his father's house outside Lexington, says that his father treated everyone—from the rich and the royal to the so-called common man—with the same respect and dignity. And everyone I talked to said the same thing of Eddie.

It so happened that when I was in Lexington, the History Center was winding up an exhibition of Man o'War memorabilia. A kind and trusting curator let me in just as the place was closing for the day, and he left me alone in that expansive room, urging me to take my time. "Just close the door behind you when you leave," he said; then he left the building.

I did take my time. I learned that Will Harbut was a native Kentuckian, born on Parker Mills Road, six miles from Lexington. I pored over the clippings, the framed art, the glass case full of Man o'War and Will Harbut memorabilia—a ceramic ashtray, a set of playing cards in a leather case, a Lucite paperweight, a tape measure, a commemorative stamp. . . . But I spent most of my time staring at the cover photograph of the September 13, 1941, issue of *The Saturday Evening Post.* There they were, Harbut on the left, Man o'War on the right, old friends embracing.

Then twenty-four years of age, the horse has buried his head in Harbut's chest and he has a soft look in his eye—like a baby curled up with his daddy. Harbut, then fifty-six, wears the tattered hat that was his trademark, and his smile conveys gladness and pride. (He once said that even were he offered the job of president of the United States, he would stick with grooming Man o'War—"the mostest horse," as he called him.) There is between horse and groom all this: trust, affection, loyalty, comfort, understanding, and a level of knowledge and intimacy that many long-married couples would envy. Will Harbut was Man o'War's valet, nurse, physical therapist, cook, caretaker, provider, lawyer, chauffeur, spokesman, and, most important, his friend.

The world of racing has many such stories that express a heartfelt connection between one horse and the human closest to him—usually the groom. Dan Williams, groom to the tragic filly Ruffian, was undone by the horse's death, Raymond Woolfe told me. "Dan loved Ruffian," he said, "in the way that Eddie Sweat loved Secretariat."

The Ruffian story is one of the saddest in all of racing, a drawn curtain around an era in racing that featured the big three of Secretariat, Seattle Slew, and Affirmed. This stunning dark bay filly— Walter Farley once remarked that, her sex and color aside, hers was the image he had in his head when he wrote *The Black Stallion* series—broke her right front leg running in 1975 in a match race at Belmont, where she is buried. Ruffian was operated on, but the poor frantic horse compounded her injuries by her thrashing as she awoke from the anesthesia. Finally, her owner—shattered by the experience—asked the vets to end the filly's suffering. Like some great Egyptian queen, her body was wrapped in white cloth and laid in a twelve-foot-square grave, her head pointing toward the finish line.

Going into that race, Ruffian was undefeated, and in nine of her ten races, she broke or equaled track records. Her *average* margin of victory in those starts was a numbing eight lengths. The *Daily Racing Form* called her "invincible," *The Blood-Horse* called her a "wonder," and the New York vet who examined her before the match race called her the most perfectly conformed horse he had ever seen. Her opponent in the match race was Foolish Pleasure, a grandson of Bold Ruler, Secretariat's sire.

On a Monday evening, when the races of the day were finished at Belmont, three dozen or so members of what was called Ruffian's "human family"—stable help, grooms, exercise riders, the jockey, the owners—looked on as a hydraulic lift gently lowered the filly into the ground. Hundreds of backstretch workers who had come to pay their own respects looked on from a discreet distance. The trainer, Frank Whiteley, fussed with two blankets laid on her body and smoothed them out. Someone tossed flowers into the grave, the ground was covered over, and a huge horseshoe wreath was laid over the top.

⌒

Enter, stage left, yet another tall chestnut horse with star quality. He is Big Ben, the only great horse I ever got close to. And the human desire to get close to greatness, I would argue, may lie at the heart of the enduring magnetism of some horses, such as Secretariat, Man o'War, and Ruffian.

Ben was 17.3 hands high, eight feet tall at the ears—so he was always looking down on humans from an imperious height. In the markings on his head, in his coloring, the expression in his eye, he looked a lot like Secretariat.

Big Ben's rider was the gifted Canadian show jumper Ian Millar. And no one would question Ian's feelings for that horse or Ian's sense of good fortune that this giant Belgian Warmblood—arguably the greatest show-jumping horse who ever lived—had come to Millar Brooke Farm, located near Perth, in southeastern Ontario. But it was Big Ben's tiny groom, Sandi Patterson, who loved, and knew, the horse best.

She slept, as a rule, in an apartment over Ben's stall, the better to hear his rustling in the dark and the better to respond when his movements broke with routine. On the road, at competitions all over Europe and North America, Sandi sometimes slept on a cot in front of his stall as a security precaution (against someone inadvertently or strategically feeding the horse something that would show up on drug testing and cause his elimination). Sandi's physical tasks around the horse were many, her hours killing, her devotion during the seven years she was charged with his care unstinting. But her most important task, and she had it round the clock, was watchfulness on a scale hard to imagine.

I do not just mean vigilance about heat in the horse's legs or a slight loss in appetite, or a change in mood or sleep patterns. All that is a given. What Sandi Patterson had to watch out for were signs, even subtle ones, of colic. The bowels of a horse are like a ninety-foot jumble of garden hose, and whatever the horse consumes must make it through that maze. A blockage, a twist in the bowel, can cause the same sort of stabbing, leveling pain that women feel at childbirth (or so some vets surmise). Colic is the number-one killer of horses, and in 1990, Sandi Patterson had to witness Big Ben's first attack. One of the terrible aspects of colic is that one attack seems to invite more, as if nature has detected a flaw or weakness and feels compelled, sooner or later, to weed it out.

Ten months later, there came a second attack, but Ben rebounded mightily from both surgeries. He was named Canadian show-jumping champion after the first one, and after the second, he won the most lucrative and hotly contested show-jumping prize in the world—the du Maurier International Grand Prix, at Calgary's Spruce Meadows. (The event is now called the CNN International, with one million dollars in prize money offered.)

In 1994, after ten years of competition, after consecutive and unprecedented World Cup titles in the late 1980s, after forty Grand Prix victories and $1.5 million in earnings, after representing Canada at three Olympic Games, it seemed that Big Ben had lost the desire to compete. For the first time in his life, the paddock beckoned to him more than the Millar Brooke horse van. Time was he would kick his stall boards if the van left without him. For five years, the old gelding enjoyed his retirement, his grass, snoozing in the sun.

Finally, a third bout of colic killed Ben the morning of Saturday,

December 11, 1999. He was twenty-three years old. A photograph in the *Ottawa Citizen* shows Sandi Patterson, Ian Millar, and his wife, Lynn Millar, at the grave site—a little hill overlooking the paddocks. The three are huddled together, huddled against cold and grief and exhaustion, and their eyes are red from crying.

Ian had chosen a spot north of the house. Just as he could look out all those years and see Ben grazing in his paddock, now he would see his grave in the distance. As they dug with the backhoe that day, they were surprised to encounter the stone foundation of the original farmhouse, which seemed to them a fitting coincidence. One old foundation would join another. They laid over the grave a massive and rugged boulder the color of dark copper—Ben's color in the rain. The stone had been picked beforehand in anticipation of this day.

Twenty-three years of age is a full lifespan for a competition horse. But knowing that a great horse's death is imminent and accepting it are two different things. "You know it's coming," Ian said at the time, "but the impact of it is fairly indescribable."

The night before he died, Ben had engaged in a boisterous game of tag around the jumps with Ian in the indoor ring. The yet-frisky old horse would rise up on his hind legs during these games, which were not for the faint of heart. Finally, play over, Ben grabbed Ian by the collar and gave him a friendly shake.

Sandi, for her part, had been an integral part of a championship team for many years. But the intensity of the experience, the virtual homelessness, all that travel had put Sandi's private life on hold. I wondered, Did she ever have second thoughts about the sacrifices made for a horse?

When I asked her just that in the summer of 2005, just days after a life-size bronze of Ian and Ben was unveiled in a park in Perth, Sandi was unequivocal: "I would not give away one second of what I did with him. As far as I was concerned—because I loved him so much—I was the luckiest person in the world. I was close to greatness, and it's still paying me back."

"How so?" I asked her.

"I wanted to live up to his expectations," Sandi replied. "My time with Ben made me a better person. Before I would do something, make some big decision, I would ask myself, Would Ben like this? Or would he be horrified?" Her answer gave me a frisson, for Tom Wade had told me virtually the same thing about Seattle Slew.

Sandi has been back to Ben's grave site only once; the spot still stirs up too much emotion. Six years after his death, she still grieves for him. Sandi remembers too well a dusk tribute at the site a month after Ben was buried. Farm staff had formed a huge horseshoe-shaped pyre of wood, which was lighted at dusk as a trio of female folk-singers from Perth sang "Wind Beneath My Wings"—a Bette Midler song that Ian had adopted years before as one that best captured their relationship. Hundreds looked on, each one in tears. Photos just inside the Millar Brooke farmhouse capture the moment's dramatic colors—the yellow of the fire, the dramatic dark blue of the sky. When I first saw the photos, I thought they were aerial shots of a volcano erupting, not a mournful good-bye to a beloved horse.

KNOWING HORSES

"Who really *knows* horses? The people who work with them—workers. In 1875, the year of the first Derby, those workers were former slaves, the men who had been entrusted with the horses' care back on the plantation, who had lived with the animals, in some cases slept under one roof with them, as Secretariat's black groom, Eddie Sweat, slept with his horse the night before the Preakness in 1973. Today, in the United States, it is getting harder to find people of any color who know horses in this way."

—John Jeremiah Sullivan,
"Horseman, Pass By" in *Harper's* magazine, October 2002

⟨ EPILOGUE ⟩

IN PRAISE OF A BOND

A GROOM'S-EYE VIEW of a champion horse; the Thoroughbred race-track as seen from the lowest rung on the ladder—that's a short, fair description of the book in hand (and, as far as I know, no one has written such a book), but it was not the book I set out to write. In the beginning, my focus was on Secretariat. But as I researched and wrote over the years, as I traveled—to Kentucky and Virginia, to South Carolina and Florida—I became as enamored of the horse's groom as I did of the horse himself.

Though I had written several horse-related books, I came to the world of Thoroughbred racing with much to learn. Mine was quite literally a journey of discovery. As I immersed myself in track lore, as my education on the blood horse continued, my focus began to shift toward the people of shed row. This was Eddie Sweat's domain, his home away from home. I began to see Secretariat through the eyes of his groom, and Eddie Sweat as perhaps the horse might have seen him.

I remember sitting in a strip-mall restaurant in Ocala, Florida, with Charlie Davis, Secretariat's exercise rider and one of Eddie Sweat's closest friends. He was getting teary-eyed as he talked about his old pal and their times on the road with Secretariat. Charlie's hot meal got cold as he described Eddie's love for that horse. Eddie, he said, was like a father to that red horse and that horse loved that man as a child loves his father.

Charlie also said—and this would remain with me—that Eddie set an example for everyone on shed row to follow. Charlie had noticed that Eddie would wash the feed buckets as if he were washing dishes for his own family, and the care and diligence he brought to all his tasks as groom got Charlie to thinking. Maybe I can do better as an exercise rider, I understood Charlie to say. Eddie had that effect on a lot of people, and that list would come to include me.

He lived his life with horses as if guided by a simple but profound mantra: Love your horse, and your horse will love you. I have thought of him countless times as I brushed my own horse. What would Eddie have done? is a question I often ask myself in response to my horse. One day while I was grooming him after a ride, Dal displayed petulance—as I lifted one foot to clean it, he shot the hoof back and forth a few times—when a second bran muffin was not forthcoming. On other days, I might have tapped him on the chest or spoken sharply to him; this time, I just gave him a look of disappointment and told him there was no need for that. His grumpiness was short-lived: I would head him off at the pass with praise whenever he refrained, and he soon stopped doing it altogether.

Simply trying to emulate one of the finest grooms who ever lived has meant a small change in my relationship with my horse. I have had Eddie and Secretariat in my head for years, and the effect has been to raise the bar in my own stable. I am a more demanding horseman but a more considerate one, too, and I dare presume, as Eddie did with Secretariat, that Saroma Dark Fox Dali understands every word I say.

When Ted McClain and Charlie Davis, when Ray Woolfe and Bill Nack spoke of the Sweat-Secretariat partnership, they sometimes found it hard to describe without emotion. And this is thirty-three years after the fact. A human and a horse had forged a rare bond, and its memory for these men is still keen and heartfelt.

A small black-and-white photograph in Woolfe's book shows Eddie leading Secretariat past the crowd and out onto the track for that last race at Woodbine on October 28, 1973. Eddie wears his porkpie hat and wild checkered pants, Secretariat a white cooler. And as they are walking, Eddie has turned to the horse and looks to be saying something, and the horse has turned his head to Eddie. They appear to be chatting. For man and horse, the onlookers arrayed on either side of them—many of them clapping and cheering—do not exist. The exquisite horse, his devoted groom, both caught in casual conversation.

When Eddie Sweat died, his family hoped and expected that someone from the track—an owner, say, or a trainer who had employed him, a jockey or two, some *white* folks of stature—would come to Rock Hill Church, near Vance, South Carolina, and speak to the black congregation on his behalf. No one did. The racetrack seemed not to have noticed his passing.

This book is not a eulogy to Eddie Sweat. I hope what I have written will be seen as a paean to the horse–human bond. Yet maybe in a small way, it *is* a eulogy. This book honors a man who honored a horse. A great man, a great horse.

~ ACKNOWLEDGMENTS ~

Kevin Hanson in Toronto had a notion many years ago that the story of Secretariat should be revisited, and that I was the one to do the revisiting. While this book bears little resemblance to the book we talked about then, the project started with our chat over coffee, and I am grateful for his faith and persistence.

Several people read various versions of the manuscript over the years, and I thank them for their diligence: my wife and perennial first editor, Ulrike Bender; my track-hound friend, David Carpenter; my eventing-coach cousin, Kathi Bayly; two trainers and veterans of the Thoroughbred racetrack—Kathie Roller-Stell and Sherrie-Lee Hawley.

The book was also blessed to have two very fine editors—Ellis Trevor at Thomas Dunne Books in New York, and Jim Gifford at HarperCollins in Toronto. Each brought to the task his high standards, his creativity, and his enthusiasm. I owe a great deal of thanks to everyone at Thomas Dunne Books, including designer Rob Grom, production editor Frances Sayers, publicist Joan Higgins, and especially copy editor Carol Edwards.

Librarians helped this book immensely, especially Phyllis Rogers at Keeneland and Jenifer Stermer at Kentucky Horse Park. It is astonishing what archival material resides in these libraries, and I hope all the clippers and keepers there go on clipping and keeping. Many newspapers and magazines helped me understand the lives of grooms and great racehorses, including the *Daily Racing Form,* the *Blood-Horse* magazine, the *Courier-Journal* in Louisville, Kentucky, the *Herald-Leader* in Lexington, Kentucky, *Sports Illustrated, Time,*

Newsweek, Practical Horseman, Western Horseman, the *Backstretch* magazine, *Thoroughbred Record, Thoroughbred Times, Mid-Atlantic Thoroughbred, Thoroughbred Daily News,* the *New York Times, Harper's* magazine, *HorseCare Magazine, Canadian Horse* magazine, *Dressage Today, Equus* magazine, the Associated Press, the *Journal-News* in Hamilton, Ohio, the *San Francisco Chronicle, Kentucky Derby* magazine, and *Spur* magazine.

Anthony J. Schefstad's Ph.D. thesis, *The Backstretch: Some Call It Home,* was invaluable for its detailed portrayal of the life of racetrack grooms.

Bill Nack and Raymond Woolfe, Jr.—the two prime biographers of Secretariat—were very generous with their time and their insights. Ray Woolfe's stunning images of Eddie Sweat and Secretariat helped shape this book, and I am grateful for their inspiration.

Thanks to: Sonny Sadinsky for the loan of the photo showing Charlie Davis at Saratoga Springs; Amy Gill for showing me around at the Fasig-Tipton sale in Lexington; Ted McClain for loaning me his box of clippings, and Penny Chenery for sending along some of hers; Carole Fletcher for helping me track down Charlie Davis in Ocala, and Gus Gray for literally taking me to him; Jimmy Gaffney for the photos; Danny Jenkins for his lessons at the starting gate; Sherrie-Lee Hawley for letting me tag along for a day (make that a dawn) in her life and for the gift of an exquisite framed photograph of Secretariat being led by Eddie Sweat; Alison Woodbury for keeping me on track; Tonja Cota for the Sweat family genealogy, and the Bogucki family—Ed, Shirley, and Katherine—for all their help.

I had remarkably good luck while researching this book. Let me illustrate. I wanted to experience a day in the life of a groom at Woodbine Race Track, so I called up an old friend, Jayne Huddleston, who is well connected in the horse world. Jayne just happened to have been a neighbor of trainer Sherrie-Lee Hawley. Hawley led me to groom Roger Broomes, who just happened to have worked next door to Eddie Sweat at Woodbine for almost a year. A rider friend in Connecticut put me on to Lexington equine nutritionist Amy Gill, who, it transpired, was once married to Ted McClain, Lucien Laurin's barn foreman and a great admirer of Eddie's. I found Charlie Davis, Secretariat's old exercise rider, through a tip from Carole Fletcher, and I only know Carole because we worked together on her memoir. Carole is pals with starter Danny Jenkins, whose pal is trainer Gus Gray, in turn, fast friend to Charlie Davis. The dominoes fell ever so neatly. I would never have found Marvin Moorer, Eddie's son, without first talking to the sculptor Ed Bogucki. (Marvin had seen Ed's bronze of Secretariat on the Internet and contacted him.) You could say that the world of horse racing is a small world and that I shouldn't be surprised by all this serendipity. I prefer to believe that all these dots were somehow already connected, and that once I chanced across the first dot the rest would light up and I would find them, as if it were meant to be.

Many people talked to me, wrote to me, told me their stories. Not everyone made it into these pages, but I owe them all a great deal. I feel especially indebted to Marvin Moorer, the son of Eddie Sweat, to Geraldine Holman, Eddie's sister, and to everyone in Eddie's family who shared their memories.

My agent, Jackie Kaiser, is, quite simply, the best. She, too, had a hand in shaping *The Horse God Built.*

My son, Kurt, and my wife, Ulrike, are the real rocks in my life, and I thank them for their good humor and for reminding me that there is life beyond horses—even great horses.

~ Sources ~

EPIGRAPH

Hotaling, Edward. *The Great Black Jockeys: The Lives and Times of the Men Who Dominated America's First National Sport.* New York: Three Rivers Press, 1999.

PROLOGUE

Nack, William. *Big Red of Meadow Stable.* New York: A. Fields Books, 1975.

Pollitzer, William S. *The Gullah People and Their African Heritage.* University of Georgia Press, Athens, Georgia, and London: 1999.

Squires, Jim. *Horse of a Different Color: A Tale of Breeding Geniuses, Dominant Females, and the Fastest Derby Winner Since Secretariat.* New York: Public Affairs, 2002.

CHAPTER 1

Smiley, Jane. *A Year at the Races: Reflections on Horses, Humans, Love, Money, and Luck.* New York: Knopf, 2004.

Woolfe, Raymond G., Jr. *Secretariat.* Lanham, Maryland, and New York: Derrydale Press, 2001.

CHAPTER 2

Sullivan, John Jeremiah. *Blood Horses: Notes of a Sportswriter's Son.* New York: Farrar, Straus and Giroux, 2004.

The editors of *Daily Racing Form. Champions: The Lives, Times, and Past Performances of the 20th Century's Greatest Thoroughbreds.* New York: Daily Racing Form Press, 2000.

CHAPTER 3

Mearns, Dan. *Seattle Slew.* Lexington: Eclipse Press, 2000.

Nusser, Susan. *In Service to the Horse: Chronicles of a Labor of Love.* New York: Little, Brown, 2004.

Kane, Jeanne, and Lisa Waltman. *The Event Groom's Handbook: Care of Horse and Rider.* London: Event Books International, 1983.

Rivas, Mim Eichler. *Beautiful Jim Key: The Lost History of a Horse and a Man Who Changed the World.* New York: William Morrow, 2005.

Scanlan, Lawrence. *Wild About Horses: Our Timeless Passion for the Horse.* New York: HarperCollins, 1998.

CHAPTER 4

Heller, Bill, with Ron Turcotte. *The Will to Win: Ron Turcotte's Ride to Glory*. Saskatoon, Canada: Fifth House, 1992.

CHAPTER 5

Haskin, Steve. *John Henry*. Lexington: Eclipse Press, 2001.

CHAPTER 6

Barich, Bill. *Laughing in the Hills*. New York: Penguin, 1981.

CHAPTER 8

Durkis, Deirdre. *Where They Sleep: Burial Sites of Thoroughbreds in the Bluegrass Country of Kentucky*. Louisville: Kentucky Derby Museum, 1998.

Zeh, Lucy. *Etched in Stone: Thoroughbred Memorials*. Lexington: The Blood-Horse, Inc., 2000.